diabetes

BREAKTHROUGHS

2010

diabetes
BREAKTHROUGHS
2010

Tips & Tools for Your Best Health

FROM THE EDITORS OF **Prevention** WITH THE STAFF OF THE JOSLIN DIABETES CENTER

RODALE

CONTENTS

Introduction   **x**

PART

1

TAKE CONTROL

Medical Breakthroughs   **2**

CHAPTER 1: Understanding Diabetes   **9**

CHAPTER 2: Dealing with Your Diagnosis   **21**

CHAPTER 3: Diabetes Drugs   **27**

CHAPTER 4: Generic Concerns   **31**

CHAPTER 5: Change That Sticks   **39**

PART

2

EAT RIGHT

Medical Breakthroughs   **46**

CHAPTER 6: Foods That Fight Diabetes   **56**

CHAPTER 7: The Box That Battles Diabetes   **65**

CHAPTER 8: Healthy Veggies with Bad Reps   **69**

CHAPTER 9: Nature's Perfect Food   **75**

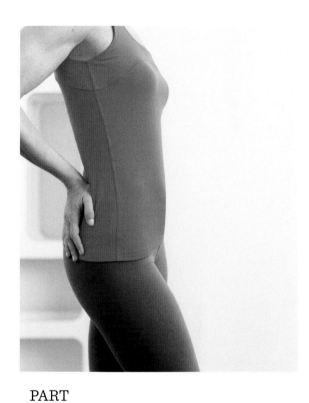

PART

3

LOSE WEIGHT

Medical Breakthroughs   **80**

CHAPTER 10: Fast-Tracked Fat Loss   **88**

CHAPTER 11: The Belly Shrinker   **102**

CHAPTER 12: The Wall Workout   **111**

CHAPTER 13: Weight Loss U   **117**

PART

4

MOVE IT

Medical Breakthroughs   **126**

CHAPTER 14: Walking Workouts
for Everybody   **132**

CHAPTER 15: Joint-Friendly Workouts   **141**

CHAPTER 16: Watch and Lose   **149**

CHAPTER 17: The Belly-Slimming Workout   **157**

CHAPTER 18: The Trouble-Spot Tamers   **169**

PART

5

STRESS LESS

Medical Breakthroughs	**176**
CHAPTER 19: The Om Workout	**182**
CHAPTER 20: Beauty Sleep	**190**
CHAPTER 21: The Slumber Diaries	**197**
CHAPTER 22: Laugh Away Stress	**205**
CHAPTER 23: Super-Simple Memory Fix	**209**

PART

6

AVOID COMPLICATIONS

Medical Breakthroughs	**214**
CHAPTER 24: Know Your Risk	**222**
CHAPTER 25: Diabetes Danger: Brain Attack	**233**

DIABETES COOKBOOK

CHAPTER 26: The Recipes	**242**	Chicken Dishes **300**
Breakfasts	**244**	Beef and Pork Dishes **310**
Appetizers and Snacks	**256**	Fish and Seafood Dishes **320**
Salads	**266**	Desserts **332**
Soups	**274**	*Photo Credits* **355**
Vegetarian and Side Dishes	**284**	*Index* **356**

INTRODUCTION

This year, *Prevention* joined forces with the staff at the Joslin Diabetes Center to bring you *Diabetes Breakthroughs 2010*. The Joslin Diabetes Center is the world's preeminent diabetes research and clinical care organization. The center was founded in 1898, and ever since then it has constantly evolved to meet the ever-changing challenges of diabetes. Joslin Diabetes Center, located in Boston and affiliated with Harvard Medical School, is on the front lines of the world epidemic of diabetes, leading the battle to conquer diabetes in all of its forms through cutting-edge research and innovative approaches to clinical care and education.

Together, we've filled this book with the latest breakthroughs for preventing, diagnosing, and treating diabetes. Plus we offer the best expert-recommended strategies or applying these break-throughs to your life—or to the life of someone you love who is battling diabetes. One good (or bad depending on how you look at it) thing about diabetes is it's a disease of self-management. That means you have a great deal of control over your own medical destiny because the foods that you eat, the exercise that you do, and the other lifestyle habits you have so greatly influence your condition. But the best news is that people with diabetes are living longer—and healthier—than ever before, thanks to improvements available for treating and managing the disease.

In part 1, "Take Control," we'll help you to do just that. You'll learn the three key steps to taking control of your diabetes. You'll also discover how healthy eating, exercise, monitoring, and medications all work together to play a role in your healthy life with diabetes. Here you'll also find an A-to-Z guide to the medications doctors prescribe for diabetes and a discussion about emerging concerns about generic drugs.

Then in part 2, "Eat Right," you'll learn why carefully considering and monitoring what you eat can help you manage your diabetes and avoid complications. You'll also find which key foods that fight diabetes to add to your shopping list today.

Because diabetes and obesity are as intertwined as macaroni and cheese, part 3 will help you to "Lose Weight." An astonishing 90 percent—9 out of 10—people who've been newly diagnosed with diabetes are overweight. Here you'll find simple ways to shed pounds, including super-simple 10-minute walking and strength workouts.

In part 4, you'll read why exercise is essential for people with diabetes. Exercise is so powerful that it can reverse the earliest symptoms of type 2 diabetes in just 1 week. Here you'll find walking workouts for every body, joint-friendly workouts, and more. Whether you need to exercise to lose weight, burn fat, or get energy, you'll find out how here.

Part 5 encourages you to "Stress Less." Stress isn't good for anyone, let alone anyone with diabetes. Here you'll find out how to find calm in minutes, ease up on stress, and get better sleep, which are all critical for good health.

Diabetes wreaks havoc with your entire body, so we've devoted part 6 to help you "Avoid Complications." For example, you'll discover the five lifestyle guidelines that slash heart attack risk by a whopping 92 percent. Even if you can only manage two of them, you'll still cut your risk by more than half. That's critical for people with diabetes because adults with diabetes have heart disease death rates about two to four times higher than adults without diabetes.

In part 7, we've gathered 100 of our most delicious, nutritious, diabetes-friendly dishes. We hope you'll love the Texas Breakfast Burritos, Creamy Veggie Dip, Quick Pasta Salad, Tuscan Chicken Soup, Savory Fruit and Nut Stuffing, Sweet and Sour Chinese Pork, Tangelo Tiramisu, and more. We hand-picked them all just for you.

Diabetes can make life a challenge, but now with the right treatment strategies and information at your fingertips, it's about to get a whole lot easier.

TAKE

Here's the latest and greatest diabetes

Medical Breakthroughs   **2**

CHAPTER 1: **Understanding Diabetes**   **9**

CHAPTER 2: **Dealing with Your Diagnosis**   **21**

CHAPTER 3: **Diabetes Drugs**   **27**

CHAPTER 4: **Generic Concerns**   **31**

CHAPTER 5: **Change That Sticks**   **39**

CONTROL

research to help you take control.

DIAGNOSTIC
Medical Breakthroughs

Receiving a diagnosis like diabetes can cause a dizzying array of emotions. You might be feeling fearful, angry, frustrated, depressed, and more—whether it's you or someone you love who has been diagnosed. But as with so many things, information is power. **Here's the latest and greatest diabetes research to help you take control.**

GET MILK (THISTLE)

Studies of milk thistle *(Silybum marianum)* show that silymarin, the herb's main compound, safely detoxifies the liver and can treat nonalcoholic fatty liver disease, which contributes to diabetes. Silymarin may also help reverse chronic liver inflammation, a suspected cause of insulin resistance, says University of North Carolina biochemist Kevin Spelman. Iraqi doctors recently saw a 20 percent drop in the fasting blood sugar of people with type 2 diabetes who took 200 milligrams of silymarin with their diabetes drug daily for 120 days.

It's important to note that not all milk thistle supplements contain enough silymarin, according to a ConsumerLab.com independent test. Two that do: Trader Darwin's, sold at Trader Joe's stores, and Thisilyn by Nature's Way. Try 200 to 500 milligrams daily, but talk with your doctor about it first.

FEELING WORSE? TRY A NURSE

Behind every good doctor is a good . . . nurse practitioner? A recent study found that family physician offices with an NP on staff improved diabetics' lifestyles better than doctor-only settings. NPs—who have specialized training to diagnose, treat, and prescribe medications—have the rep of being better focused on disease prevention than physicians.

Finding an NP just got easier: The new Web site www.npfinder.com locates NPs nationwide and provides directions to their practices.

DIAL *D* FOR DIABETES CONTROL

Monitoring your glucose can be easier and more convenient with the newly available GlucoPhone by HealthPia America. It comes equipped with a slot to insert a standard glucose test strip, and it's also a working cell phone. The phone displays glucose readings and records them in an online database. You and your doctor can view them by computer or text message.

You can learn more at their Web site, www.glucophone.net.

DON'T LET DIABETES DRUGS LEAVE YOU DEFICIENT

Like dozens of chronic health conditions, diabetes and, often, the drugs that treat the condition have a common side effect: They reduce vitamin levels. Nature Made's Rx Essentials, a line of daily

The percentage of American Academy of Nurse Practitioners members who have a master's degree or doctorate:

96

supplements ($13 per bottle, 30 to 60 tablets), are formulated to offset such shortfalls. Multivitamins are generally safe to take with prescriptions, says *Prevention* advisor David Katz, MD, MPH.

But foods can replenish these vitamins just as well. Here, tips from nutritionist Sari Greaves, RD, of New York Presbyterian Hospital/Weill Cornell.

If you take drugs for diabetes such as metformin, Glucophage, and Glucovance: Fill your vitamin gap with vitamin B_{12} by eating more fortified cereals, lean beef, and fish. Also, fill your vitamin gap with folate/folic acid by eating more fortified cereals, asparagus, okra, spinach, turnip greens, broccoli, beans and lentils, orange juice, and tomato juice.

If you take drugs for cholesterol, such as Lipitor and Zocor: Fill your vitamin gap with Coenzyme Q10, which is a natural cell compound that's also sometimes known as CoQ10. You'll find it in organ meats such as heart, liver, and kidney. Heart-healthy options include beef, soy oil, sardines, mackerel, and peanuts.

If you take drugs for heartburn/acid reflux, such as Nexium and Prilosec: Fill your vitamin gap with calcium. Get more of it in low-fat or fat-free dairy products, tofu, sardines, salmon, fortified juices, and leafy greens such as kale, broccoli, and bok choy.

If you take drugs for depression, such as Zoloft, Lexapro, and Prozac: Fill your vitamin gap with B vitamins riboflavin, niacin, B_6, and thiamine. Eat more whole

The Diabetes Epidemic

According to the American Diabetes Association, 23.6 million people in the United States, or 8 percent of the population, have diabetes. The total prevalence of diabetes increased 13.5 percent from 2005 to 2007.

One spot of good news: Only 24 percent of diabetes is undiagnosed, down from 30 percent in 2005 and 50 percent 10 years ago.

Common Rx Soundalikes

Take special care if you're ever prescribed any of the following medications, which sound a lot like other medications.

IF YOU'RE PRESCRIBED	MAKE SURE IT'S NOT
Actos for type 2 diabetes	Actonel for osteoporosis
Celebrex for arthritis	Celexa for depression
Prilosec for acid reflux	Prozac for depression
HESpan to thicken blood	Heparin to thin blood
Metformin for type 2 diabetes	Metronidazole, an antibiotic
Sulfasalazine for ulcerative colitis	Sulfadiazine, an antibiotic

grain products, pork loin, low-fat or fat-free dairy products, eggs, lean meat, skinless poultry, fish, beans and lentils, and tofu. Also, fill your vitamin gap with folate/folic acid by eating more fortified cereals, asparagus, okra, spinach, turnip greens, broccoli, beans and lentils, orange juice, and tomato juice.

If you take drugs for arthritis, such as naproxen and ibuprofen: Fill your vitamin gap with vitamin D by eating fortified low-fat or fat-free milk and cereal, fatty fish (such as salmon, mackerel, tuna, sardines, and herring), and eggs. Also, fill your vitamin gap with folate/folic acid by eating more fortified cereals, asparagus, okra, spinach, turnip greens, broccoli, beans and lentils, orange juice, and tomato juice.

■ PREVENT MED MIX-UPS

The names of more than 1,400 drugs are frighteningly similar to those of others, creating potentially troubling confusion, according to a study by the United States Pharmacopeia (USP), a scientific organization. Here are four ways to avoid this simple mistake. Also see "Common Rx Soundalikes" above—all of which have been dispensed incorrectly and actually harmed patients, according to USP.

1. When your doctor gives you a new prescription, write down the drug name and dosage on a separate sheet of paper from your prescription and read it back to your doctor to confirm. Then, when your pharmacist fills the prescription, check this information against the pill bottle with your pharmacist present. (You're entitled by law to receive free pharmacy counseling every time you begin a new medication.)

2. If you're given a prescription for a generic drug rather than a brand name, confirm the generic's brand-name equivalent and indication with your pharmacist after receiving your meds. Many prescriptions are filled with generics, meaning the drug name on a bottle label could be different from the one that your physician wrote down.

3. Most pharmacies include an information sheet along with the medication. Verify the medication's "indication for use," which means the symptoms that it treats, before taking it.

THE POWER OF PREVENTION

Even if you have prediabetes, that doesn't necessarily mean you'll go on to develop diabetes. Studies have shown that people with prediabetes who lose weight and increase their physical activity can delay—or even completely prevent—diabetes, returning their blood glucose levels to normal.

The Diabetes Prevention Program, which is a large prevention study of people at high risk for diabetes, showed that lifestyle intervention reduced developing diabetes by 58 percent during a 3-year period. For people age 60 and older, the reduction was even greater—71 percent.

4. Still unsure? Search for your drug by name online in *Prevention*'s Drug Encyclopedia on the government's MedLine Plus database at www.nlm.nih.gov. And call your doctor before taking the first pill if you still have doubts.

■ STAY SAFE ON YOUR MEDS

Here experts Joe Graedon, MS, and Teresa Graedon, PhD, coauthors of *Best Choices from the People's Pharmacy,*

answer critical questions to help you take your medications safely.

How common are unanticipated reactions to medication? Unfortunately, we hear about it all the time. Some people find that a medication does wonders, while others suffer debilitating pain not mentioned on the package insert. If these reactions are underreported, doctors won't begin to associate the drug with the symptom.

What unlisted side effects have you helped uncover? The new anti-smoking pill is touted as a "miracle" cure, but we've heard accounts of depression and suicidal thoughts—even in people with no history of psychological problems. These reactions are not mentioned in ads, and they're not easy to find in the prescribing info.

What should you do if this happens to you? Talk with your doctor. One study concluded that millions of side effects could be prevented if patients told their physicians about the physical and psychological symptoms that they experienced after starting a medication. Then, if necessary, your doctor can adjust your treatment.

THE EXPERTS

Joe and Teresa Graedon are Prevention *advisors, drug-safety experts, and founders of the People's Pharmacy, which provides information on treatments for everyday conditions, from home remedies to prescription drugs. Joe, a pharmacologist, and Terry, a medical anthropologist, have cowritten a dozen books on the subject, and their nationally syndicated column is in its third decade, and their popular Web site has million of users. Every year, they answer thousands of questions from fans about using prescription drugs safely and effectively.*

■ MIND YOUR MEDS

Having a hard time keeping up with your medication schedule? Here are three handy helpers.

First, to improve prescription adherence, physicians at the University of California, San Francisco, have devised a computer-based weekly calendar called a Visual Medication Schedule. It features

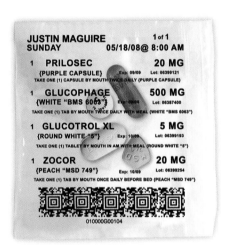

color images of medications paired with daily instructions that can be printed out on one sheet. A UCSF study proves it boosts drug compliance. To share the idea with your doctor, download a sample VMS at www.prevention.com/vms.

Two new custom pharmacy services make it easy to adhere to your medication schedule. The DailyMed dispensing system (www.dailymedrx.com) is a mail-order pharmacy that organizes your prescription, vitamin, and supplement pills in plastic pouches bearing the drug name, date, and time of day to take. Daily Med costs $15 per month and is free for the first month. A similar service, onePAC, offers the same customized pill packets via mail order or your local pharmacist for $10 to $20 per month (depending on location). Print the information at www.myonepac.org and give it to your pharmacist to enroll.

Understanding

DIABETES

Learn more about diabetes and how you can take simple steps toward better health.

I f you have diabetes, you're not alone. About 24 million people (that's 8 percent of the population) in the United States have diabetes. Almost six million of those people don't know they have diabetes. And another 57 million have prediabetes. Despite the grim statistics and the eye-opening fact that more and more people are being diagnosed with diabetes, there *is* good news: People with diabetes are living longer and healthier lives than ever before, thanks to improvements in treatment and management. And there's more good news: while you might be feeling overwhelmed by having diabetes, you don't have to manage it alone. There are three key steps to taking control of your diabetes:

Step 1: Know Diabetes

The first step in taking control of your diabetes is to understand what diabetes is. Diabetes means that your body does not use *glucose* (sugar) the way it should; as a result glucose can build up in the blood stream. High levels of glucose are primarily responsible for causing diabetes complications. There are two main types of diabetes: type 1 and type 2. Type 1 diabetes occurs when a person does not make any insulin—so people with type 1 diabetes must take insulin, either through injections or a pump, to survive. People with type 2 diabetes, the most common type, still make insulin, but not enough, and the insulin they do make does not work as well to convert food into energy. Some people with type 2 diabetes can control their diabetes through meal planning, weight management, and physical activity. But over time, most people with type 2 diabetes will need to take diabetes pills and/or insulin.

By the way, anyone, young and old alike, can get either type 1 or type 2 diabetes. It used to be thought that only children got type 1 diabetes and older adults got type 2 diabetes. However, in recent years more children, adolescents, and young adults are getting type 2 diabetes, and it's not uncommon for people in their forties to develop type 1 diabetes.

Yet another type of diabetes is called *gestational diabetes*. This type of diabetes occurs during pregnancy and almost always goes away once the baby is born. Women who have gestational diabetes, however, have a greater chance of developing type 2 diabetes later in life.

Step 2: Know Yourself

The second step to diabetes control is to learn as much about your own diabetes as you can. This means learning about the various tests that tell you how your diabetes is doing and what the numbers mean. These tests include A1C, blood pressure, cholesterol, and microalbumin numbers. It also means learning ways to eat more healthfully and to be more active. Use the Goal Tracker on page 20 to help stay on track.

Step 3: Know Your Treatment Plan

Work with your provider and other members of your healthcare team to create a diabetes treatment plan. This plan will be your road map to good control. Because your diabetes can change over time, your treatment plan will probably need to change, too. One important way to make sure it's working is to keep your appointments with your healthcare team and stay up to date on the latest diabetes treatments. Yes, it can seem like a lot of time and effort is needed to manage diabetes. In fact, diabetes is usually referred to as a condition of "self-management" because truly, most of the work is up to you! It's your responsibility to let your team know if something isn't working, if you have questions about your diabetes, or if you are interested in new medications or devices. Speaking of "team," you might be wondering what that means. Your healthcare team is most often made up of your physician (your primary care physician and/or an endocrinologist) or nurse practitioner and usually a dietitian and diabetes educator. Other members of your healthcare team could include a podiatrist, pharmacist, and mental health counselor. But don't forget that you might have other team members, too—your spouse, your children, a caregiver, a neighbor, or a co-worker—anyone who helps or supports you in your diabetes management.

Now that you know the three steps to taking control of your diabetes, read on to learn how healthy eating, physical activity, monitoring, medications, and knowing your numbers all play a role in living healthfully with diabetes.

NOTES FROM JOSLIN | Here is some good news: If your A1C is higher than your goal, lowering it by just 1 percent will lower your risk for complications by 40 percent!

Healthy Eating

Healthy eating is important for everyone, but especially if you have diabetes. Learning to control carbohydrates (carbs) is a first step. Why? Because foods containing carbs have the most impact on blood glucose. This doesn't mean, though, that you should stop eating carbs or that they're somehow bad for you. Carbs are essential for good health because they give you energy and fuel for your body.

If you are overweight, losing just 5 to 10 percent of your body weight can lead to a big improvement in glucose control. (That's 10 to 20 pounds if you weigh 200 pounds.) While losing any amount of weight can be challenging for some people, the good news here is that you don't have to get to an unrealistic "ideal" weight

(or the weight you were at in high school) to reap health benefits. Weight loss can also help lower your blood pressure and your cholesterol.

One way to get started with healthy eating is to ask your provider for a referral to a registered dietitian (RD) who specializes in developing meal plans for people with diabetes. A meal plan can be designed especially for you based on your eating preferences, lifestyle, and medication plan.

You'll also want to control your carbs which are found in:

- Rice, pasta, and noodles

- Beans, peas, and lentils

- Breads and cereals

- Fruit and juices

- Vegetables

- Milk and yogurt

- Desserts and sweets

Here's what you can do.

- Eat smaller portions. Weighing and measuring foods can help.

- Eat about the same amount of carb foods each day.

- Try to eat at the same time each day and don't skip meals.

- Choose whole grain breads and cereals. They contain more nutrients

and fiber than the refined, white grains.

- Fill half your plate with nonstarchy vegetables such as broccoli, spinach, and carrots. They're low in carbs and good sources of fiber.

- Aim for 2 to 3 small servings of fruit a day, and choose whole fruit instead of juice or dried fruit.

- Choose lean meats and skinless poultry and try to eat fish (not fried!) twice a week.

- Read labels! Look at serving size and total carbohydrate. One carb serving contains 15 grams of carb.

- Meet with a registered dietitian to create an individualized meal plan.

physical activity lessens the chances of getting certain diseases, such as heart disease. Try to include some type of activity in your daily routine.

Here's what you can do.

- Check with your healthcare provider to make sure it's safe to start being more active.

- Choose activities that you enjoy, or even try something new and fun, such as ballroom dancing, yoga, or a Pilates class.

- Aim for 30 to 45 minutes of activity four to six times a week. It doesn't need to be done in one session. Three 10-minute walks a day has the same benefit as walking for 30 minutes.

- Consider using a pedometer to measure your steps. The goal for most adults is to take 10,000 steps each day. Make excuses to walk more.

Activity Ideas

- Walking
- Bicycling
- Dancing
- Taking stairs
- Swimming
- Chair exercises
- Yoga or tai-chi

Be Active

Activity is great medicine! Being active can do wonders for your diabetes by lowering your blood glucose, blood pressure, and cholesterol; helping you lose weight; and making you feel better overall. Plus,

Know Your Numbers

MONITOR BLOOD GLUCOSE

Checking blood glucose (BG) is one of the best ways to know if your diabetes treatment plan is working. Your blood glucose numbers help you and your healthcare team make decisions for your daily diabetes management. If you're not checking your blood glucose, talk to your healthcare team about how to get started and when and how often to check.

A1C	Estimated Average BG	Estimated BG Range
12	298	240–347
11	269	217–314
10	240	193–282
9	212	170–249
8	183	147–217
7	154	123–185
6	126	100–154
5	97	76–120

Here's what you can do.

- Talk with a diabetes educator about different types of meters. If you have a meter, double check that you are using it properly.

- Ask your healthcare provider for target BG goals and how often to check BG. Goals for most people with diabetes are:

  - Before meals: 70 to 130
  - Two to three hours after meals: less than 180
  - Bedtime: 90 to 150

- Check more often if you:

  - Are sick
  - Make a change in the way you eat, your activity, or your medicines
  - Are pregnant (or thinking about becoming pregnant)
  - See that your glucose levels run above or below target
  - Travel to different time zones

- Write down your glucose results in a log book. Look for patterns of high or low readings. Bring your log book to each visit with your healthcare provider.

A1C AND AVERAGE GLUCOSE

While checking blood glucose is an important part of your day-to-day diabetes management, the best way to know how your diabetes is doing over time is to get a blood test called the A1C test. This test, which should be done every 3 to 6 months by your healthcare provider, is a measure of your average blood glucose levels over the past 2 to 3 months. It gives you an even better picture of your glucose control than you would get by just looking at numbers on your meter alone.

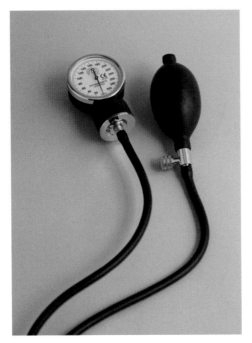

The goal with glucose, as with the A1C, is to get the average down as low as is safely possible. Less than 154 mg/dl (an A1C of 7 percent) is the goal for most people.

Here's what you can do.

- Find out when your last A1C test was done and write down the result.

- Know your A1C goal.

- If your A1C is above your goal, talk with your healthcare team about making changes in your meal plan, activity plan, or medicines.

For most people, the A1C goal is less than 7 percent. For comparison purposes, a person without diabetes will have a result between 4 and 6 percent.

When you check your blood glucose with your meter, you're looking at a snapshot of your glucose at that exact moment. If you could check your blood glucose every minute of every day over the same 2- to 3-month period and average the results, this would be your A1C. While it would of course be impossible to check that often, you can get an idea of how your A1C compares to your daily blood glucose numbers by looking at a number called your "estimated average blood glucose." See the chart on page 15 to determine how your A1C compares to your estimated average blood glucose.

Your blood pressure (BP) tells you about the pressures inside your arteries. The top number should be below 130 and the bottom number below 80. Both of these numbers are important for your health. Keeping your BP below 130/80 not only reduces your risk for heart disease, but also lowers your risk for eye and kidney disease, too.

Here's what you can do.

- Have your BP checked at every visit with a healthcare provider and write down the result.

- If your BP is above your target, consider buying a home monitor. The more information you and your provider have, the better.

- Talk with your provider about what you can do to help lower your blood pressure, including:
  - Losing weight, if you need to
  - Eating fewer foods that are high in sodium
  - Eating more fruits and vegetables
  - Being more active
  - Reducing stress by using techniques such as yoga, meditation, or relaxation exercises
  - Taking a medication that will help lower your BP

CHOLESTEROL COUNTS

One of the downsides of having diabetes is that you have a higher risk for heart and blood vessel disease. But once again, here's where you can take control and lower your risk of heart disease. In addition to keeping tabs on your blood pressure, you should also know your cholesterol results and what steps you can take to lower cholesterol if not at target. Once a year, have a *lipid profile.* (This is a series of blood tests that measure your cholesterol and triglyceride levels.) Compare your results to those targets:

LDL cholesterol (the lousy/bad cholesterol): Under 100
HDL cholesterol (the healthy / good cholesterol): Over 45 for men, over 55 for women
Triglycerides (blood fats): Under 150

Here's what you can do.

- Find out when your last lipid profile was done and write down the results.

- Focus on choosing healthy fats, such as those in fish, olive oil, canola oil, nuts, and seeds.

- Lay off the bad fats (saturated and trans fats) that are found in beef, dairy products, and some processed and fast foods.

- Fit more high-fiber foods, such as oatmeal, fruits, and vegetables, into your eating plan.

- Be more active. Regular activity can lower your risk of heart disease.

- Talk with your provider about medicines that can lower bad cholesterol or raise good cholesterol.

MICROALBUMIN

You might not be familiar with the microalbumin test, but it happens to be one of the most important tests for people with diabetes. People with diabetes are at risk for kidney problems. Fortunately, your provider has a way to catch any kidney problems early on by measuring your urine for small amounts of protein, called microalbumin. Think of the microalbumin test as a gauge for how well your kidneys are working. The goal for microalbumin is less than 30, and this test should be done at least once a year.

Here's what you can do.

- Keep your A1C, glucose, and blood pressure in your target range as much as possible.

- Ask your provider about medicines called ACE inhibitors or ARBs that can help keep your microalbumin from rising—and also help control your blood pressure.

- If you smoke or use tobacco products, make a plan to quit.

Understand Your Diabetes Medicines

Diabetes medicines are sometimes needed to help keep blood glucose in target. These medicines work along with (not in place of!) a healthy meal plan and regular physical activity.

Why do some people with diabetes need medication while others don't? Much of it depends on the type of diabetes you have and how long you've had diabetes. For example, if you have type 1 diabetes, you have to take insulin to survive; pills will not work for you. If you have type 2 diabetes and have had it for a short while, you might be able to successfully manage it by using a meal plan, reaching and staying at a healthy weight, and doing physical activity most days of the week. However, over time, people with type 2 diabetes will usually need some type of diabetes pills or insulin to control glucose

levels. This is the natural progression of the disease. Also, it's important to note that if you have type 2 diabetes and have to start insulin, it does not mean that you now have type 1 diabetes. You still have type 2 diabetes but you need to take insulin to help manage it. Medications for type 2 diabetes include:

Diabetes pills: There are several different types of pills. Each type, or class, of pills works in a slightly different way. Many people start with one type but eventually need to add a second or even a third type of pill.

Insulin: Insulin is a hormone made by the body. You need to replace your insulin if you don't have enough or if the insulin you make isn't working. Insulin is injected with a syringe, an insulin pen, or an insulin pump.

Other injectables: There are other injectable medicines that replace other hormones (like insulin) that you may be lacking. They work with your diabetes pills or insulin to help control blood glucose. One of the side effects is that they may lead to weight loss!

As explained earlier, many people with type 2 diabetes will eventually need to take insulin. Having to take insulin does not mean you're a "failure" or that your diabetes is getting worse; it's just changing. Some people are afraid that taking insulin injections will hurt. Insulin injections are actually less painful than doing a fingerstick with your meter because the needles are smaller than the lancets.

Insulin is a safe, effective, natural medicine with very few side effects. In fact, insulin is one of the best ways to control diabetes. If your healthcare team has suggested that you start taking insulin, be sure that you ask about any fears or concerns that you may have. You'll most likely find that starting insulin is not as bad as you thought it would be!

Here's what you can do.

- Learn about your medicine: how it works, how and when to take it, and any side effects.

- Take your medication as directed; if you can't for any reason, let your provider know.

- Ask about new types of medicines.

- Bring your medicines, along with any vitamins and supplements you are taking, to appointments with your provider. Keep a list of what you take, the dose, and when you take it.

- Make sure someone close to you knows about your medicines in case of an emergency.

- Stay on top of any lab tests, such as blood work, that you may need to be done while you're taking a particular medication.

- If you need to have an X-ray or outpatient procedure, find out if you need to stop taking your diabetes medicine for a short time.

Eyes, Feet, and More

In addition to the lab tests mentioned previously, there are two very important exams that you'll want to be sure you have done every year: a dilated eye exam by an ophthalmologist and a thorough foot exam by your provider or podiatrist. The dilated eye exam is done to check your retina for small blood vessels that could be damaged by high glucose levels. And your provider should check your feet for sensation and blood flow. By the way, a good way to remind your provider to check your feet is to take your shoes and socks off at every visit!

Here are a few other important steps to take to keep healthy with diabetes:

- See your dentist at least twice a year.

- Get a flu shot every year.

- Make a plan to stop smoking if you smoke or use other tobacco products.

- Tell your provider if you are feeling sad or depressed. Depression is two to three times more common among those with diabetes and can be treated.

My Personal Diabetes Goal Tracker

Keep track of the goals you want to set for yourself by writing them down.

	Target goal	My last result
A1C	Under 7%	
Blood pressure	Under 130/80	
LDL cholesterol	Under 100; under 70 for some	
HDL cholesterol	Over 45 for men, over 55 for women	
Triglycerides	Under 150	
Microalbumin	Under 30	
Body Mass Index (BMI)	18.5—24.9	
Asian populations:	Less than or equal to 23	
Waist circumference	Less than or equal to 40" for men, less than 35" for women	
Asian populations:	Less than or equal to 35" for men; less than or equal to 31" for women	
Eye exam	Once a year	
Foot check	Every visit	
Flu shot	Once a year	
Smoking	No smoking	

Dealing with Your
DIAGNOSIS

After you receive a shocking diagnosis like diabetes, **your mind can be a powerful ally**. Here's how to tap your mind's incredible power to heal in the hours, days, and months ahead.

I t's the moment everyone dreads: The door closes, and your doctor says, "I have some bad news." Learning that you have a serious illness can be devastating enough. But the emotional and psychological tsunami that strikes just moments after can often make you feel worse than the disease itself.

Modern medicine offers plenty of great medical care for most serious illnesses, but too often, treatment of the accompanying anger, fear, grief, and feelings of helplessness gets short shrift. Modern medicine offers plenty of great medical care for most serious illnesses, but too often, treatment of the accompanying anger, grief, and feelings of helplessness gets short shrift. People with diabetes are at greater risk for depression. According to the American Diabetes Association, 10 to 30 percent of people with diabetes also have depression. Plus, poor diabetes control can cause symptoms that look like depression.

Unfair as it seems, it's up to you to identify how vulnerable you are. In a University of South Florida study of 15 of the world's leading cancer centers, just 8 reported screening some patients for distress, and only 3 looked for signs of distress in all patients.

There are real benefits to collecting your wits early on and developing a psychological protection plan. "Getting a handle on your emotional state at diagnosis will ultimately help you evaluate and choose the most appropriate course of treatment," says Nancy E. Adler, PhD, a psychologist at the University of California, San Francisco. Becoming engaged in the treatment process might even result in less pain, fewer symptoms, and more energy throughout the healing process, say experts who study the mind-body connection.

The following hour-by-hour, week-by-week psychological battle plan will take you from Kleenex-clutching zombie to well-balanced warrior.

The First 5 Minutes: You're in Shock

Just take it all in. "The immediate reaction to any serious diagnosis is usually shock, disbelief, and denial," says Barry J. Jacobs, PsyD, author of *The Emotional Survival Guide for Caregivers*. "Many patients are simply overwhelmed and feel like they can't absorb any information."

If you suspect you'll be getting some scary news from your doctor, you'd be wise to bring a friend or family member along to the appointment, or at least have a tape recorder or a notebook handy. Otherwise, focus on just one thing: the next step. Ask your doctor if you need another test, a follow-up visit, or a referral to a specialist. And before you leave, ask for his or her direct contact information so you can ask questions after you've processed the news.

The First 24 Hours: You Seize Control

Don't commit to treatment yet. At first, snap decisions can feel right—after all, they make you feel as if you're in charge. And some illnesses, such as diabetes, require prompt action. But do some research. Simple Internet searches and talking with a friend's doctor or other medical professionals can open up options and change your perspective. "Getting involved in the treatment selection process, rather than immediately acting on recommendations, may result in better long-term satisfaction," says Karen Weihs, MD, who has developed a comprehensive model for cancer patients' mental health care at the Arizona Cancer Center in Tucson.

The First Week: You Hit a Slump

Identify your feelings. In the early days, you might swing from feeling angry to afraid or feel both. Writing about these swirling emotions can help you cope with them. The University of Texas M.D. Anderson Cancer Center suggests writing for 15 minutes twice a week.

"Exploring your deepest thoughts and feelings is more effective than just writing about what you did that day," says Dr. Weihs. You can even tear up the paper or stick it in a drawer when you're done. "It's the self-expression alone that's helpful," she says.

You might also start a blog—the 21st-century version of the leather-bound diary. The nonprofit Web site www.caringbridge.org, geared toward patients, offers this service at no cost; set your blog to "public" or "private," or allow only a few select visitors. Another option: Sign up for personal blogging at www.prevention.com. (Registration is free.)

Recruit your "A" team. Choose at least one person to be your go-to partner for emotional support, and choose another person to help you deal with more practical matters, such as assisting with transportation, tracking appointments, and researching treatments. By separating these needs—emotional and practical—you'll be more likely to pay attention to how you're progressing on both fronts.

Investigate "self-management" programs. These programs offer a variety of psychological and social support options that will help you stay calm, make more thoughtful decisions, and just feel better day to day. Typically, they are available through the patient resources or social services office in your hospital or treatment center.

ID YOUR PATIENT PERSONALITY

Psychologists lump people who have been recently diagnosed with conditions such as diabetes into two broad categories: blunters and monitors. The population is about evenly split between monitors and blunters, although women are slightly more likely to be monitors, says Suzanne M. Miller, PhD, director of psychosocial and behavioral medicine at Fox Chase Cancer Center in Philadelphia.

Knowing your tendencies might help predict potential pitfalls in how you interpret information about your illness, and that knowledge might enable you to outwit those pitfalls.

BLUNTERS These folks take a relaxed approach to health care, and they are more likely to avoid detail and less likely to follow up with tests and treatments. They could therefore miss out on critical information.

TIP: Enlist a monitor ally to help you track appointments.

MONITORS These people are more likely to want to learn the details of a health condition and its treatment, prefer plenty of choices, tend to visit doctors more often, and are more likely to suffer from stress and anxiety.

TIP: Recruit a blunter partner to help you take a more relaxed approach.

"In the very beginning, patients have to make a lot of decisions, like whether and when a second opinion is warranted, or if a clinical trial or off-label drug use is an appropriate option. It's like learning a new language. A social worker or other professional can help sort it out," explains Kim Thiboldeaux, president and CEO of the Wellness Community (www.thewellness community.org), which pioneered these types of programs 25 years ago.

If your hospital or treatment center doesn't offer these services, search the Internet for professional-led groups. Web-based therapies are just as effective as in-house programs in treating depression, anxiety, and stress. The Stanford Patient Education Research Center offers 6-week online workshops for people with diabetes, heart or lung diseases, or arthritis. Visit them at http://patienteducation. stanford.edu.

In the Weeks Ahead:
You Make a Comeback

Embrace your inner grouch. Don't fall for the myth that relentless optimism is key to survival. This concept gained popularity in the 1980s, fueled by studies showing that people with "a fighting spirit" were more likely to survive.

"I've had patients ask me to help them develop a positive attitude so they can shrink a tumor," says William Breitbart, MD, chief of psychiatry services at Memorial Sloan-Kettering Cancer Center in New York City.

But a 2002 University of Glasgow analysis of 26 studies involving thousands of cancer patients found little to no correlation between attitude and survival or recurrence. New research from the University of Pennsylvania School of Medicine came to a similar conclusion. Researchers now believe that emotional authenticity is more beneficial. In other words, if you feel angry, embrace it.

But if you're still feeling blue a month after diagnosis, you may be experiencing clinical depression. Look out for lack of pleasure in activities you usually find enjoyable, along with sleep and appetite disturbances. If you notice these signs, request a referral to a counselor experienced in treating individuals coping with medical problems.

Resist redefining yourself. After receiving a diagnosis like diabetes, it's easy to lose your identity in the shadow of the disease. You're suddenly no longer you, but your disease. You're a diabetic. However, it's not necessary—or wise—to automatically start referring to yourself as a "fighter" or "survivor," especially if you don't feel like one, explains Terri Ades, director of cancer information for the American Cancer Society. Choose language that reflects how you feel (the exact words are up to you)—not the way you suspect others want you to feel.

As your treatment gains traction, it's okay to turn daily conversation toward something "normal." It isn't necessary to lead a running dialogue on your condition and its progress if all you really want to do is have a good, hard laugh.

| NOTES FROM JOSLIN | It can be overwhelming to find out you have diabetes because there is so much to learn and do to successfully manage this condition. You can prevent feeling overwhelmed by making sure you have a diabetes treatment plan (think of this as your personal road map that helps you with food, activity, medication, and monitoring) that is clear and reasonable for you. |

Diabetes

DRUGS

Diabetes medications can help you manage your blood sugar and avoid complications. **Here's your A-to-Z guide.**

Type 2 diabetes is a metabolic problem that affects your body's ability to respond to insulin, which is a hormone produced in the pancreas that regulates the delivery of blood glucose (blood sugar) to your body's organs and tissues.

Doctors generally encourage people with diabetes to manage their condition through diet, exercise, and weight loss. And sometimes those are enough. But other times, these measures aren't able to bring blood sugar levels back to normal. That's when doctors prescribe medications.

In this chapter, we'll discuss the medications that doctors prescribe to treat diabetes and related conditions such as unhealthy blood sugar, glucose, and insulin levels. Read carefully, because some of the drugs, many of which stimulate the pancreas, regulate insulin, aid in digestion, or help break down food, may only be used in combination with proper diet and exercise. That part is up to you!

Acarbose

Brand name(s): Prandase (Canada), Precose (United States)
Acarbose works by slowing the action of certain chemicals that break down food and release glucose into your blood. Slowing food digestion helps keep blood glucose from skyrocketing after meals.

Exenatide Injection

Brand name(s): Byetta
Exenatide is used in combination with metformin and/or a sulfonylurea medication to treat people who have type 2 diabetes. Exenatide is in a class of medications called incretin mimetics. It works by stimulating the pancreas to secrete insulin when blood sugar levels are high. Exenatide also slows the emptying of the stomach, and it also causes a decrease in appetite.

Glimepiride

Brand name(s): Amaryl
Glimepiride is used in combination with diet and exercise to treat type 2 diabetes. Glimepiride stimulates your pancreas to make more insulin and also makes your body more sensitive to insulin. Glimepiride may be used with or without insulin.

Glyburide

Brand name(s): Diabeta, Glynase, Micronase
Glyburide is used to treat type 2 diabetes, particularly in people whose diabetes cannot be controlled by diet alone. Glyburide lowers blood sugar by stimulating the pancreas to secrete insulin and by helping the body use insulin efficiently.

Glyburide and Metformin

Brand name(s): Glucovance

The combination of glyburide and metformin is used to treat type 2 diabetes in people whose diabetes cannot be controlled by diet and exercise alone. Glyburide belongs to a class of drugs called sulfonylureas, and metformin is in a class of drugs called biguanides. Glyburide lowers blood sugar by stimulating the pancreas. Metformin helps your body regulate the amount of glucose in your blood. It decreases the amount of glucose you get from your diet and the amount made by your liver. It also helps your body use its own insulin more effectively.

Insulin

Brand name(s): Apidra, Humalog, Humulin, Lantus, Lente, Iletin, Novolin, NovoLog, Velosulin, various others

In a person with diabetes, the pancreas does not produce enough insulin for the body's needs, so additional insulin is required. It must be injected because stomach acid would destroy it if taken by mouth. Insulin controls, but does not cure, diabetes. It must be taken regularly.

People with diabetes gradually develop serious nerve, blood vessel, kidney, and eye problems, especially if the diabetes is not controlled properly.

Miglitol

Brand name(s): Glyset

Miglitol is used, alone or with other drugs, to treat type 2 diabetes, particularly in people whose diabetes cannot be controlled by diet alone. It slows the breakdown and absorption of table sugar and other complex sugars in the small intestine. This process results in decreased blood sugar levels (hypoglycemia) following meals.

Nateglinide Oral

Brand name(s): Starlix

Nateglinide is used alone or in combination with other medications to treat type 2 diabetes in people whose diabetes cannot be controlled by diet and exercise alone. Nateglinide belongs to a class of drugs called meglitinides. Nateglinide helps your body regulate the amount of glucose in your blood. It decreases the amount of glucose by stimulating the pancreas to release insulin.

NOTES FROM JOSLIN | Different types of diabetes pills work in different ways. Some people with type 2 diabetes take one, two, or even three types of pills. Some even take diabetes pills along with insulin, especially if the pancreas's ability to make insulin is reduced. Overall the goal is to either help your body use its own insulin more effectively or give it extra insulin if needed.

Pioglitazone

Brand name(s): Actos

Pioglitazone is used, alone or in combination with other medications, to treat type 2 diabetes in people whose diabetes cannot be controlled by diet and exercise alone. Pioglitazone is in a class of drugs called thiazolidinediones. It works by increasing the body's sensitivity to insulin.

Pramlintide Injection

Brand name(s): Symlin

Pramlintide is only used to treat people whose blood sugar couldn't be controlled by insulin or insulin and an oral medication for diabetes. Pramlintide is in a class of medications called antihyperglycemics. It slows the movement of food through the stomach, preventing blood sugar from rising too high after a meal, and may decrease appetite and cause weight loss.

Repaglinide

Brand name(s): Prandin

Repaglinide helps your body regulate the amount of glucose in your blood. It decreases the amount of glucose by stimulating the pancreas to release insulin.

Rosiglitazone

Brand name(s): Avandia, Avandaryl, Avandamet

Rosiglitazone is used along with a diet and exercise program and sometimes with other medications to treat type 2 diabetes. It is in the thiazolidinedione class of medications. It works by increasing the body's sensitivity to insulin.

Sitagliptin

Brand name(s): Januvia

Sitagliptin is used along with diet and exercise and sometimes other medications to lower blood sugar levels in patients with type 2 diabetes. It is in a class of medications called dipeptidyl peptidase-4 (DPP-4) inhibitors. It works by increasing the amounts of natural substances that lower blood sugar.

Tolazamide

Brand name(s): Tolinase

Doctors prescribe tolazamide for type 2 diabetes, particularly in people whose diabetes cannot be controlled by diet alone. The drug lowers blood sugar by stimulating the pancreas to secrete insulin and by helping the body use insulin efficiently.

Tolbutamide

Brand name(s): Orinase

Tolbutamide is generally used for people whose type 2 diabetes cannot be controlled by diet alone. This medication decreases blood sugar by stimulating the pancreas to secrete insulin and also by helping the body use insulin efficiently.

Generic

CONCERNS

Because people with diabetes often need to take multiple medications, many choose generics to save money. However, **these money-saving alternatives might not always be as effective as brand names**, according to an alarming new study. *Prevention*'s exclusive, must-read report by Joe Graedon, MS, and Teresa Graedon, PhD, will give you all the facts you need to protect your health.

Antidepressants have helped Holly Smith-West weather some very rough times. When she was diagnosed with hepatitis C, they kept her going during chemotherapy. Then they helped her cope with the death of her husband, who had type 1 diabetes and died on Christmas Eve, 2003, while awaiting a kidney transplant. With Wellbutrin, she says, "I found joy again." That is, until early last year, when Medicare required her to switch to Budeprion, a generic form of the drug.

"I slowly felt my depression start to return," says Smith-West, 54. "I would get up in the morning and think, I have a whole day ahead of me of things I can't deal with. I didn't want to die. I just didn't want to be alive the way I was."

Smith-West had no idea why her medication suddenly stopped relieving her symptoms. But one evening, she was talking to her sister, who took Wellbutrin to manage the symptoms of chronic fatigue syndrome. Her prescription, too, had been changed to Budeprion, and her CFS symptoms had started to return.

That night, Smith-West went online. With a few clicks, she found the People's Pharmacy Web site and read dozens of postings from others who'd had problems with a generic form of Wellbutrin. "They all sounded just like me!" she says. "I called my doctor and went back on Wellbutrin, and I started to feel better right away."

For years, insurance companies have been working hard to get people to switch to generics. Medicare, too, has been coaxing its clients toward these cheaper drugs. And those efforts are succeeding: Americans fill 1 billion prescriptions for generics yearly and count on them to work as well as brand-name medications. But at the People's Pharmacy, we've worried about generics for years now. At our Web site, we've heard from hundreds of people who've had difficulties with some of these substitutes. They've told us, for example, that their normally manageable blood pressure spiked when they switched to a generic drug, or that the pain of bone cancer was made bearable by a prescription painkiller, but it became excruciating when they had to rely on a generic. Or that

THE EXPERTS_____

Our authors, Joe and Teresa Graedon, are Prevention *advisors, drug-safety experts, and founders of the People's Pharmacy, which provides information on treatments for everyday conditions, from home remedies to prescription drugs. Joe, a pharmacologist, and Terry, a medical anthropologist, have cowritten a dozen books on the subject, and their nationally syndicated column is in its third decade. Their popular Web site has million of users. Every year, they answer thousands of questions from fans about using prescription drugs safely and effectively.*

Nine Ways to Take Generics Safely

If your doctor or pharmacy switches you to a generic, this checklist will help you stay safe and ensure that you're getting the correct dose.

1 Ask if your drug has a "narrow therapeutic index" (NTI). This means the dose needed for the medicine to work isn't much lower than the dose that can cause side effects. If your doctor says this is true of your drug, ask him to specify "do not substitute" or "dispense as written" on your prescription.

2 Track your progress. Keep careful records of your blood sugar checks. If you're on blood pressure meds, buy a home blood pressure monitor, take readings a couple of times a day for a while, and write them down. Also, keep results of lab tests. Bring these records to your doctor if you suspect that your drugs aren't doing their jobs.

3 Pay attention to how you feel. This is especially important if a medication is for a condition with no lab tests, such as depression.

4 "Challenge" your generic meds. If you suspect it isn't up to snuff, ask your doctor to put you on the brand-name drug for a month; then try the generic again. (Researchers call this a drug challenge.) The exercise might help convince your insurance company to charge you the generic co-pay for your brand-name drug.

5 Be prepared to appeal. If your insurance company has decreed that it will cover only the generic version of your medication, you might need your doctor to go to bat for you. This can be a drawn-out procedure, but it's often worth the effort.

6 Pay out of pocket, but shop around. Insurance company won't budge? If you decide to pony up for the brand, a discount pharmacy can save you money. ConsumerLab.com's sister site, PharmacyChecker.com, searches out the best prices from pharmacies that meet rigorous, posted standards.

7 Ask the pharmacist for the name of the manufacturer. Not all generics behave the same way, and if you keep track, you might find that you have better results with a drug from a particular manufacturer. However, because your drugstore can switch makers whenever it finds a better deal, you may have to call around to find the particular generic you want.

8 Switch versions. If a once-a-day formulation isn't working for you, a drug designed to be taken two or three times daily might be better.

9 Report problems to the FDA. The agency is supposed to investigate drugs with a pattern of problems reported to www.fda.gov/medwatch—though budget shortfalls mean that many reports go nowhere.

their depression returned with a vengeance when they were moved to a generic antidepressant, as Smith-West experienced for herself.

Reports like hers concerned us so much that in the summer of 2007 we approached ConsumerLab.com, an independent company that since its founding in 1999 has tested more than 2,000 products, such as

herbal supplements, vitamins, and functional foods. We asked for help: Would the firm compare long-acting Wellbutrin with generic versions of the drug? Tod Cooperman, MD, ConsumerLab.com's president, agreed.

Now the results are in, and a long-simmering worry has broken into open debate. The study shows that some generics performed respectably: Two generic versions of Wellbutrin (Global Pharmaceuticals' bupropion SR 200 and Watson Pharmaceuticals' bupropion SR 150) were roughly comparable to the brand. But a common Wellbutrin XL 300 substitute, Budeprion XL 300, behaved very differently in the test tube from the brand-name drug. And that suggests a problem we believe goes far beyond a single misbehaving antidepressant.

We want to be clear: We love the idea of generics. They're much more affordable than brand-name drugs—costing between 30 and 80 percent as much, on average—while the Food and Drug Administration (FDA) requires that they have the same active ingredient as the brand-name drug. And although other components, such as fillers, can differ from those in the drug they replace, FDA regulations are supposed to ensure that the generic is equally safe and effective. So even before 1984, when Congress made it easier to bring plain-wrap substitutes to market, we saw these drugs as a great advance.

These days, 63 percent of all US

WHERE IS THE SAFETY NET?

Why some bad generics might make it to market

When we began to investigate the safety and efficacy of generics, we were shocked to find that generic drugs get minimal monitoring. We quizzed FDA officials on their system in 2002. (When we recently asked for an update, we were told that the process hadn't changed, though the numbers vary from year to year.) That year, the FDA selected 50 or 60 different drugs—brand-name and generic—for a spot test. The agency got two or three batches of bottles for each of those drugs and sent them to a lab for analysis. That's not a typo: The agency tested 50 or 60 drugs. Yet in 2006 alone, people filled more than 3.3 billion brand-name and generic prescriptions.

The FDA is also supposed to send inspectors to each drug-manufacturing plant every 2 years. However, Nicholas Buhay, director of the division of manufacturing and product quality at the FDA, acknowledged that the agency doesn't have enough inspectors to meet that goal. Some companies are inspected only every 3 or 4 years. And the agency generally doesn't have authority to inspect overseas manufacturing facilities at all.

That's a major hole in the safety net, because 80 percent of the raw materials for prescription drugs now come from outside the United States, according to Congressman Bart Stupak, who chairs a committee on the safety of these imports. India and China supply almost half the imports. In other words, when it comes to what's on pharmacy shelves, drug companies are on the honor system. That's true even though generic manufacturers have a powerful incentive to cut costs, because price is their major selling point.

The recent study by ConsumerLab.com raises the question of whether the FDA's approval process ensures that generics truly act the same as their brand-name counterparts. To get a new brand-name drug approved, it's typically tested in hundreds or sometimes thousands of people. Development costs run into the hundreds of millions of dollars, and the company is rewarded with a period of patent protection: 20 years from the time the patent is submitted.

The generic manufacturer doesn't have to prove all over again that the drug works. In fact, drug testing is generally required only on 24 to 36 people for a brief period of time. As long as the pills contain the same active ingredient as the brand-name version, in roughly the same amount, and it gets into the bloodstream in a comparable manner, the meds are good to go.

prescriptions are for the no-frills versions. But our feelings have changed. The reason: Over the past 6 or 7 years, we've heard hundreds of complaints from people who've had bad experiences with generic drugs. And although we're in fairly frequent contact with FDA officials, their responses have left us more concerned, not less.

One of the first stories that caught our attention came from a mother who told us that Ritalin normally controlled her son's ADHD, but when she gave him a generic pill, his teachers—who were unaware of the drug switch—would complain about his behavior. (She noticed a difference, as well.) And pharmacists told us they'd been fielding similar complaints from parents.

Comments like these were scattershot—a dozen or so complaints about the generic version of the antidepressant Zoloft, a half dozen from people whose heartburn started acting up after they switched from Prilosec to its generic counterpart, omeprazole. But early last year, we began getting a lot of questions and complaints about a new generic drug: Budeprion XL 300, distributed by Teva Pharmaceutical Industries. It's used in place of GlaxoSmithKline's Wellbutrin XL 300. (XL indicates that these are extended-release formulations. This means that you take just one pill a day, whereas other forms of Wellbutrin and its generics require two or even three pills a day.) We've received more than 250 letters, e-mails, and postings to our Web site about this pill, and they share a shocking similarity. The writers were all doing fine on Wellbutrin XL 300. But when they switched to Budeprion XL 300, many felt like they had fallen off a cliff.

The people experienced the classic symptoms of depression. Some even said they felt suicidal. Others reported common antidepressant side effects, including anxiety, irritability, nausea, headaches, dizziness, and trouble sleeping.

On March 20, 2007, we contacted the FDA with our concerns. Both Robert J. Temple, MD, director of the Office of Medical Policy at the Center for Drug Evaluation and Research, and Gary J. Buehler, RPh, director of the Office of Generic Drugs, told us that the agency

would look into it. But the FDA moves slowly, and we were anxious to get to the bottom of this, so we teamed up with ConsumerLab.com to take a close look at Wellbutrin XL 300 and its equivalent, Budeprion XL 300, as well as two generics for sustained-release Wellbutrin. ConsumerLab.com bought samples of each drug to test, using two labs to double-check the results.

Budeprion XL 300 contained the right amount of the active ingredient, bupropion, but it released it at a substantially different rate than the brand-name drug did. In the laboratories' test tubes, Wellbutrin XL 300 released the chemical slowly for the first few hours, while Budeprion XL 300 released the drug far more quickly. In fact, within the first 2 hours, Budeprion delivered more than four times as much drug as Wellbutrin—34 percent of Budeprion's active ingredient, compared with just 8 percent of Wellbutrin's. Within 4 hours, the generic pill had released about half of the crucial chemical, while the brand name had given up only one-quarter.

Granted, the pills were in a test tube, not a person. But the findings suggest that people on generic Budeprion XL 300 get hit fast with a big dose of the antidepressant—perhaps enough to raise the risk of known side effects such as nausea and anxiety. Even more important, the results raise the possibility that hours later, there may be too little of the drug in the bloodstream to prevent depression from returning. That pattern, of course, is exactly what our readers have described to us.

Teva Pharmaceuticals, the company behind Budeprion XL 300, says it followed the government's testing guidelines. "All of our products meet the FDA's regulations governing the review and approval of generic pharmaceuticals," said Denise Bradley, director of communications and community relations, in an e-mail. Bradley also said that ConsumerLab.com's testing methodology isn't "currently approved by the FDA for comparisons of generic products and is, therefore, inappropriate."

However, says ConsumerLab.com's Dr. Cooperman, ConsumerLab.com used the method the FDA required when GlaxoSmithKline tested the original Wellbutrin XL 300—and that the FDA required when Budeprion XL 300 was approved, according to publicly available documents.

"The results for the two products were shockingly different," Dr. Cooperman says. "And if the drug is releasing so much faster in the dissolution test, it's hard to imagine that it wouldn't be doing the same in the gut. The test is designed to simulate the gut."

It's impossible for us to know what's responsible for the way Budeprion dissolves. But experts say it can be tricky for a drug manufacturer to get a pill to release its active ingredient at the right time and at the right speed—especially for extended-release formulations. In Wellbutrin XL 300, the drug is released gradually through a membrane over the course of the day. This design is still under patent, however, and it wasn't used in Budeprion XL 300. Instead, that drug depends on something called a matrix technology, which means that the active ingredient is released as the pill gradually disintegrates. Some researchers worry that this kind of system is inherently less predictable. Food might affect the way the pill behaves in the stomach, and in some cases, this could lead to "dose dumping"— too much active ingredient getting into the bloodstream too fast.

The ConsumerLab.com results are worrisome, says Ray Woosley, MD, PhD. Woosley, once a candidate for the position of FDA commissioner, who is president and chairman of the board of the non-profit Critical Path Institute, which partners with the FDA and the pharmaceutical industry to speed development of safe drugs. "That's a huge difference for a drug like this, and could make switching from one formulation to the other a problem," he says. "It could well explain the adverse events people have described."

Meanwhile, the FDA is paying attention, though progress is still hard to discern. Whereas Buehler's earlier e-mails told us, "We are investigating," his message on November 8, 2007, said, "This is a high priority for [the] FDA, and we are working diligently on it."

For the full ConsumerLab.com report (available by subscription), go to www. consumerlab.com.

CHANGE
That Sticks

When you've been diagnosed with diabetes, it's likely your **doctors are going to urge you to make big changes in your diet, your activity level, and your life.** Here's the new thinking on resolutions—and the science that guarantees you'll stick with every last one.

This is the moment you've been looking forward to: You've been diagnosed with diabetes, and you're committed to gaining back control of your health, jumping headfirst into a vigorous campaign to eat less, exercise more, and practice the de-stressing techniques that will make you happier, healthier, and more productive than ever. This time you really will change. You've never been more motivated and committed. Ready? On your mark, get set . . . Stop!

Sorry, but there's a good chance you're getting ahead of yourself, according to a revolutionary new theory of change. Only about 20 percent of people who need to ditch bad habits for good ones are actually ready to do so, says psychologist James Prochaska, PhD, coauthor of *Changing for Good*. Before you take your inaugural predawn power walk or mix your first high-protein shake, you must progress through three essential preparatory stages, he says. If you do, you have an excellent chance of making those new habits stick.

Dr. Prochaska, director of the Cancer Prevention Research Center at the University of Rhode Island, has identified five key stages of change. In the first, you admit to having a vague sense that you need to alter your behavior; in the second, you intend to do so, but not right now. By the third stage, you're arranging all the details that will kick off the fourth, or action, stage. In the fifth, you maintain your new routines until they blend seamlessly into your lifestyle.

The first three stages require the most mental prep. Here's how to ID where you are in the process—and take steps necessary to make your goal a lifelong reality.

Step 1: Precontemplation

You're here if: You have the nagging feeling that you really do need to, say, start exercising and eating better. But where should you start?

What you might be thinking: My friends disapprove of my bad habits, but I just can't stop. I know I should, but I just don't know how.

HOW TO MOVE TO STEP 2

Tune in to your excuses. When a friend invites you to a yoga class, how do you respond? Do you decline the invite, blaming a busy schedule? Your bad back? Facing your excuses is the first step toward overcoming them.

Tally the benefits of change. If you lost weight, you'd be able to better manage your diabetes and lower your risk of heart disease and hypertension. You'd also boost your energy, feel more attractive, and fit easily into your clothes. And the upside of maintaining the status quo . . . ? Case closed.

Ask for help. Let your friends know you're struggling with your decision and that pushing you is exactly what you

don't need. What is helpful: gently pointing out your delaying tactics.

Step 2: Contemplation

You're here if: You know you have to modify your behavior but don't know how, and you're still afraid of failing.

What you might be thinking: Okay, so now it's time for me to act. No. No. I'm serious. I'm going to change . . . right after my birthday.

Educate yourself. Read articles and books about the new habit you want to cultivate. For instance, doing cardio burns calories, and it helps stave off memory loss. Also, get a reality check from your doctor: Unlike your spouse, who may not mind the 30 pounds you've gained, your doc should tell you bluntly about how excess weight may be harming your health.

Work through ambivalence. When you fall back on a familiar excuse, you should ask yourself, Is this true? Do you really have no time to work out when in fact you watch reruns of *Law and Order* twice a week? Connect your interest in changing with something you value. For example, if dropping 20 pounds means you have more energy to join your spouse and kids on their yearly ski trips.

Dip your toe in the water. Want to start a walking program—some day? Do a test

The average number of years you add to your life if you eat lots of fruits and vegetables, don't smoke, exercise regularly, and drink in moderation, compared with people who don't follow such habits:

14

run now by going for a short brisk walk to see how it feels. "It's like warming up your engine," Dr. Prochaska says. "By taking those small steps, you'll be motivated to launch your plan."

Step 3: Preparation

You're here if: You're ready to undertake the hard work required to, for example, lose weight, shape up, or manage stress better, and you're taking small steps to commit to the effort for at least 6 months.

What you might be thinking: I did it! I bought the treadmill and picked the diet plan. My husband will walk the dog every morning so I can exercise. No more excuses. Tomorrow is the day!

MOVE TO THE STARTING LINE

Make room for your goal. You may need to reorganize your kids' schedules or delegate certain household responsibilities. Then pencil in cooking, exercise, or meditating on your daily calendar just as you would a meeting, says Maryann Troiani, PsyD, a psychologist in Barrington, Illinois, and coauthor of *Spontaneous Optimism.*

Map out a plan. If you're going to upgrade your diet, should you see a nutritionist? Stock up on certain foods? "If you can't write down your plan or explain it to a 10-year-old, you're not ready," says John C. Norcross, PhD, a professor of psychology at the University of Scranton and coauthor of *Changing for Good.* Anticipate potential obstacles. For example, if a work deadline will interfere with your exercise schedule, map out a short lunchtime walk.

Take your plan public. Set a start date and clue in family and close friends. "Once you say it out loud, it becomes a commitment that other people know about, which creates pressure on you to follow through," Dr. Norcross says.

Now that you've laid the necessary groundwork, you surely will. So, are you ready? Get set . . .

Now go!

NOTES FROM JOSLIN | Keeping track of the dates and results of important diabetes tests, such as your A1C, cholesterol, and blood pressure, can help you remember when you need your next test—and help you and your provider know if and when to make changes to your diabetes treatment plan. Write the information down and keep it somewhere handy, such as in your wallet or on your refrigerator so that you can chart your progress.

Medical Breakthroughs		**46**
CHAPTER 6:	Foods That Fight Diabetes	**56**
CHAPTER 7:	The Box That Battles Diabetes	**65**
CHAPTER 8:	Healthy Veggies with Bad Reps	**69**
CHAPTER 9:	Nature's Perfect Food	**75**

EAT

What you eat can dramatically offset

PART **2**

RIGHT

your diabetes—for better or for worse.

NUTRITION
Medical Breakthroughs

Even though people with diabetes have the same basic nutrition needs as everyone else, what you eat is critical for managing your diabetes. Carefully considering and monitoring what you eat can help you manage your diabetes and avoid complications. **Here's the latest diabetes nutrition news.**

■ STEEP YOURSELF IN BETTER HEALTH

The health benefits of tea keep mounting: New studies suggest that the soothing beverage may help stabilize blood sugar levels and even protect against osteoporosis, in addition to its well-touted cardiovascular benefits.

There are countless varieties (experts say tea is the most commonly consumed beverage in the world after water), and some are better for you than others. Here's the latest on what to sip and what to skip.

Rooibos: Made from the South African red bush plant, with a sweet, nutty flavor, this tea is rich in several rare polyphenols that have potent antioxidant and cancer-fighting power, according to a report from nutrition researchers at Tufts University.

White tea: Made by lightly processing the same tea leaves used to make black and green tea, white tea retains a high concentration of catechins, which are the powerful antioxidants found in fresh leaves. It has a mild, pleasant taste. Also research suggests that white tea has strong antibacterial and antiviral properties.

Chai: Traditionally, this black tea is blended with spices such as digestion-promoting cardamom and served sweetened and lightened with milk. However some cafés prepare it from a powdered mix or concentrate, which can be loaded with sugar as well as creamers that are filled with saturated or trans fat. Instead, look for freshly brewed chai and add your own milk and sweetener. (We use a splash of soy milk and 1 teaspoon of honey.)

Pu-erh: Though it's reported to be popular among celebrities as a way to shed pounds, there is no evidence that this postfermented tea works as a weight-loss aid.

It does, however, contain high levels of caffeine. Large amounts of caffeine from any source can cause serious side effects, ranging from headaches to abnormal heart rhythms. To make matters worse, caffeine can raise your blood sugar levels, as you'll read in "Steer Clear of Caffeine" at right.

Kombucha: Traditionally home brewed by fermenting yeast and bacteria in sweetened black tea, this hot health-food store pick (devotees say it's a cure-all) can bring on side effects from nausea to lead poisoning. The drink can become contaminated with microorganisms, making it especially dangerous (and potentially fatal) for people with compromised immune systems.

Once you've selected your tea, here's an easy way to multiply it's disease-fighting benefits: Simply add a splash of citrus juice. A new study published in the journal *Molecular Nutrition and Food Research* found that adding 2 to 3 tablespoons of citrus juice (orange, grapefruit, lemon, or lime) to 1 cup of green tea improves the stability of catechins (antioxidants that help prevent cancer, stroke, and heart disease), increasing the amount that is available for digestion by as much as five times. Most teas are high in these compounds, but because they're unstable in nonacidic environments like your intestines, less than 20 percent is typically absorbed.

Mario Ferruzzi, PhD, lead researcher and assistant professor of food science at Purdue University, suggests steeping one tea bag in 1 cup of boiling water for 3 to 5 minutes before you add the juice to ensure high antioxidant levels.

■ STEER CLEAR OF CAFFEINE

Cutting back on caffeinated coffee (or tea) may help people with diabetes control blood sugar, which of course is your top stay-healthy strategy.

Duke University Medical Center researchers tracked the ebbs and flows in blood sugar levels in 10 coffee drinkers with type 2 diabetes for 72 hours. On days when the subjects consumed 4 cups' worth of caffeine, blood sugar levels increased by 8 percent. Though other studies have shown coffee consumption to prevent diabetes, researchers say the effect might be different in people who already have the condition.

"If you're a coffee or tea drinker with type 2 diabetes, it makes sense to quit," says study author James Lane, PhD.

To avoid withdrawal headaches, taper

The number, in thousands, of cancer deaths in 2007 linked to low vitamin D levels, according to William B. Grant, PhD, Sunlight, Nutrition and Health Research Center:

257

off over a few weeks. Transition gradually by drinking a "half-caf" blend. Brands include Green Mountain Coffee Roasters and Eight O'Clock Coffee.

■ BECOME A DEVOTEE OF D

The "D" in vitamin D doesn't stand for "deficiency," but it might as well. Current guidelines call for 200 to 600 IU daily. However, many researchers now believe that we may need up to 1,000 IU or more—from D-rich foods such as fish and low-fat fortified dairy products, 10 to 15 minutes of direct sunlight daily, and supplements. New studies show that stocking up on the "sunshine vitamin" may improve your health in a variety of ways. Here's why getting more D in your diet is such a bright idea.

Getting Enough D Can...

Deter diabetes. In one study of more than 83,000 women, those with the highest intakes of calcium and vitamin D had the lowest risk of developing type 2 diabetes.

Relieve backaches. In a group of 360 people with chronic back pain, symptoms were improved in 95 percent of those who took a high dose of vitamin D daily for 3 months.

Ward off cancer. Higher levels of vitamin D may cut in half your risk of getting breast, colon, or rectal cancer; consuming 300 IU or more daily helped reduce pancreatic cancer risk up to 44 percent, as compared with those who consumed less than 150 IU daily.

Being D-Deficient Can...

Damage your heart. Inadequate amounts of vitamin D may increase the risk of peripheral artery disease by a huge 80 percent.

Weaken bones. Eighty-five percent of women hospitalized for osteoporotic hip fractures have a vitamin D deficiency, according to Brigham and Women's Hospital in Boston.

Increase the blues. Blood levels of D were 14 percent lower in depressed individuals, a recent study discovered.

Shorten your life. Among 13,331 adults, a deficiency boosted premature death risk by 26 percent.

▪ GIVE MACADAMIAS A SHOT

This tropical nut is surprisingly smart for your heart! Macadamia nuts might have a bad rap because of their high calorie count, but a moderate serving can help keep your arteries clear. A new study found that adding $1\frac{1}{2}$ ounces (the size of a shot glass, about 305 calories' worth) of macadamia nuts daily to a typical diet lowered total cholesterol and "bad" LDL by about 9 percent each after 5 weeks. And the results weren't due to weight loss; the subjects weighed the same over the course of the study.

You could enjoy the nuts plain or crush them and dust salads, vegetables, and yogurt.

▪ HAVE YOUR FRIES AND STAY SLIM, TOO

Even guilty pleasures can be healthful with the right cooking method. Case in point: Half of all US moms think that french fries can be part of a well-balanced diet, according to a recent Gallup poll.

We agree—depending on the choices you make. Potatoes eaten with the skin are packed with vitamin C and are one of the best sources of potassium and fiber. Plus potatoes can be a part of a diabetes-

The percentage of french fries consumed away from home:

88

healthy diet. (See "Healthy Veggies with Bad Reps" on page 69.) Chefs around the country are experimenting with healthier prep methods that use better-for-you oils or even skip the deep fryer altogether.

Here's how to get your french fry fix, without the whopping fat and calorie counts—not to mention the drive-thru.

Buy them frozen. Some companies make frozen fries with gourmet ingredients and good-for-you fats. Look for those with no more than 120 calories and 3.5 grams of fat per 3-ounce serving. We like Alexia Olive Oil & Sea Salt Oven Fries, Ian's Sweet Potato Fries, and Cascadian Farm Organic Wedge Cut Oven Fries.

Get 'em to go. Some fast-food chains now offer baked "air fries." One 3-ounce serving has about 180 calories, 6 grams of fat, and 1 gram of saturated fat. Find them at Topz (California, Michigan, Texas), KnowFat! (Massachusetts, Minnesota), and EVOS (Florida, Nevada).

Make your own. You can cook an antioxidant indulgence from scratch with our recipe for Rainbow Fries. You'll need the following:

5 blue (or purple) potatoes (about $^3/_4$ pound)

1 medium sweet potato (about $^1/_2$ pound)

3 teaspoons olive oil

Salt

Pepper

First, preheat the oven to 425°F. Cut the blue potatoes lengthwise into $^1/_2$-inch wedges and then soak them in cold water for 45 minutes. In the meantime, cut the sweet potato into $^1/_2$-inch wedges.

Next, drain the water from the blue potatoes, dry them, and place them in a medium-size bowl. Add the sweet potatoes, olive oil, and salt and pepper to taste. Toss to mix.

Lay the the potato wedges on a baking sheet and bake for 40 minutes, turning once, until they're browned.

Makes 4 servings; per serving: 114 calories, 3 grams protein, 18 grams carbohydrate, 3.5 grams fat, 0.5 gram saturated fat, 0 milligrams cholesterol, 4 grams fiber, 25 milligrams sodium.

■ DON'T GET A POP BELLY

Do you drink diet soda to keep off the pounds? Try another tactic. Soda may increase your risk of metabolic syndrome, which is a group of symptoms that includes high levels of belly fat, blood sugar, and cholesterol. People who consumed one diet soda daily had a 34 percent higher risk of the syndrome than those who abstained, according to a new University of Minnesota study of nearly 10,000 adults ages 45 to 64.

Although more research is needed to determine whether the diet drinkers' high rates of metabolic syndrome are the result of the soda or a shared behavior (such as overeating), it can't hurt to cut down on diet drinks. To satisfy a sweet tooth for just a few calories, mix fresh-cut fruit (such as berries or citrus) with seltzer water.

▪ PICK MORE PRODUCE

It's a common misconception that people with diabetes can't eat sweet produce such as oranges and carrots. Don't be misled.

Not all sugars are created equal. The two main classes are naturally occurring (from Mother Nature) and added (by food companies). Don't limit the former. For example, although an orange can contain 12 grams of sugar, it also provides vitamins, minerals, and antioxidants. Plus, natural sugar doesn't raise diabetes risk in the same way added sugar does. No health organization recommends limiting natural sugar, so keep filling your cart with colorful produce.

Added sugars, on the other hand, shouldn't exceed 10 percent of your total calories, according to the World Health Organization. That's approximately 40 to 45 grams per day.

The only way to tell if a food contains added sugar is to scan the ingredients list. But sugar isn't always listed as simply "sugar." Be on the lookout also for the following: brown sugar, corn sweetener, corn syrup, dextrose, glucose, high fructose corn syrup, invert sugar, malt syrup, molasses, and sucrose.

▪ DRINK (JUST A LITTLE) TO YOUR HEALTH

Here's the straight-up truth: Drinking some alcohol every day can be good for heart health, but we know even just an extra couple of nips can raise the risk of diabetes, heart disease, and stroke. So how much is just right? Exactly one drink per day for women and two per day for men, say University of Missouri cardiologists. One drink means 13 to 15 grams of alcohol—a 12-ounce bottle of beer, a 5-ounce glass of wine (five glasses to a 750-milliliter bottle), or a shot glass ($1\frac{1}{2}$ ounces) of 80-proof liquor.

▪ SATISFY YOUR SWEET TOOTH

Eating fattening foods that are low in nutrients, such as candy, might damage your heart as much as your waistline. When Boston University researchers tracked the diets of nearly 1,300 heart disease–free women, they found that those who ate lots of empty calories had a significant increase in the thickness of their

Number of grams of heart-healthy fiber in a shot glass' worth of macadamia nuts:

$3\frac{1}{2}$

carotid artery walls, which is a predictor of cardiovascular disease, compared with women who favored nutrient-rich foods. Satisfy your sweet tooth and protect your ticker with the following tasty substitutes.

Empty-calorie snack: Bag of fruity gummy candy

Instead try: $1/2$ cup unsweetened mixed dried fruit, such as apples, nectarines, and figs

Empty-calorie snack: Slice of apple pie

Instead try: One diced apple tossed with 2 teaspoons brown sugar and apple pie spices, microwaved and topped with toasted oats

Empty-calorie snack: Chocolate candy bar

Instead try: Two medium strawberries dipped in dark chocolate

Empty-calorie snack: Cinnamon roll

Instead try: One packet of instant plain oatmeal prepared and topped with 1 tablespoon pecans, 1 teaspoon cinnamon, and 1 teaspoon maple syrup

■ SAVE YOUR SIGHT

Preventing poor eyesight as you get older may be as simple as cutting more refined carbohydrates out of your diet. Among 3,977 women and men age 55 and older, those who ate above-average amounts of white bread, white rice, and other foods with a high glycemic index were 17 percent more likely to develop age-related macular degeneration, reports scientists at the USDA Human Nutrition Research Center on Aging at Tufts University.

To protect your eyes, cut back on soda and sugary sweets, advise the study authors, and stick to whole wheat versions of pasta, bread, and rice.

EATING RIGHT WITH DIABETES— IT'S ALL ABOUT CHOICES

Managing your diabetes is really about making choices, and choosing what foods you will eat is one of the most important choices you'll need to make. Ask anyone you know who has diabetes, and they'll be more than happy to give you advice on what to eat. But chances are, everyone's advice will be a little bit different. Why? Isn't there a special diet that everyone with diabetes needs to follow? Fortunately, the answer is "no." Gone are the days of the restrictive, so-called diabetic diets. Instead, the "diet" that's right for you is one that is based on the way you usually eat, your food preferences, your schedule, and many other factors.

More good news: People with diabetes don't need to eat special foods. What is helpful, however, is to use a meal plan to help guide your food choices and portions. A meal plan is an individualized tool that's based on the way you usually eat. Its main purpose is to help you keep your blood glucose within your target range while at the same time allowing you to enjoy your favorite foods and special treats. If you don't have a meal plan, ask your healthcare provider for a referral to a registered dietitian. He or she will work with you to develop a meal plan that's right for you.

In the meantime, here are a few things you can do to get started with healthy eating before you see a dietitian.

- Eat meals at regular times each day and don't skip meals, especially if you take mealtime insulin or certain diabetes pills that can cause low blood glucose (hypoglycemia).
- Eat about the same amount of carbohydrate foods each day. Carbohydrate, or carb, is found in bread, pasta, and cereal (starchy foods); fruits and vegetables; legumes and beans; milk and yogurt; and sweets and desserts. A good way to get started with "carb counting" is to aim for 3 or 4 carb choices per meal if you're a woman, and 4 or 5 carb choices per meal if you're a man. One carb choice contains 15 grams of carbohydrate. If you eat snacks, aim for 15 to 30 grams of carb per snack.
- Eat a variety of foods, including
  - Fresh fruits and vegetables
  - Whole grain breads, cereals, rice, pasta, legumes, and beans

- Low-fat milk and yogurt
- Lean cuts of meat, poultry, and fish
- Heart-healthy oils and fats

▢ Cut back on foods high in saturated and trans fat; choose healthier fats and oils instead, such as olive oil and canola oil and include at least two fish meals (not fried fish sticks!) in your menu every week for healthy omega-3 fatty acids.

▢ Write down what you eat and drink for a few days before you see the dietitian. See if you can relate your food choices or portions to your blood glucose levels.

CHAPTER
6

Foods That Fight

DIABETES

What you eat dramatically affects how you feel.
Here you'll discover how three women turned the tide on
their diabetes, lowered their blood pressure, or slashed
their cholesterol, all with simple yet powerful changes to
their diets—and all in just a few weeks.

I t's such an amazing claim that it's hard to believe: You can beat some of the most dangerous medical conditions around simply by eating right and exercising. But this promise isn't snake oil or even an exaggeration: It's scientific fact. Studies done at leading research centers show that food can do what drugs often can't: Restore your health and vitality.

The following determined women triumphed over ailments that plague millions of Americans: diabetes, high blood pressure, and high cholesterol. Instead of giving in to a lifetime of prescription drugs, they took control of their health by adopting diets that have been proven to fight disease. The eating plans (plus moderate exercise for two of the regimens) demanded commitment. But the results were so fast and dramatic, they inspired the women to stick with the changes. Each woman discovered, to her astonishment, that her new routine quickly stopped feeling like work and became a way of life. Today they are all healthier and fitter and are feeling great.

You can eat your way to better health. These stories show you how.

The Problem: Diabetes

The food cure: The Pritikin Diet can reverse type 2 diabetes in 3 weeks.

Seven years ago, Andrea Coogle, now 45, developed gestational diabetes while pregnant. Her blood sugar returned to normal after she gave birth, but it shot up again a few months later, and the Tampa audiologist was diagnosed with type 2 diabetes. Coogle went on the diabetes medication metformin (Glucophage). But she felt drained and depressed, and she steadily gained weight.

In 2004, Coogle's brother visited from New York. Stunned by how she'd changed, he insisted on treating her to a week at the Pritikin Longevity Center & Spa in Aventura, Florida. She went reluctantly and sobbed when she arrived, ashamed of a life she felt had spun out of control.

"I kept thinking: What am I doing here?" she recalls. "I didn't realize that it would be the turning point of my life."

Coogle had always eaten whatever was convenient: muffins, fast food, hot dogs. At the Pritikin center, she was fed a super-low-fat, near-vegetarian diet. For 2 days her stomach ached. She dragged herself to the gym and hated every minute.

But on day 3, the pangs stopped, and Coogle began to enjoy the treadmill and elliptical trainer. And as her tastebuds adjusted, the meals seemed more appetizing. On the fourth day, she learned that her weight had dropped, and her blood sugar had, too. That moment made her a

3 RULES TO GET STARTED

EAT PLENTY OF FRUITS AND VEGETABLES—in fact, go wild with them. But limit juice to 1 cup daily; it doesn't fill you up as much, so you'll consume more—and take in too many calories.

CHOOSE FISH OVER POULTRY OR MEAT. Stick to one small serving daily—about the size of your palm and the thickness of a deck of cards. Otherwise, go for beans and other veggie protein sources.

GET PLENTY OF EXERCISE. An hour a day is optimal for preventing or reversing insulin resistance. The workout doesn't have to be strenuous. Brisk walking is fine.

convert. By the week's end, Coogle had lost 10 pounds, and her blood sugar had fallen by 7 percent.

"I was amazed," she says.

The Pritikin diet is spartan. It offers a lot of choices, but all are very low in fat. Nevertheless, Coogle says that it's not hard to stick with it. She keeps her kitchen stocked with organic produce and whole grains, and she cooks from scratch four or five times a week, instead of grabbing takeout. (She adds small amounts of meat and salt for her family.) Coogle knew she needed support, so she joined Weight Watchers and a gym, and she works out three times a week.

Coogle's fasting glucose levels have fallen from about 180 mg/dl to about 112 (from diabetic to prediabetic range), and she's dropped 55 pounds. She's thrilled about her weight loss and the fact that she's halved her diabetes meds. Coogle's goals are to lose a few more pounds and get off diabetes medication entirely.

"I weigh myself every day," she says. "I'm constantly monitoring my blood sugars. I got it in my mind that this isn't a diet—it's forever. And with that mindset, I've won the battle."

HOW THE DIET WORKS

The Pritikin program is even stricter than the healthy eating plans recommended by leading medical organizations: It emphasizes many of the same foods, such as fresh produce and whole grains, but it permits only tiny amounts of animal protein (preferably fish or shellfish). Dairy must be fat free, and little added sugar, salt, or caffeine is allowed.

The public has always associated the Pritikin diet with cardiovascular health, partly because inventor Nathan Pritikin created the program 30 years ago to reverse his own heart disease. But studies have long shown that the Pritikin regimen of diet and exercise also lowers blood sugar in type 2 diabetics, in most cases so much that they no longer need medication. The results come fast, even without major weight loss, says Christian Roberts, PhD, an adjunct assistant professor of physiological science at UCLA. In 2006, Dr. Roberts studied blood samples from 13 men with diabetes on the Pritikin regimen and found that in just 3 weeks their blood sugar dropped almost 20 percent, on average. Six of the men were no longer classified as diabetic when they left the spa.

"Type 2 diabetes is basically an excess-calorie disease," says James J. Kenney, PhD, RD, nutrition research specialist at the Pritikin center. "If calories and weight go down, insulin resistance goes way down, too. That's why diet and exercise are so effective."

Try it! A taste of Pritikin: Begin your day with oatmeal sprinkled with cinnamon and chopped raw apple.

Follow the plan: To find recipes and menu plans, go to www.prevention.com/foodcure.

The Problem: High Cholesterol

The food cure: The Portfolio Diet lowers bad cholesterol as effectively as drugs.

Rosalba Erdelyi, 61, watched her mother struggle for decades with high cholesterol, high blood pressure, and

NOTES FROM JOSLIN | An important way to help you make changes that stick is to set SMART goals: These are goals that are specific, measurable, attainable, realistic, and timely. If your goals aren't SMART, chances are they're not the right goals for you!

other medical problems. As Rosalba's mom's kidneys and liver began to fail, her mother blamed her many meds, not underlying disease. "I remember her telling me: 'Avoid taking medication if you can,'" Erdelyi says.

When Erdelyi was 45, her own cholesterol began creeping up, and her doctor suggested she go on a statin drug. She said she'd cut her cholesterol with diet and exercise instead. "He told me, 'You won't be able to do it on your own.' I decided to prove I could."

She tried oat bran and cut way back on red meat. But her cholesterol kept rising. So, in 2005, she volunteered for a study of the Portfolio Diet, developed by David Jenkins, MD, PhD, DSc, a nutritional sciences researcher at the nearby University of Toronto.

Dr. Jenkins is known as the father of the glycemic index, which ranks foods by their effect on blood sugar levels. But one day, as news mounted about the cholesterol-cutting power of different foods, his wife, a dietitian, posed a question: Why not roll all the good stuff into one meal plan? Dr. Jenkins decided to try it.

The vegan Portfolio Diet is a radical departure from a typical Western diet. It relies on four categories of foods known to help prevent heart disease: soy, nuts, plant sterols, and foods high in "viscous," or sticky, fiber. No meat, fish, or dairy is allowed. The only permissible sweet is a dollop of fruit jam.

The Portfolio Diet produces striking

THREE RULES TO GET STARTED

HAVE AN OUNCE OF ALMONDS OR OTHER NUTS (about a handful) as a daily snack.

DITCH OR AT LEAST REDUCE MEAT, POULTRY, AND FISH. Dr. Jenkins found that the less animal protein people ate, the more their cholesterol dropped. Try a tofu stir-fry instead.

SWITCH TO SOY MILK. Many "beginners" prefer the taste of flavored soy milk.

results fast, working about as well as statins for people with moderately high cholesterol. A 2003 study of 46 adults found the diet slashed LDL 28.6 percent in just 4 weeks.

For Erdelyi, the plan took some adjustment—mostly because of the foods she had to add. The large amounts of fiber made her gassy at first. But following the plan has become second nature. "If I eat something like a steak, I don't even enjoy it anymore," she says. Besides, her results keep her going. Her total cholesterol sank 21 percent, from 260 mg/dl to 205 mg/dl, which was enough to keep her off medication.

"I have a lot of energy," she says. "I don't have side effects of medication. And I've accomplished something I set out to do."

HOW THE DIET WORKS

Portfolio is the most demanding of the three diet plans discussed here. It excludes dairy, meat, poultry, fish, and eggs. Instead, it's heavy on soybeans, soy milk, and tofu, which are all thought to reduce cholesterol production. Plant sterols, which are found in fortified orange juice and margarine, block cholesterol absorption. And eggplant, oatmeal, and other foods high in viscous fiber prompt the liver to pull cholesterol out of the blood.

Portfolio isn't everyone's cup of tea. Only about one-third of people in a 2006 study followed it completely after a year. But people who stuck to the program only 60 percent of the time got good results.

"If you're on the cusp of statin therapy, you might want to try the diet first," Dr. Jenkins says. "You can tell within 2 weeks if it works for you."

Try it! A taste of Portfolio: Blend together 1 cup of vanilla or chocolate soy milk with $1/4$ cup of soy isolate powder.

Follow the plan: To find recipes and menu plans, go to www.prevention.com/foodcure.

The Problem: High Blood Pressure

The food cure: Dietary Approaches to Stop Hypertension (DASH) is as effective as medication for many patients, but without the side effects.

Judy Hecker, 52, always struggled with her weight, but after back surgery and a hysterectomy in the mid-1990s laid her up for more than a year, the pounds piled

3 RULES TO GET STARTED

INSTEAD OF TOSSING A CUP OF ROMAINE LETTUCE INTO A SALAD, USE 2 CUPS or switch to spinach, which is higher in potassium and calcium. Just don't increase the salad dressing.

IF YOU LIVE ON TAKEOUT AND PACKAGED FOODS, make a commitment to cook at least one meal a week. That's the only sure way to control fat, salt, and sugar. Salmon delivers potassium; pair it with magnesium-heavy potatoes and artichokes.

USE CANOLA OR OLIVE OIL IN COOKING—but sparingly, to keep fat levels low. Replace butter with yogurt, fresh herbs, or unsalted spice blends instead.

on. Depressed and constantly fatigued, she needed two medications for her very high blood pressure, along with beta-blockers for her heart.

Hecker and her husband used to take their boat to catch crabs in a bay not far from their home outside Portland, Oregon, but by 2002, she couldn't enjoy it anymore. "I got to the point where I couldn't even climb into the boat," she recalls. That's when she had a mild heart attack. Now she had to slim down and get healthy. So when she heard that Kaiser Permanente researchers were launching a weight loss study using the DASH diet, she signed up. "At first I was skeptical," she admits. But after just 4 weeks, the pounds had started to come off, and her blood pressure was dropping. "When I saw it was working, it gave me hope that I could heal my body."

Hecker initially found it tough to give up a few favorite treats, such as Doritos and ice cream. But the diet, which is high in fruits, vegetables, nuts, and low-fat dairy products, fit right into her life. "It was easy to eat all the fruits and vegetables," she says. "And once you start eating them, you really crave them."

The exercise required by the study was more of a challenge. Hecker and the other volunteers began with 30 minutes of walking two or three times a week, but she quickly realized that the more she worked out, the faster she lost weight. Now she strength-trains twice a week and works out on a treadmill for 30 to 45

minutes three times week. She also goes for frequent walks in the steep hills near her home, and she and her husband have taken up golfing and hiking.

"I feel great," she says. "It's really a whole new life."

Hecker's dream to get off blood pressure medication became reality in only 3 months, after she'd lost just 10 pounds. Her blood pressure now measures 104/59 mmHg, from a high of 210/186 mmHg. A 15 percent blockage in her artery has cleared. And Hecker's weight is down nearly 50 pounds.

Although the study is over, Hecker is sticking with the DASH plan.

"If I keep losing, I'll be able to go out on the boat with my husband and get up on the rocks," she says. "That's my new goal—to climb that jetty again."

HOW THE DIET WORKS

The DASH diet focuses on old-fashioned, wholesome fare: more fruits, vegetables, whole grains, and low-fat dairy products than what's found in the typical American diet—and less red meat, sweets, added sugar, and sugary drinks. DASH is rich in protein and fiber, as well as potassium, magnesium, and calcium, which are all minerals known to help control blood pressure.

Scientists developed DASH on a hunch. Studies had shown that magnesium, potassium, and calcium helped regulate blood pressure, but supplements never seemed to work as well. So researchers at a number of major institutions created and tested a diet loaded with foods that contain those minerals.

It's likely that DASH's nutrients help blood vessels relax. Studies show that the diet lowers blood pressure dramatically and fast, says Njeri Karanja, PhD, senior investigator at the Kaiser Permanente Center for Health Research in Portland, one of the institutions that helped design and test the eating plan.

"The size of the reduction is amazing," Dr. Karanja says—big enough to get many people with high blood pressure out of the danger range. Scientists say that if everyone followed the diet, Americans would have 15 percent less coronary heart disease and 27 percent fewer strokes.

Try it! A taste of DASH: Make a modified Waldorf salad. Toss together unsalted nuts, fruit, feta cheese, and spinach or lettuce. Mix with walnut oil and lemon juice.

Follow the plan: To find recipes and menu plans, go to www.prevention.com/foodcure.

The Box That Battles
DIABETES

Cereal is healthy and satisfying and fights diabetes, to boot. But only if you shop smart. Here's how:

Here's an eye-opening fact about breakfast: People who skip it are 4½ times as likely to be obese as those who always eat it. Here's another: A new Harvard health study found that people who consumed whole grain cereal seven or more times per week had the lowest incidence of heart failure.

Still not excited? Yet another study from the University of Minnesota reported that the risk of all coronary events was reduced by 10 percent for each 10 grams of grain fiber consumed per day. And because cereal is one of the best sources of these lifesaving whole grains, that means a single daily serving has the potential to slash your risk of heart disease, the number one killer of women. A higher whole grain intake is also linked to lower rates of type 2 diabetes, breast cancer, high blood pressure, and stroke.

And then there's this: Cereal is fast and convenient and comes in a gazillion varieties. But that's also its potential downfall. If you don't know what to look for, you could end up with a bowl full of empty calories instead of a nutritional powerhouse. To make sure you're getting the most bang for your cereal buck, follow these tips.

Be a fiber fiend. Look for the words "high fiber" on the box. That ensures at least 5 grams per serving. But don't stop there. Check the label. In some brands, the benefits of fiber are overshadowed by the addition of refined grains, added sugar, or cholesterol-raising fats.

Go "whole" hog. Where that fiber comes from matters, too, so check the ingredient list to find out exactly what those flakes or squares are made from. Millet, amaranth, quinoa, and oats are always whole grain, but if you don't see the word "whole"

Cereals That Follow the Rules and Taste Great, Too!

HEALTH VALLEY
Organic Fiber 7 Multigrain Flakes Cereal
160 calories
7 grams of fiber per 1 cup

UNCLE SAM CEREAL
Original Whole Wheat Flakes
190 calories
10 grams of fiber per ¾ cup

KASHI
7 Whole Grain Flakes
180 calories
6 grams of fiber per 1 cup

CASCADIAN FARM
Raisin Bran
180 calories
6 grams of fiber per 1 cup

NATURE'S PATH ORGANIC
Optimum Slim Cereal
200 calories
11 grams of fiber per 1 cup

in front of wheat, corn, barley, and rice, these grains have been refined.

Watch for hidden sugar. The "total sugars" listing doesn't distinguish between added and naturally occurring sugars. You don't need to avoid the natural sugars found in nutrient-rich whole grains and fruits. (See "Pick More Produce" on page 52.) But added sugars tack on extra calories without vitamins or minerals and can wreak havoc on your blood sugar and energy levels. The best way to tell is to scan the ingredients again. The following terms represent added sugars: brown sugar, corn sweetener, corn syrup, dextrose, fructose, high fructose corn syrup, invert sugar, maltose, malt syrup, molasses, sugar, and sucrose. Ingredients are listed by weight, so skip cereals that list any of these within the first three ingredients.

Avoid sugar alcohols or artificial sweeteners. They're sometimes added to boost sweetness without calories. We're not fans of anything artificial, and sugar alcohols can bloat your belly, so we recommend avoiding them. Steer clear of cereals containing sucralose, aspartame, sorbitol, mannitol, xylitol, maltitol, maltitol syrup, lactitol, and erythritol. Instead, add natural sweetness by topping your cereal with fresh fruit.

NOTES FROM JOSLIN | The best diet for you if you have diabetes is one that fits with your lifestyle, helps you meet your diabetes treatment goals, and is one you can follow long-term.

HEALTHY VEGGIES

with Bad Reps

Myths about nutrition for diabetes abound: White potatoes make you fat! Carrots are made of sugar! These and other myths about the produce you grew up on, busted!

I f the low-carb diet craze of the early 2000s left you believing that potatoes equal pounds and corn and carrots are no better than candy, it's time to wake up and taste the produce. Truth is, even vegetables you may think of as nutritional duds are packed with vitamins, minerals, and phytochemicals, not to mention varied colors, flavors, and textures. If you've been avoiding these "produce outcasts," your diet—and health—are missing out. Here, we debunk the biggest myths about a few unfairly maligned vegetables—and provide easy and healthful ways to eat more of them.

White Potatoes Make You Fat

The truth: One medium baked potato has only 161 calories, plus 4 grams of filling fiber. For an added bonus: Chilled, cooked potatoes are packed with resistant starch, which is a fibrous substance that could help you lose weight.

Never heard of resistant starch? You're in good company. Resistant starch is a type of dietary fiber that is naturally found in many foods that are rich in carbohydrates, including beans, grains, and potatoes. Resistant starch is so-called because it "resists" digestion in the body. Although you could actually say that about many types of fiber, what makes resistant starch so special is the powerful impact it has on health, and on weight loss.

Here's how resistant starch can help you lose weight: Resistant starch fills you up, reduces your hunger, and increases your body's ability to burn fat. Its health benefits are truly impressive as well. Studies show resistant fiber improves blood sugar control, boosts immunity, and may even reduce your cancer risk.

"If you keep portion sizes in check—no more than one medium potato in a given meal—and eat the fiber-rich skin, potatoes make a satisfying, low-cal, nutrient-rich side dish," says Michelle Dudash, RD, a Gilbert, Arizona–based nutritionist. Potatoes also:

Fight disease. When scientists from the

USDA's Agricultural Research Service tested more than 100 varieties of potato, they discovered 60 different vitamins and phytochemicals. For starters, they found flavonoids, which are credited with improving heart health and protecting against lung and prostate cancers, including quercetin, which might boost immunity.

Help maintain healthy blood pressure. Potatoes are loaded with kukoamines, which are plant chemicals that help lower blood pressure, found the USDA researchers. In addition, one medium baked potato (including the skin) provides 20 percent of your daily potassium, which is a known hypertension fighter.

Try this: To make a fat-burning potato salad, boil new potatoes in water until cooked through. Cut into $1/2$-inch slices and then quarter. Toss with olive oil, red wine vinegar, Dijon mustard, and chopped fresh parsley, and chill. Or for a hearty meal, skip the sour cream, butter, and cheese, and top a baked russet potato with vegetarian chili.

Iceberg Lettuce Has No Nutrients

The truth: It has plenty of good-for-you compounds. Just because darker varieties have a few more is no reason to banish it! Iceberg also:

Boosts bones. Just 1 cup of shredded iceberg lettuce delivers nearly 20 percent of your daily dose of vitamin K, which is a nutrient many women don't get enough of. When Harvard University researchers tracked the diets of more than 72,000 women, those who ate one or more servings a day of any type of lettuce (they're all rich in the vitamin) had the lowest rates of hip fracture.

Protects your sight. Iceberg lettuce is a good source of vitamin A (just 1 cup supplies 15 percent of your daily dose), needed to keep your vision sharp.

Inches you toward "five-a-day." If iceberg is your favorite lettuce, don't hesitate to use it as the base of a tossed salad. "Any lettuce that keeps you eating salads is a great vehicle for getting more produce into your day," says Dawn Jackson Blatner, RD, a spokesperson for the American Dietetic Association. Remember: Even the most nutrient-rich lettuce does you no good if it ends up in the trash.

Try it: Grilled! For a unique, smoky flavor, halve or quarter a head of lettuce and grill just long enough for the telltale marks to form (about 4 to 5 minutes). Remove from heat, core, chop, and dress. For an Asian twist, toss with sesame oil, grated fresh ginger, minced garlic, and rice wine vinegar.

Carrots Are Loaded with Sugar

The truth: One cup of chopped raw carrots contains just 52 calories and a mere 12 grams of carbohydrates. Only half of the carbs are from natural sugar; the rest are

(continued on page 74)

The Veggie Factor

Adding the right amount to your diet single-handedly fights type 2 diabetes, stroke, heart disease, and cancer. But to get the maximum anti-aging protection and disease prevention, you need to not only eat the right number of servings per week, but also include variety, and lots of it.

That's the main message behind an often overlooked but critical recommendation within the latest USDA Dietary Guidelines report. This new research reveals that eating about 14 cups of vegetables per week, from a wide range of veggie groups, raises blood levels of many protective antioxidants. In addition to their well-documented ability to fight and reduce the risk of disease, antioxidants may help preserve your long-term memory and learning capabilities, even as you get older.

Numerous studies also link a higher veggie intake to a reduced risk of stroke,

cardiovascular disease, cancer, type 2 diabetes, and obesity. That's why the strongest recommendation from the USDA's report is a greater consumption of a wide variety of vegetables—advice that's mirrored by every major health organization, including the American Heart Association, American Institute for Cancer Research, and American Diabetes Association.

Convinced, but still struggling to work all this produce into your real-life diet? Then follow our plan, which includes suggestions on how to sneak in vegetables, a breakdown of the five essential veggie "groups," and a cheat sheet for quick reference. You'll be fulfilling your 14-cup quota in no time.

EASY WAYS TO SNEAK IN VEGGIES

Swap noodle soup for bean or lentil

Serve chicken or fish over a bed of corn or wilted greens instead of rice

Use salsa or marinara sauce for dipping

Add mashed beans or chopped mushrooms to lean ground beef or turkey

Trade half your pasta portion for chopped veggies

EAT 14 CUPS OF VEGETABLES A WEEK

That might seem like a lot, but it's easier than it sounds. Researchers have divided the entire vegetable spectrum into five "groups" (yes, beans are a veggie!) and broken down your exact weekly needs.

DARK GREENS
Servings: 2 cups per week
Sources: Spinach; broccoli; romaine;

mesclun; collard, turnip, and mustard greens

Payoff: Better lung health, stronger bones, a stronger immune system, lower blood pressure, reduced inflammation, and a healthier brain.

ORANGE VEGETABLES

Servings: $1\frac{1}{2}$ cups per week

Sources: Carrots, sweet potatoes, winter squash, pumpkin

Payoff: Better blood sugar control, vision, and lung health; high in cancer-fighting carotenoids.

BEANS

Servings: $2\frac{1}{2}$ cups per week

Sources: Pinto beans, kidney beans, black beans, lentils, edamame, chickpeas, tofu

Payoff: Lower rates of type 2 diabetes, heart disease, high blood pressure, and breast and colon cancers.

STARCHY VEGETABLES

Servings: $2\frac{1}{2}$ cups per week

Sources: White potatoes, corn, green peas

Payoff: The nutrients in this group range from vitamins A, C, B_6, and folate to potassium and magnesium, and each vegetable is rich in unique antioxidants, such as cancer-fighting isoflavones in peas and blood pressure–lowering kukoamines in potatoes.

WILDCARD

Servings: $5\frac{1}{2}$ cups per week

Sources: Artichokes, asparagus, brussels sprouts, cabbage, cauliflower, eggplant, green beans, mushrooms, onions, bell peppers, tomatoes, wax beans, zucchini

Payoff: This eclectic group ensures a broad spectrum of nutrients and antioxidants that protect every system in your body, including beta-carotene in bell peppers and quercetin, which is a natural anti-inflammatory, in onions.

ONE WEEK AT A GLANCE

This simple plan will help you reach your vegetable quota in no time.

Monday
Lunch 1 cup dark greens
Dinner $\frac{3}{4}$ cup starchy veggies

Tuesday
Lunch $\frac{1}{2}$ cup orange veggies
Dinner $\frac{1}{2}$ cup beans

Wednesday
Lunch 1 cup dark greens and $\frac{1}{2}$ cup beans
Dinner $1\frac{1}{2}$ cups wildcard

Thursday
Lunch 1 cup wildcard
Dinner 1 cup beans

Friday
Lunch 1 cup wildcard
Dinner $\frac{3}{4}$ cup starchy veggies

Saturday
Lunch 1 cup wildcard
Dinner 1 cup orange veggies

Sunday
Lunch $\frac{1}{2}$ cup beans
Dinner 1 cup starchy veggies and 1 cup wildcard

from heart-healthy fiber and complex carbohydrates. That's fewer than you'd get in a cup of milk or a medium-size piece of fruit. Plus, the sugar in carrots comes packaged with vitamins, minerals, and fiber, unlike the excessive empty calories you'd get from foods with added sugar, such as a candy bar or cookies. Carrots also:

Benefit blood sugar: Fiber and beta-carotene, both of which are linked to improved blood sugar control, are abundant in carrots.

Improve your eyes: One-half cup of carrots has more than four times the amount of vision-boosting vitamin A that you need in one day.

Promote colon health: Carrots are packed with falcarinol, which is a phytochemical that may help protect you against colon cancer.

Try this: Toss grated carrots into marinara sauce and simmer for added depth and a meaty texture (minus the fat found in beef), shred into tuna salad, or roast slices and add them to pizzas or sandwiches.

Celery Is Just Water

The truth: Before the 1500s, celery was used as a medicine to treat a long list of ailments. Its devotees were on to something. The crunchy veggie has a unique combination of disease-preventing vitamins, minerals, and phytochemicals. Celery also:

Keeps your blood pressure down. Celery contains pthalides, rare compounds that lower your blood pressure by relaxing artery walls.

Lowers cancer risk. This veggie packs a dose of apigenin, a potent phytochemical that protects against cancer by inhibiting gene mutations.

Helps you stay slim. Celery sticks can satisfy an urge to munch with virtually no calories. One large rib has just 10 calories and 1 gram of filling fiber.

Try this: Make a mirepoix, which is a flavorful base for soups, stews, and sauces that's often used in French cooking. Combine equal amounts of finely chopped celery, onions, and carrots. Sauté them in olive oil until just softened.

| NOTES FROM JOSLIN | Starting off the day by eating a whole-grain, high-fiber cereal might just help keep your weight down; studies show that the more whole grains one consumes, the lower the rate of weight gain. |

9

NATURE'S
Perfect Food

Beans might not be glamorous, but they're part of the foundation of the American Diabetes Association's diabetes food pyramid for many reasons. They have the highest antioxidant content, period. Plus they're delicious and low cal, and they fill you up fast. **Here's how to eat—and enjoy—beans more.**

If we could eat only one food for the rest of our lives, it would definitely be beans. We love the way they taste, and they also fill us up for hours. Plus, bean eaters are associated with smaller waist sizes and a 22 percent lower risk of obesity. They also take in less "bad" fat and one-third more fiber than those who avoid these nutritional gems.

One cup of beans provides a whopping 13 grams of fiber—which is half of what we need daily—with no saturated fat. Beans are loaded with protein (about 15 grams per cup) and dozens of key nutrients, including calcium, potassium, and magnesium. Studies also tie beans to a reduced risk of type 2 diabetes, heart disease, high blood pressure, and breast and colon cancers. Surprisingly, red, pinto, and kidney beans are the highest antioxidant food, beating out both blueberries and cranberries.

The latest Dietary Guidelines advise eating $2\frac{1}{2}$ cups every week, and the canned varieties do count! Keep bloating (and embarrassing gas) to a minimum by popping a Beano supplement before you eat or sipping peppermint tea after. Here are our bean shopping tips.

Buy canned: They're just as healthy. You may have heard that bagged beans are best, but they need to be soaked and then

Health Benefits: Bean by Bean

The key nutrients in each bean vary by type. Give your body a broader range and reap the anti-aging and disease-fighting benefits by mixing it up.

Pinto: The fiber in these beans helps stabilize blood sugar, lowering the risk of type 2 diabetes.

Black: These beans are rich in anthocyanins, which are the same heart disease- and cancer-fighting antioxidants that are found in grapes and cranberries.

Garbanzo (chickpeas): A recent study found that a chickpea-fortified diet slashed "bad" LDL cholesterol levels by almost 5 percent.

Kidney: The thiamine (vitamine B_1) in this bean protects both memory and brain function. A deficiency of this critical vitamin has been linked to Alzheimer's disease.

Navy: These beans pack lots of potassium, which regulates blood pressure and normal heart contractions.

boiled for hours. Bagged beans are generally less expensive (about $1 per 16-ounce bag versus $1.50 for a 15-ounce can) and have no added ingredients, including salt. But canned varieties, which are ready to eat, can be just as nutritious.

Go for low sodium. Canned low-sodium beans are exactly the same price, with two-thirds less sodium. That's a decrease from about 720 milligrams per cup to 220 milligrams. Rinsing beans in a colander under cold water for 1 minute will wash away about a quarter of the sodium.

Look for vegetarian versions. Baked and refried are two of our personal favorites because both are seasoned and versatile. Luckily, you can easily find vegetarian versions of each these days. Choosing vegetarian refried beans reduces the saturated fat content from 16 percent of the daily value to zero per cup and adds a bonus 2 grams of protein, and they taste just as delicious.

Avoid dented or bulging cans. Small dents and dings are okay, but if you find a badly dented or swollen can in your cupboard, or if a can spurts liquid when opened, toss it out right away while wearing disposable gloves. These are all possible signs of botulism, which is a potentially deadly form of food poisoning that generated canned-food recalls as recently as last summer. If you're ever unsure, think, When in doubt, throw it out. For more on food recalls, visit www.recalls.gov/food.html. For info on how to discard contaminated cans, check www.cdc.gov/botulism/botulism_faq.htm.

BEAN-BASED POWER MEALS

Cup for cup, beans provide about twice as much fiber as most veggies, and you can count them as either a protein or vegetable in your meals. Use these fast fixes to fill up for fewer than 300 calories and fewer than 30 carbs.

TACO SALAD: Top 2 cups bagged baby greens with $1/2$ cup rinsed and drained, no-salt-added, canned black beans. Top with $1/4$ cup fresh salsa, sprinkle with reduced-fat shredded Cheddar cheese, and garnish with 2 tablespoons chopped avocado.

Per serving: 208 cal, 13 g pro, 27 g carb, 6 g fat, 2.1 g sat fat, 10 g fiber, 499 mg sodium

MEDITERRANEAN BEAN BOATS: Spoon 2 tablespoons rinsed and drained canned garbanzo beans into each of 4 large romaine lettuce leaves. Top each with a few strips of jarred roasted red pepper and garnish with chopped onions (1 tablespoon) and pine nuts (1 tablespoon).

Per serving: 110 cal, 3 g pro, 12 g carb, 6.3 g fat, 0.5 g sat fat, 3 g fiber, 120 mg sodium

RUSTIC BEAN SAUTÉ: In a medium skillet, simmer $1/2$ cup rinsed and drained, no-salt-added, canned kidney beans with 1 cup canned Italian-style tomatoes and 1 cup frozen cut green beans. When heated through, transfer to a dish and dust with 1 tablespoon grated Parmesan or Romano cheese.

Per serving: 194 cal, 12 g pro, 29 g carb, 1.4 g fat, 0.9 g sat fat, 9 g fiber, 386 mg sodium

PART 3

LOSE

Here's the latest research on weight loss and

Medical Breakthroughs **80**

CHAPTER 10: Fast-Tracked Fat Loss **88**

CHAPTER 11: The Belly Shrinker **102**

CHAPTER 12: The Wall Workout **111**

CHAPTER 13: Weight Loss U **117**

WEIGHT

diabetes to help you do just that.

WEIGHT LOSS
Medical Breakthroughs

Diabetes and obesity are as intertwined as macaroni and cheese: An astonishing **90 percent** of people newly diagnosed with diabetes are overweight. But if you're overweight, losing some of that weight can help you better manage your condition and avoid complications such as high blood pressure and high cholesterol. **Here's the latest research on weight loss and diabetes to help you do just that.**

■ WATCH OUT FOR "SKINNY FAT"

Think you were born lucky if you've managed to maintain your weight without exercise? Hold off on feeling smug.

In a Mayo Clinic study of 1,101 women (average age of 41), 54 percent qualified as "normal weight obese." That means despite a healthy weight on the scale, their body fat measured more than 30 percent.

The less-than-healthy result: nearly triple the risk of prediabetes, four times the risk of metabolic syndrome, double the risk of high triglycerides, and a 20 percent jump in high blood pressure. Researchers suggest checking body fat either at a health club or by asking your doctor to measure it. The same machine that tests bone density can test body composition.

If your number is high (and even if it's not!), regular cardio and strength training can help you lose fat and maintain lean muscle mass.

■ ENJOY THE INCREDIBLE, EDIBLE EGG

Trying to whittle your waistline? You might want to rethink your morning meal.

Recent research found that men and

intake to less than 300 milligrams per day (below 200 milligrams per day for people with heart disease and high LDL cholesterol), try scrambling an egg yolk (around 210 milligrams cholesterol) with two egg whites for a high-protein, cholesterol-conscious breakfast.

■ DROP 21 POUNDS THE FRENCH WAY

A recent study comparing the habits of nearly 300 Parisians and Chicagoans explains one possible reason why more than 20 percent of Americans fell into the overweight category, compared with just 5 percent in the French group, who weighed 21 pounds less on average. When it comes to putting their forks down, our croissant-loving counterparts are more likely to rely on internal cues, including feeling full, wanting to save room for dessert, or not liking the taste of a food. Americans, on the other hand, tend to be triggered by external cues, such as stopping when the food is gone or a TV show is over.

women who ate two eggs for breakfast as part of a low-calorie diet lost 65 percent more weight and had a 61 percent greater reduction in body mass index (BMI) than their counterparts who started the day with an equal-calorie bagel breakfast. Eggs, which are a high-quality protein, kept people more satisfied until their next meal, which helped them stick to and succeed on a reduced-calorie diet.

Because the American Heart Association recommends keeping cholesterol

■ SLIM, FAST

Good news for good posture: It can help you lose weight faster. Slumping during cardio ups your heart rate, a study shows, making your workout feel harder. Pulling back your shoulder blades lets you take in more oxygen, so picking up the pace feels easier; you'll also burn more calories.

■ LIFT AWAY BELLY FAT

Strength training is one of the best ways to offset a widening waistline as you age, reports a University of Pennsylvania study. Overweight women ages 25 to 44 who lifted weights twice a week lost about 4 percent of body fat over 2 years and avoided 66 percent of the abdominal fat gained by their less active peers—without any additional exercise or dieting. Less belly fat doesn't just mean a flatter stomach. It also reduces your risk of heart disease. For the ultimate boost to your figure and your health, pair cardio with weights.

■ DOWNLOAD A BIGGER CALORIE BURN

Although any music helps boost your stride, a new study from Ghent University in Belgium proves that the right tempo pushes you to speed up, so you work off calories faster. The following three Web sites specialize in pace-perfect tunes.

You want: Familiar songs

MyWalkingMusic.com lets you customize popular songs to your walking speed without ruining the quality of the music. ($1 per download)

You want: Someone else to play DJ

Podrunner provides hour-long podcasts of high-energy instrumental and vocal music at jogger and walker-friendly tempos. (Free; www.djsteveboy.com/podrunner.html and www.itunes.com)

You want: Your own music

BeaTunes.com features a downloadable program that lets you sort all of your existing songs by beats per minute (BPM). (Free 14-day trial, then $25 for unlimited use)

■ ZAP CALORIES THE EASY WAY

Here's some motivation: Walking uphill increases your calorie burn by 10 percent for each degree of incline, says the American College of Sports Medicine. Try this routine on a treadmill—or any hill that takes at least 3 minutes to climb—to blast 207 calories (based on a 150-pound person) in 35 minutes.

Time: 0:00–3:00

Treadmill: Walk at an easy pace with no incline.

Time: 3:00–5:00

THE PERFECT WALKING PLAYLIST

PACE: Warm-up (about 3 MPH)
DOWNLOAD THIS: "Monday, Monday" (The Mamas and The Papas)
BPM: 115

PACE: Moderate (about 3.5 MPH)
DOWNLOAD THIS: "All Shook Up" (Elvis Presley)
BPM: 125

PACE: Brisk (about 4 MPH)
Download this: "Love Shack" (The B-52's)
BPM: 135

PACE: Fast (about 4.5 MPH)
DOWNLOAD THIS: "Don't Cha" (Pussycat Dolls)
BPM: 145

PACE: Very fast (about 5 MPH)
DOWNLOAD THIS: "Crazy Little Thing Called Love" (Queen)
BPM: 160

Treadmill: Walk at a brisk pace with no incline.

Time: 5:00–8:00

Treadmill: Increase grade to 5 percent; maintain speed.

Outdoors: Head uphill.

Time: 8:00–10:00

Treadmill: Lower incline; walk briskly.

Outdoors: Turn around; walk briskly downhill.

Time: 10:00–30:00

Treadmill: Repeat minutes 4 more times.

Outdoors: 5:00–10:00

Time: 30:00–33:00

Treadmill: Increase grade to 5 percent; maintain speed.

Outdoors: Head uphill.

Time: 33:00–35:00

Treadmill: Lower incline, walking at an easy pace.

Outdoors: Turn around; walk slowly downhill.

■ SET A GOAL TO LOSE BIG

Want the best body of your life? Then set a goal that transcends weight loss. In a study of first-time marathoners, those who concentrated on losing weight were 70 percent more likely to drop out of a training program than those who sought to improve self-esteem or achieve a personal best.

But you don't have to run. Go to www.prevention.com/team to learn how you can walk a half or full marathon—whatever your fitness. You'll get inspired—plus sleep more soundly, boost your energy, feel amazing, and maybe drop a few pounds along the way.

More calories per person consumed on Saturday than weekdays, on average, according to the Washington University School of Medicine:

236

■ FIND A FRIEND IN WEIGHT LOSS

If the scale hasn't budged since you turned 40, try making an appointment with a registered dietitian. In a University of Minnesota study, researchers instructed 26 middle-aged adults to meet with a dietitian weekly for nearly 3 months. Those who attended all scheduled sessions lost 67 percent more weight than those who skipped out on appointments.

Even better news: Although not all dietitians accept health insurance, many plans do offer partial or full coverage for affiliated practitioners, depending on your needs. Call your provider to find out what your plan includes.

■ DON'T GIVE YOUR DIET THE WEEKEND OFF

Be wary of what you eat on Saturday. Your waistline could end up with a case of the Mondays in the weeks ahead, say researchers. Using food diaries, exercise monitors, and a series of weigh-ins, they tracked 48 adults (ages 50 to 60) and found that participants consumed more calories on Saturday than on any other day of the week. Over a year, the extra noshing would add up to 9 more pounds.

■ KEEP YOUR EYES ON YOUR PLATE

Ratcheting up workouts can help you shed pounds faster—if you keep tabs on your diet. Researchers at Pennington Biomedical Research Center in Baton Rouge, Louisiana, found that women who exercised more than 3 hours a week lost half the weight expected based on the calories they burned. The likely culprit? They compensated for their workouts by eating more.

To avoid unconsciously increasing your food intake, write down what you eat. (Try the free program at www.prevention.com/healthtracker.) If you need an energy boost before or after exercising, stick to a single 100-calorie snack such as a banana or half a Luna bar.

WEIGHT LOSS AND DIABETES

Diabetes and being overweight often go hand-in-hand. The extra pounds you carry around makes your heart and lungs work harder, and they can also make it harder for your body to use insulin. The good news is that losing even a small amount of weight will help the insulin your body makes be more effective. Weight loss will also help your diabetes medicines work better, and you may be able to take less of them.

However, no one ever said losing weight was easy. It requires effort, and, as you've probably heard, there are no quick diets that work! As the saying goes, slow-and-steady wins the race—at least when it comes to weight loss. But many people who need to lose weight are confused by all the misinformation that is out there. So, before you start on a weight loss plan—or as you evaluate the one you are already on—make sure you can separate fact from myth. These tips from the experts at Joslin Diabetes Center will help you become a successful loser!

Myth: You should lose to your "ideal body weight" or what you weighed when you were 20.
Fact: Losing just 5 to 10 percent of your starting weight is usually enough to make a big improvement in your diabetes control.

So, if you weigh 200 pounds, for example, that would mean a weight loss goal of just 10 to 20 pounds.

Myth: Skipping breakfast can help cut calories and help you lose weight faster.
Fact: Most successful losers eat breakfast every day. Eating smaller, frequent meals will help you from overeating and may help even out blood glucose levels, too.

Myth: A high-protein, low-carbohydrate diet is the best way to lose weight.
Fact: There is no one best way. Different people will be successful with different approaches. Some people lose weight on their own by cutting back, joining a group program, or trying an online Internet approach. Whichever approach you choose, key elements for success include aiming to lose 1 to 2 pounds a week, finding a meal plan you can stick with for the long-term, and fitting in about 60 minutes of physical activity a day (not necessarily all at once).

Myth: Special diet foods are needed for a weight loss program.
Fact: Although there are many low-calorie foods that may be a helpful part of a weight loss meal plan, you do not need to buy special foods. In fact, some foods labeled

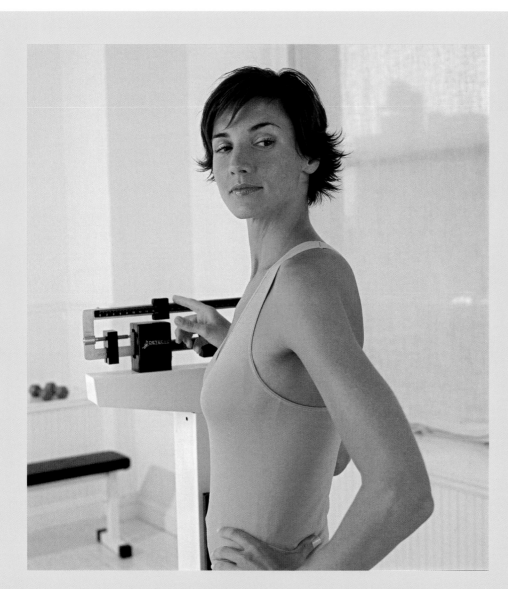

as "diet" or "dietetic" are not necessarily low in calories or carbohydrate. Aim to eat lots of non-starchy vegetables, fruits, and whole grains, as the fiber will help you feel full. Eating a little extra lean protein (such as grilled skinless chicken, fish, or low-fat cheese) can help you feel full longer as well, and it won't raise your blood glucose levels. Some people find that using a liquid meal replacement shake or portion-controlled frozen meal can help control calories for one or two meals a day.

CHAPTER
10

Fast-Tracked
FAT LOSS

What's the first step toward controlling your weight to help control your diabetes? Lacing up your walking shoes. Here, you'll find **super-simple 10-minute walking and strength workouts** that slim you down and tone all your trouble spots.

Are you ready to take the first step toward losing weight and managing your diabetes? Then start walking! Studies show that walking can lower blood sugar by helping your body process insulin better. Start with short interval walks that kick-start your fat burn. Then practice total-body strength moves to reshape your body and prepare it for harder workouts ahead.

Lack of time is no longer an excuse for skipping a workout. Just ask fitness guru, Chris Freytag, who developed this super-effective program that will shape you up on your schedule. As a working mother of three who drives carpools, corrects homework, and travels up to 2 weeks each month, Chris knows a thing—or five— about living a hectic lifestyle and keeping trim. Her secret weapon: do-anywhere 10-minute routines that burn calories and tone every trouble spot. Even better, the latest research shows that short workouts are as effective as traditional half-hour workouts. Almost instantly, you'll have more energy. Within 2 weeks, you'll feel stronger and look firmer. Within 6 weeks, you could lose up to 10 pounds!

Put It All Together

What you need: A pair of supportive walking shoes, a set of 5- to 8-pound dumbbells, a chair or low table, and an exercise mat or a soft, carpeted area

How to do it: Choose your goal: Lose weight, get toned, or boost energy and get healthier. Each one has a target number of sessions you need to complete each week. (See the "Goal Setting" chart on page 91.) You'll mix and match our various 10-minute cardio workouts and our 10-minute firming routines weekly to achieve your desired results.

When to do it: Ideally, aim to fit in two or three sessions throughout each day, but if you can't, simply adjust your workouts over the week. For example, if you have time for only one or two workouts one day, double up another day when you have more time. Just try to get all your sessions in by the end of the week.

For faster results: We have 1-minute toners that you can do intermittently almost anywhere to shape up in less time, or use them on days when you can't fit in a full 10-minute workout.

Why 10-Minute Workouts Are Better

Here are the plan's benefits.

You'll lose 30 percent more fat. Women who performed 10-minute bouts of exercise throughout the day lost nearly a third more weight than those who exercised in one 30- to 40-minute chunk three times a week, reports a University of Pittsburgh study.

You'll cut your heart attack risk in half. All it takes is accumulating an hour of walking a week. (You can do that!)

You'll shrink your belly in less time. Women ages 31 to 57 who squeezed in three 10-minute walks most days of the week lost nearly twice as many inches off their waistlines as those who did single 30-minute sessions, according to British research.

You'll get fit faster. Men and women who did two 15-minute workouts 4 days a week improved their cardiovascular endurance twice as much as those who worked out in a single 30-minute routine 4 days a week.

Mini-workouts deliver such powerful results because you're more likely to do them, say experts.

THE EXPERT _____

Chris Freytag, writer and model for our story, created this exclusive workout based on her book and new DVD, both titled Shortcuts to Big Weight Loss *(available at www.prevention.com/shop).*

Goal Setting

Do These to Lose Weight	Do These to Get Toned	Do These to Boost Energy and Get Healthier
5 Energy-Boosters (See page 92.)	3 Energy-Boosters (See page 92.)	4 Energy-Boosters (See page 92.)
6 Calorie-Burners (See page 92.)	2 Calorie-Burners (See page 92.)	4 Calorie-Burners (See page 92.)
4 Toning Walks (See page 93.)	6 Toning Walks (See page 93.)	4 Toning Walks (See page 93.)
2 Butt & Thigh Firmers (See page 94.)	3 Butt & Thigh Firmers (See page 94.)	1 Butt & Thigh Firmer (See page 94.)
2 Arm Sculptors (See page 97.)	3 Arm Sculptors (See page 97.)	1 Arm Sculptor (See page 97.)
2 Belly Flatteners (See page 99.)	3 Belly Flatteners (See page 99.)	1 Belly Flattener (See page 99.)
Total: 21 sessions each week	Total: 20 sessions each week	Total: 15 sessions each week

10-MINUTE **WALKING WORKOUTS**

Each of these three 10-minute routines revs up your calorie burn. We've tailored them even further for variety and to help you reach your specific goal. All three maximize every minute of your workout time by getting your heart rate up quickly and keeping you in the optimal fat-burning zone throughout the 10-minute routine. Intensity levels are based on a 1-to-10 scale, with 1 being how you'd feel standing still and 10 how you'd feel sprinting. And because the workout is short, you'll have more energy to give it your all the entire time and burn more fat in the process.

Calorie-Burner

Minutes	Activity	Intensity
0:00	Warm-up	4
1:00	Moderate-pace walk: You can talk in sentences	5
4:00	Pump it up: Fast walk, almost breathless	9
5:00	Moderate-pace walk	5
6:00	Pump it up: Fast walk	9
7:00	Moderate-pace walk	5
8:00	Pump it up: Fast walk	9
9:00	Moderate to cool-down pace	5-4
10:00	Finish	

Energy-Booster

Minutes	Activity	Intensity
0:00	Warm-up	4
1:00	Moderate-pace walk: You can talk in sentences	5
4:00	Pick up the pace	6
7:00	Brisk but not breathless; power-walk pace	7
9:00	Moderate to cooldown pace	5
10:00	Finish	5-4

Toning Walk

Minutes	Activity	Intensity
0:00	*Warm-up*	4
1:00	Moderate-pace walk: You can talk in short sentences	5
3:00	Hit the stairs	8
5:00	Moderate-pace walk	5
6:00	Hit the stairs	8
8:00	Moderate-pace walk	5
9:00	Moderate to cool-down pace	5-4
10:00	Finish	

1-Minute Toner	**UPPER ARMS:** At the store: Bend elbows, curling grocery bags toward shoulders. Hold for a second, then slowly lower.

NOTES FROM JOSLIN

People who have been successful at not regaining weight say that maintaining their fitness program is the main reason for their success. In fact, most successful losers fit in at least an hour of activity each day in order to keep that weight off.

10-MINUTE **STRENGTH ROUTINES**

These sculpting workouts do double duty. Each includes 1-minute cardio bursts so you can rev your calorie burn while you tone.

Butt & Thigh Firmer

Warm up by marching in place while swinging your arms at your sides for 30 seconds. Rest 10 to 20 seconds between exercises. Repeat routine twice.

Activity	Repetitions
One-Legged Lunges	8 times with each leg
Cardio Burst: Side-to-Side Shuffle	1 minute
Clock Work	4 clocks with each leg
Cardio Burst: Side-to-Side Shuffle	1 minute
Monster Squats	8 times with each leg

One-Legged Lunges

> Place your left foot on a chair or table behind you so your leg is extended and you're balancing on your right leg.
> Bend your right knee, lowering into a lunge, with your front knee behind your toes.
> Press into your right foot standing back up.

Clock Work

> Stand with your feet together.
> Step your left foot forward (12 o'clock position) 2 to 3 feet, bend your knees, and lower into a lunge, keeping your front knee behind your toes, as shown.
> Don't lean forward.
> Press into your left foot and stand back up, with your feet together.
> Step your left foot out to the side (9 o'clock position), with your feet hip-width apart
> Bend your knees and hips and sit back into a squat, with your knees behind your toes and your chest lifted.
> Stand back up, with your feet together.
> Step your left foot behind you (6 o'clock position), lower into a lunge, then stand back up.
> Repeat with your right leg, stepping to 3 o'clock position for a squat.

Cardio Burst	**SIDE-TO-SIDE SHUFFLE:** Sit back into a squat, with arms bent in front of you and your elbows by your sides. Shuffle 10 to 15 feet to the right, moving right foot then left foot. Return shuffling to left.

Monster Squats

> Stand with your feet wider than shoulder-width apart, with your toes pointing out slightly and your arms relaxed at your sides.

> Sit back into a squat, keeping your knees behind your toes.

> As you stand up, raise your left knee out to the side, placing your foot back on the floor as you lower into the next squat, lifting your right leg.

1-Minute Toner	**UPPER BODY:** At home or in the office: Do standing push-ups. Place your hands on a desk or counter and bend your elbows, lowering your chest, then push back up.

10-MINUTE **ARM SCULPTOR**

Warm up by marching in place while "swimming" your arms as if you were doing the breaststroke for 30 seconds. Rest 10 to 20 seconds between exercises. Repeat routine twice.

Activity	Repetitions
Supported Curls	15 times with each arm
Cardio Burst: Mountain Climbers	1 minute
Side Plank Push-Ups	8 times with each side
Cardio Burst: Mountain Climbers	1 minute
T-Stand Rows with Kickbacks	15 times, balancing on left leg first time through and right leg second time through

Supported Curls

> Sit in a chair with your feet a few inches apart.
> Holding a dumbbell in each hand, lean forward from your hips with your elbows on your thighs, palms up.
> Bend your left elbow, curling the dumbbell toward your shoulder.
> Keep your upper arm still.
> Hold for a second, then lower and repeat with your right arm.
> Continue alternating arms.

Cardio Burst	**MOUNTAIN CLIMBERS:** Get in a push-up position with your hands on the seat of a chair. Bring your right foot forward 10 to 12 inches, knee bent. Jump quickly, switching feet as if you were climbing a mountain.

Side Plank Push-Ups

> Start on your knees with your hands beneath your shoulders and your body in line from your head to your knees.
> With your elbows out to the sides, lower your chest almost to the floor.
> Straighten your arms, pushing back up, then raise your left arm overhead, rolling your body to the left to form a side plank.
> Lower and repeat on the right.

T-Stand Rows with Kickbacks

> Stand with your feet together, a dumbbell in each hand.
> Hinge forward at your hips and raise your right leg behind you, with your arms hanging beneath your shoulders and your palms in.
> Tighten your glutes and abs to stay balanced.
> Bend your elbows toward the ceiling and squeeze your shoulder blades together, pulling the dumbbells toward your rib cage.
> Keeping your upper arms still, press the dumbbells back and straighten your arms.
> Hold for a second, then reverse direction.

10-MINUTE **BELLY FLATTENER**

Warm up by marching in place while slowly twisting your torso from side to side, arms bent in front of you, for 30 seconds. Rest 10 to 20 seconds between exercises. Repeat routine twice.

Activity	Repetitions
Crisscrosses	12 reps
Cardio Burst: Bob 'n' Weave	1 minute
Full-Body Roll-Ups	5 to 8 times
Cardio Burst: Bob 'n' Weave	1 minute
Windmills	8 times on each side

Crisscrosses

> Lie faceup with your knees above your hips, with your calves parallel to the floor and your hands behind your head.
> Contract your abs, raising your head and shoulders off the floor as you extend your right leg.
> Twist to the left, bringing your right elbow and left knee toward each other.
> Don't pull on your neck; the work should come from your abs.
> Hold for a second, then switch sides, twisting to the right. (That's 1 rep.)

Cardio Burst	**BOB 'N' WEAVE:** Stand with your feet shoulder-width apart and your arms bent. Squat and dip your head and torso to the right as you stand back up, like you're ducking under something. Repeat to the left.

Full-Body Roll-Ups

> Lie faceup with your legs extended and your arms overhead.

> Contract your transverse abdominis (the deep ab muscle that runs between your hip bones) as you inhale and raise your arms up toward the ceiling.

> Exhale as you tuck your chin and roll up, pulling your navel toward your spine.

> Curl forward with your arms extending in front of you.

> Inhale as you stay rounded.

> Slowly and with control, reverse directions, uncurling your body as you exhale and lower to the floor, one vertebra at a time.

> Keep your feet on the floor the entire time.

1-Minute Toner	**BELLY AND BUTT:** In the car or standing in line: Alternate between contracting your abs and glutes, holding for 30 seconds each.

Windmills

> Kneel with your right leg extended to the side, with your arms out to the sides and your palms up.

> Bend your torso to the left, placing your left hand on the floor, raising your right hand overhead, and lifting your right leg off the floor.

> Hold for a second, then return to the starting position.

CHAPTER

11

The Belly

SHRINKER

Once you've gotten into the walking habit, you're ready to step it up a notch. Here you'll find three longer routines to **shrink your waist by up to 2 inches and help you drop a size** in 30 days, all of which will help you better control your blood sugar.

Forget crunches. For a workout that really flattens your belly, get up and move your feet. Studies show walking is one of the best ways to shed belly fat, in less time than you think. Researchers reviewed 40 years of studies on exercise and belly fat and found that just $2\frac{1}{2}$ hours of brisk walking a week—about 20 minutes a day—can shrink your belly by about 1 inch in 4 weeks.

All walking burns belly fat, but for best results, crank up your weekly MET (metabolic equivalent) hours—the number of calories you burn. "Shaking up the intensity with on-again, off-again bursts of energy will give you the most time-efficient, calorie-burning workout possible," says exercise physiologist Peggy Pletcher of Source Endurance, an online coaching service based in Austin, Texas.

Walk 20 minutes a day with our workout, and your waistline may shrink an inch; double it and double your results. Or go an hour and lose inches everywhere. Try our belly-flattening strength moves and smart eating tips in part 2, and you could drop a size or more this month!

What to Do

6 or 7 days a week: Do one of the Flat Belly Walks, following our pace guidelines at right. If your goal is to whittle your waist-

THE EXPERTS_____
Exercise physiologist Peggy Pletcher, consultant for Source Endurance, an online fitness coaching service, helped design the walking plans. Celebrity trainer Valerie Waters developed the firming moves.

line with the bare minimum of exercise, follow Plan 1 on page 105. If you have more time and want to rev up your results, dive into Plan 2 on page 105. To shed inches all over, go with Plan 3 on page 106.

3 days a week: Do the 4 Belly Flattening moves on pages 107–110. It'll only take about 10 minutes, but you'll see improvement in core strength—vital to helping power through your walks—in a flash. Do 2 sets of each of the given reps 3 days a week.

FIND THE RIGHT PACE

Use a scale of 1 to 10. It's the best way to determine how hard you should be working, with 1 being very easy and 10 an all-out effort. If you're on a treadmill, try our suggested speeds, but adjust the speed according to your effort level.

Warm-up/cooldown: 2 to 3 (treadmill at 3 mph). You can chat with ease.

Brisk pace: 4 to 5 (3.5 to 3.8 mph). Your breathing is pleasantly harder. You can still talk, but with pauses.

Push pace: 6 to 7 (4 mph). You're doing some huffing and puffing and giving one- to two-word replies.

Power pace: 8 to 9 (4.2 to 4.5 mph or uphill at 3.5 mph). No talking possible.

3 FLAT BELLY WALKS

Plan 1: Speedy Waist Whittler

Time: 20 minutes a day, 7 days a week

What you'll lose: Up to 1 inch off your belly in 1 month

Time	Pace
Start	Warm-up
3:00	Brisk pace
6:00	Push pace
9:00	Brisk
12:00	Power pace
13:00	Push
15:00	Brisk
18:00	Cooldown
20:00	Finish

Total calories burned: About 100*
*Based on a 150-pound person

Plan 2: Lose-a-Size Tummy Trimmer

Time: 40 minutes, 6 days a week

What you'll lose: Up to 2 inches off your waist (a pants size) in just a month

Time	Pace
Start	Warm-up
3:00	Brisk pace
6:00	Push pace
13:00	Power pace
15:00	Repeat minutes 3 through 15 (brisk walk for 3 minutes, push for 7 minutes, power for 2 minutes)
27:00	Brisk
37:00	Cooldown
40:00	Finish

Total calories burned: About 200*

Plan 3: Total-Body Fat Blaster

Time: 60 minutes, 6 days a week

What you'll lose: Up to 3 pounds plus inches off your hips, butt, and thighs this month.

Note: If you're doing this workout indoors on a treadmill, start with a 3 percent incline for the hills, working up to 5 percent. If you're outside, try to find a loop with two hills about midway through that will take you about 5 to 6 minutes to climb.

Time	Pace
Start	Warm-up
3:00	Brisk pace
5:00	Push pace
20:00	Brisk
22:00	Uphill
28:00	Brisk
32:00	Uphill brisk
38:00	Brisk
42:00	Push
57:00	Cooldown
60:00	Finish

Total calories burned: About 330*

THE BELLY FLATTENING MOVES

"Walking can help you lose fat, but to really pull in your waist and flatten your belly, you need to strengthen the muscles that support your core," says celebrity trainer Valerie Waters of Brentwood, California, author of *Red Carpet Ready*. Key among these: the deep transverse abdominals, which act like a corset to hold your waist in and support your spine. Because there's no floor work and no equipment required, you can do this speedy 10-minute routine anywhere, anytime—even midway through your walks.

Rowing Twist

Firms: Obliques, hips, glutes

- Stand with your feet hip-width apart.
- Extend your arms out from your chest at shoulder height, with your palms together, facing in, and your fingers interlaced.
- Pull your navel toward your spine and sweep your arms toward the right as if rowing a boat, bending your right elbow back and twisting your torso to the right.
- Simultaneously raise your right knee to hip level (pictured here).
- Pause, then return to the starting position.
- Repeat on the opposite side.
- Do 20 reps per side.

Leaning Plank

Firms: Abs, shoulders, glutes, outer and inner thighs

> Place your hands shoulder-width apart on a bench or low wall and walk your feet back, balancing on the balls of your feet so your body forms a line from your head to your heels.
> Pull your right knee toward your chest (pictured here).
> Hold for 5 to 10 seconds.
> Return to the starting position.
> Bring your right knee out to the side toward your right elbow.
> Hold for 5 to 10 seconds.
> Return to the start.
> Pull your right knee across your body toward your left elbow.
> Hold for 5 to 10 seconds.
> Return to the starting position.
> Switch legs and repeat the series on the opposite side.

Scoops

Firms: Abs

> Sit on the edge of a bench or low wall.
> Place your hands beside your butt and lean back, raising your knees to your chest.
> Pull your navel toward your spine and slowly straighten your legs downward until they are nearly extended, then pull your knees toward your chest in a scooping motion, as though forming a C, keeping your abs engaged throughout (pictured here).
> Do 20 reps.

NOTES FROM JOSLIN | The bathroom scale tells only part of the story; measure your waist to check your progress. Men should aim for a waist circumference of less than 40 inches, and women, less than 35 inches. The bigger your waist, the higher your risk for type 2 diabetes and heart disease.

THE BELLY FLATTENING MOVES (CONT.)

Sweeping Kick

Firms: Abs, glutes, hamstrings

> Stand with your feet together, with your arms extended out to the sides at shoulder height, pulling your navel toward your spine.
> Lift your left leg forward while rounding your back slightly, sweeping your arms in front of your chest (pictured here).
> Return to the starting position and repeat on the opposite side.
> Do 20 reps per side, alternating sides.

Hunger-Fighting Foods

Find out the fiber content and other nutritional info of all your favorite foods at **www.prevention.com/fiberup.**

The Wall

WORKOUT

Walking is terrific for your health—and for your diabetes. But to really see health and fitness gains, you need more. Here's a great workout to add to your routine to help build muscle and strength.

The newest way to shape up your belly, butt, and thighs without stressing your joints: Flip your workout upside down! These five ballet-inspired moves use one piece of equipment you're sure to have in your home—a wall—to gently increase your flexibility and range of motion.

The result: You'll isolate the tough-to-reach muscles that pull in your belly, lift your backside, and trim your thighs. The perfect complement to weight-bearing exercises like walking, inverted moves use gravity to naturally boost circulation and provide an instant energizing rush. They also give your knees and hips a break from the pounding of upright life.

THE EXPERT

Ellen Barrett, certified personal trainer, Pilates expert, and star of Prevention's Flat Belly Diet Workout *DVDs (available at www.flatbellydiet. com), developed this routine.*

NOTES FROM JOSLIN

For many years, people with diabetes were discouraged from doing strength training. It was thought to cause or contribute to other diabetes problems, such as diabetic eye and kidney disease. However, research has shown that resistance training can improve glucose levels, aid in weight loss, and lower blood pressure.

Workout at a Glance

WHAT YOU NEED: Open wall space (4 to 6 feet) and a mat. A resistance band is optional.

HOW TO DO IT: Perform the routine barefoot four or five times a week. Do 10 slow, controlled reps of each move. Start with the Main Move. If that's too difficult, do the Make it Easier variation. Not challenging enough? Try the Make it Harder version.

FOR FASTER RESULTS: Do 2 sets of each exercise and add 30 minutes or more of cardio most days of the week.

Wall Bridge

Tones your back and butt

> Lie on your back with your butt against a wall, your arms at your sides, your knees bent, and your feet planted 3 to 4 feet up the wall.

> Exhale and peel your lower and mid back off the floor, keeping your shoulder blades down so your body forms a nearly straight line from your chest to your knees.

> Hold for a deep inhale, then exhale and slowly roll back down.

> **Make it harder:** Cross your right ankle over your left knee so only your left foot is on the wall, then roll up, pause, and lower.

> Do the full number of reps, then switch feet.

> **Make it easier:** Don't use the wall.

> Keep your feet flat on the floor as you lift into a bridge; pause and slowly lower.

Windshield Wipers

Tones your inner and outer thighs

> From the Wall Bridge starting position, extend your legs straight up against the wall so your body forms an L.

> Inhale and slowly lower your left leg down the wall like a clock arm toward 9 o'clock; exhale and then return to the starting position.

> Repeat with your right leg, sweeping toward 3 o'clock.

> Continue to alternate your legs until you've completed all reps.

> **Make it harder:** Wrap an exercise band around your left foot and hold both ends beside the opposite hip for added resistance as you sweep your left foot down the wall.

> Do all reps, then switch legs and repeat.

> **Make it easier:** Move 3 to 6 inches away from the wall so your torso and legs form a wider angle.

Toe Reaches

Tones your abs

> Return to the Windshield Wipers starting position with your hands on your belly.

> Keeping your abs tight and chin tucked slightly toward your chest, lift your head, shoulders, and upper back, reaching your right hand toward your left foot.

> Lower and repeat reaching your left hand to your right foot.

> Continue to alternate until you've completed all reps.

> **Make it harder:** Stack your feet with your left heel against your right toes.

> Reach your right hand to the left side of your feet, then reach your left hand to the right side.

> Do the full number of reps on each side.

> **Make it easier:** Lift only your head and shoulders off the floor as you reach toward your knees.

Wall Scissor

Tones your butt and backs of thighs

> From the Toe Reaches starting position, bend your knees to plant feet on the wall.
> Peel back off the floor, keeping your shoulder blades down, and step your feet up the wall so your body forms a diagonal.
> Bend your elbows and support your lower back with your hands; keep your shoulder blades, upper arms, and head on the floor.
> Lower your left leg toward your head, keeping your legs straight and abs tight.
> Return to the wall and lower your right leg.
> Alternate until you've completed all reps.
> **Make it harder:** As you lower your leg, pause and pulse an inch or two for 2 or 3 times before returning it to the wall.
> **Make it easier:** Scoot your body 3 to 6 inches away from the wall so the wall supports more of your weight.

Knee Press

Tones your butt and fronts and backs of thighs

> Lie on your back with your butt against the wall, your knees bent, and your feet planted 3 to 4 feet up the wall.
> Peel your lower and mid back off of the floor and cross your left ankle over your right knee.
> Squeeze your butt and front of thigh to press your left knee toward the wall.
> Do 20 pulses, then lower your body and repeat on the opposite side.
> **Make it harder:** As you press your knee, engage your abs to lift and lower your hips a couple of inches with each rep.
> **Make it easier:** Do the move with your feet and back on the floor.

13

Weight

LOSS U

Perhaps as you're on your weight loss journey, you've hit a bump in the road. What to do? Get back to basics and go back to school. **Here's what top schools teach about dropping pounds and keeping them off:** the methods, science, and alumni success stories from four cutting-edge academic weight loss programs.

On the very campuses where students order in late-night pizza, specialized weight loss centers on the front lines of diet, exercise, and behavioral research help thousands of people drop pounds safely and effectively every year. Here, we review the philosophy behind four of the leading university-based weight loss programs, feature participants who have successfully lost weight and kept it off, and highlight key tips that you can use to reach your weight loss goal.

Duke University

Diet & Fitness Center, Durham, NC

Weight loss philosophy: Abandon the strict diet mindset

Chronic dieters tend to have a "been there, done that" mentality. So the first task for participants who enter the Duke Diet & Fitness Center program is to leave that thinking behind them. For the next 4 weeks, dieters live near campus and meet with specialists to gain new understanding about how to lose weight and keep it off for good. The key—and where Duke's program differs from so many popular diets—small, sustainable changes. To help participants incorporate these new lessons into their daily routines, registered dietitians give demos on healthful cooking techniques, lead grocery store tours, and walk participants through restaurant outings. Individuals also attend "mindful eating" classes, where behavior experts shed light on concepts such as hunger and satiety. Exercise specialists tailor gym-based, outdoor, or at-home activities to fit each person's lifestyle.

In a 2005 study, 80 percent of Duke's Diet & Fitness Center graduates reported improved quality of life: better stamina, self-confidence, and mobility. The center's research finds that participants lose, on average, up to 5 percent of their body weight during their first month. A year later, they've lost on average 10 percent of their original body weight.

LESSONS LEARNED

Move more. In addition to traditional workouts, try to sneak in some activity: Stand up while chatting on the phone; talk to coworkers face-to-face not via e-mail; stretch during TV commercials.

Monitor your meals. Before you sit down, make a conscious decision about how much you're going to have instead of eating until you're full. (The brain takes 20 minutes to register a full stomach.)

Fill up on fiber. Swap your old standbys with their whole grain equivalents. The fiber slows digestion, which keeps you fuller longer. Breads, pasta, tortillas, and waffles all come in multigrain or whole wheat versions.

Susan Ray, 48
Virginia Beach, VA
Pounds lost: 85
Height: 5′4¹⁄₂″
Weight now: 140 pounds

I was in a bad marriage and depressed, so I turned to food for support. I tried to diet with extreme measures, like severely cutting calories, but even if I lost some weight, I couldn't keep it off. Then I landed in the hospital with what I thought was a heart attack, and I was terrified—and upset that my weight could have been the cause. It was just an anxiety attack, but it was a wake-up call. I started making changes; one was signing up at the Duke Diet & Fitness Center.

There I found the root cause behind my habits. I was burying my emotions in food. Once I realized that, I regained control and started taking baby steps toward weight loss. The nutritionists offered creative ways to include more produce in my diet. Grating vegetables into everything is one of my favorite tricks. Food can be enjoyable and healthful if you use it to nourish your body instead of to bury your emotions. I will never yo-yo diet again.

University of Alabama

EatRight Program, Birmingham, AL

Weight loss philosophy: Liberate yourself from food

In the EatRight Optifast program, participants with 50 pounds or more to lose put regular food on hold for 12 weeks and drink Optifast shakes for breakfast, lunch, dinner, and snacks. The physicians

who developed EatRight chose to incorporate shakes into their plan because they believe that such an extreme change frees chronic dieters from unhealthy patterns, so they can consider how they've been eating—and why. Participants are required to get medical clearance before starting and have blood checked every other week. (Supervision is imperative because meal-replacement diets can cause rapid weight loss and put stress on the body.) After this 12-week kick start, many participants are ready to renew their relationships with food. For 6 weeks, they transition back to food, and then they move on to the EatRight Lifestyle program, which is a 12-week eating plan that favors filling, low-calorie, high-volume choices such as fruits, vegetables, and nonfat yogurt.

In the journal *Obesity* (2006), UAB reported data on graduates who were followed for a little over 2 years. What they found: More than 75 percent of the participants maintained their weight loss, which was an average of 4 to 5 percent of their starting body weight.

LESSONS LEARNED

Break out of your patterns. While we can't recommend subsisting on shakes without a doctor's supervision, there are other ways to liberate yourself from poor eating habits. Try replacing the meal you're most likely to overeat with a healthful, preportioned frozen dinner.

Think sneakers, not snacks. For example, if you always take an afternoon cookie break, try going for a walk instead. You might learn that what you really crave is a break from your workday.

Fill up on soup. Minestrone, chicken noodle, and split pea soups are EatRight foods—a lot of volume for just a few calories. Sip a cup before your meal so you feel fuller on fewer calories.

REAL-LIFE RESULTS

Karen Matthews, 54
Montgomery, AL
Pounds lost: 100
Height: 5'8"
Weight now: 172 pounds

I didn't have a problem with my weight until I hit 40. In a short period of time, I lost both parents and my brother. Angry and sad, I turned to food to cope, and my weight escalated. I tried a few diets, but nothing worked. Eventually I tore the meniscus in my right knee and needed surgery. The pain in my joints, plus the realization that the person in the mirror was not the real me, prompted me to join the EatRight Optifast program.

The shakes forced me to think about why I ate when I wasn't hungry. Truth is, I was drowning my sorrows in what I called "happiness pie." I'd overdose on sweets when I felt sad. I began to understand why I used food to mask the pain, and I learned strategies to manage my feelings. I used to vacuum when I was upset, but I find it's even better to take a walk. I lost 100 pounds and shaved

ticipants to wear pedometers and track how many steps they walk daily (in addition to other exercise). This motivates dieters to incorporate more activity, even if it's small changes such as taking the stairs instead of the elevator. Leaders also teach participants to replace self-defeating thoughts (I totally blew it by having that ice cream) with positive ones (I ate five different veggies today!).

A recent study published in the *Journal of Physical Activity and Health* found that after the first 16 weeks, participants lost about 6 percent of their body weight. In the next 12 weeks, weight loss jumped to about 11 percent.

LESSONS LEARNED

Patrol your portions. Learn how to eyeball the right serving sizes. For example, half a baseball is equivalent to a serving of pasta, a checkbook is 3 ounces of fish, and a CD is an ideal waffle.

Find out your true calorie needs. One diet does not fit all. Visit www.prevention.com/caloriecounter for an estimate of how many calories you should be eating each day, tailored to your weight, height, and activity level.

Buddy up! Partner with a friend or coworker who's also trying to lose weight to share motivation—and treat yourself with the same kindness and empathy you offer that person. Face-to-face contact isn't a requirement. Visit www.prevention.com/forum and search weight loss to connect with others online.

100 points off of my cholesterol number in 9 months. A clean house is nice, but being thin is better!

University of Colorado

Colorado Weigh, Denver, CO

Weight loss strategy: Calorie control, physical activity, and positive self-talk

Experts at Colorado Weigh use bioelectrical impedance, which is a high-tech way to measure the number of calories their participants need every day. Each person gets an individual eating plan based in part on that number. At weekly group meetings with dietitians, participants learn skills to keep portions in check. The leaders also encourage par-

little of it even though I was overweight. Reality hit when my 7-year-old daughter wanted me to take her on a hike. It killed me to say no, but I could hardly climb a staircase, let alone a mountain. I was too young to be so unhealthy. Something had to change.

When Colorado Weigh started a program at my office, I teamed up with several colleagues, and we all tackled weight loss together. I quickly began losing 1 to 2 pounds each week. I started preportioning snack foods because I tend to overeat them; I could put away a whole bag of Goldfish crackers in a sitting.

I wore a pedometer and scheduled breaks in my day to walk. When it was impossible to go outside, I'd use exercise bands while I helped my daughter with her homework. When it got tough, I remembered that being healthy enough to see her grow up is worth every bit of effort!

University of Vermont

Vtrim, Burlington, VT

Weight loss philosophy: No weight loss goals necessary

A diet program that requires you to give up the drive to lose weight seems contradictory. But according to the researchers who created Vtrim, it's better to make health your goal; then—one at a time—adjust the habits that stand in your way. Their holistic approach focuses on wellness. For example, the goal to exercise 4 days a week replaces

Be a pedometer pro. This small gadget sits on your waistband and clocks how many steps you take. Aim for 10,000 daily. For more tips on wearing a pedometer, visit www.prevention.com/pedometer.

REAL-LIFE RESULTS

Lupe Reyther, 34
Denver, CO
Pounds lost: 42
Height: 5'4"
Weight now: 140 pounds
I used to eat lots of fast food and think

the desire to be a size 6. Pounds come off as a side effect. All Vtrim participants write in a food journal to keep track of every morsel of food they eat, from morning coffee to supermarket samples to bites off their children's plates. At the end of each week, the participants meet with nutrition specialists to look for patterns in their diets and identify simple ways to cut calories.

According to studies published in the journals *Obesity* and *Annals of Behavioral Medicine,* Vtrim participants can expect to lose about 20 pounds after 6 months. A year later, they'll have kept off two-thirds of the weight they lost.

LESSONS LEARNED

Identify your weak spot. Does a spoonful of ice cream always turn into a pint? Allow yourself one serving—go out for a small cone, or buy a portion-controlled treat at the grocery store. The next time you're faced with a pint, it should be easier to moderate how much you're eating.

Set nonweight goals. Aim to exercise every other day, take the stairs, or eat 5 cups of produce daily.

Review your diet each week. Keeping track of your diet can help you lose twice as much weight, found a recent study in the *American Journal of Preventive Medicine.* Jot down everything you eat for a week, look for simple ways to shave calories, and incorporate those changes the next week.

REAL-LIFE RESULTS

Nancy Rabinowitz, 56
Burlington, VT
Pounds lost: 42
Height: 5'8$\frac{1}{2}$"
Weight now: 145 pounds

I was at a healthy weight for most of my life. Then, when I turned 46, I got married. I was so happy, but that contentment turned into complacency as I started eating more, exercising less, and generally not taking care of myself. Fifty-four pounds later, running errands was a challenge. My asthma got worse, and I had no energy. Then reality hit: a pair of size 16 jeans that no longer fit.

Everything changed when I started Vtrim. A goal of mine was to give up added sugar for 4 months, which meant no sweets—my trigger foods. Eventually, I incorporated them into my diet again and had far less of an urge to overeat.

Journaling helped keep me honest. If I wanted a steak, fine; I just had to write it down and not overdo other foods. My favorite part is that the journals serve as a record of how far I've come.

NOTES FROM JOSLIN | Get support. Members of the National Weight Control Registry who continued bimonthly support group meetings maintained their weight loss, whereas those who didn't attend meetings regained almost half of the weight they lost.

Medical Breakthroughs **126**

CHAPTER 14: Walking Workouts for Everybody **132**

CHAPTER 15: Joint-Friendly Workouts **141**

CHAPTER 16: Watch and Lose **149**

CHAPTER 17: The Belly-Slimming Workout **157**

CHAPTER 18: The Trouble-Spot Tamers **169**

MOVE

Exercise? What can't it do?

PART

IT

Here's the latest exercise news.

EXERCISE
Medical Breakthroughs

Our bodies were made to move, and for people with diabetes activity is essential. Here's why: First, exercise makes your body more sensitive to insulin. Second, exercise burns calories, helping you lose weight. Third, exercise helps you avoid diabetes complications, such as high blood pressure and high cholesterol—and even some cancers. Fourth, exercise improves your mental health by giving you more energy, helping you sleep better, and relieving your stress. Exercise? What can't it do? **Here's the latest exercise news.**

■ REDUCE DIABETES RISK IN 7 DAYS

You can reverse the earliest symptoms of type 2 diabetes in just 1 week, finds a University of Michigan study. Sedentary, prediabetic adults who walked for an hour daily improved their sensitivity to insulin by 59 percent and their ability to produce insulin by 31 percent in as little as 7 days; both indicate improved ability to regulate blood sugar.

Keep exercising over time, and you could lower your risk of developing diabetes by 58 percent, especially if you drop a few pounds along the way.

■ SWEAT OFTEN—LIVE YOUNGER

Need a reason to prioritize your workout? University of Toronto researchers found that exercise may be your best anti-aging tool, based on a review of 69 studies.

The percentage of age-related weight gain that can be prevented with exercise, according to the *American Journal of Epidemiology:*

63

Adults who did about an hour of moderate activity (such as walking or bicycling) most days of the week from their middle years into their eighties and nineties kept their hearts and lungs as healthy as those of less active folks up to 12 years their junior; plus, their chances of needing assisted living dropped to that of someone a decade younger.

■ TAKE A (FAT-BURNING) BREAK

Exercisers who rested for 20 minutes halfway through an hour-long cycling session burned more than 20 percent more fat than those who did an hour straight, reports a University of Tokyo study. A mid-workout pause appears to cause fat-burning hormones to function more effectively, say study authors. Try this:

Begin exercising when you get home; then prepare dinner and finish your workout as it cooks. If a 20-minute break isn't convenient, a longer one works, too. Researchers speculate the benefits will be similar.

■ WALK OFF 10+ POUNDS

Smart pedometer wearers burn more than 100 extra calories a day, according to Stanford University research. That's up to 12 pounds a year! Here's how they do it.

Set goals. Walkers who aimed for 10,000 steps a day netted four times as many steps daily (about 1.15 miles more) as those who didn't try for a specific number.

Log your steps. Adults who jotted down their tally added an extra 1.25 miles of daily walking, while those who didn't keep tabs added less than half a mile.

Stay consistent. Regular wear is key to results. Try a device that can be worn with any outfit, such as the Tanita Step 3 Axes pedometer ($35; www.tanita.com). It stores in your pocket or hangs on a lanyard.

■ GET FIT FAST AFTER 40

Surprise: You can actually get better results from embarking on an exercise program now than when you were in college, say Brazilian researchers. Sedentary women over age 60 who did the same twice-weekly strength and cardio regimen as women ages 18 to 35 boosted their aerobic endurance 20 percent more, providing additional oxygen to fuel calorie-burning muscle and lowering their heart disease risk. Plus, both groups gained strength at exactly the same rate, and the older women were no more likely to get injured.

Start now: The more fit you are in your forties, the easier it will be to maintain at 60 and beyond.

■ TAKE 10 YEARS OFF YOUR HEART

Brisk walking can actually reverse the aging of your ticker, reveals a yearlong Washington University study of overweight 50- to 60-year-olds. Those who walked off 240 to 300 calories a day (about 45 to 60 minutes at a brisk pace, based on a 150-pound person) lost an average of 22 pounds without dieting, and their hearts pumped blood and nutrients as efficiently as people in their thirties and forties.

WALK AWAY FROM HIGH BLOOD PRESSURE

If you're going to talk the talk on healthier living, then walk the walk—at least three times a week, to be exact. Researchers at Queen's University Belfast in Ireland had 93 healthy adults ages 40 to 61 complete at least three half-hour brisk walks per week. The walkers saw average drops of at least 5 points in systolic blood pressure and 1 inch off their waistlines in 3 months—without any dietary changes. Participants were even allowed to break the walks into smaller chunks (of no less than 10 minutes), so long as they totaled 30 minutes daily, at least 3 days a week. A stroll at lunch and 10 minutes before and after work should enable you to reap the benefits.

GET ENERGIZED

To do everything with more gusto, make one of your daily musts a short walk, suggests research presented to the American Heart Association. Women who walked briskly for a minimum of 70 minutes a week (or just 10 minutes a day) for 6 months reported 18 percent more energy than their sedentary peers did. They also felt more clearheaded and confident, had fewer aches, and hoisted groceries and climbed stairs more easily. Walking about 20 minutes three or four times a week provides the same boost, the study found.

PUMP UP YOUR WORKOUT

Moderate-tempo tunes may pump up your workouts more than fast-paced ones, finds a British study. Aim for songs that have 115 to 120 beats per minute, such as "All I Wanna Do" by Sheryl Crow

TRICK YOURSELF THIN

Visualizing your workout can help you finish strong every time, a study finds. Enlist your brain to help you burn maximum calories with these tips from researcher Sandra Short, PhD.

Start by picturing your sneakers. Concrete objects are easier to visualize, helping put you in the exercise mindset.

Next see the finish. Imagine yourself invigorated and proud as you complete your routine.

Halfway through visualize your calorie burn. Picture a pint of ice cream emptying with every step.

The Price of Inactivity

According to the American Diabetes Association, people with diabetes age 60 years or older are two to three times more likely to report an inability to walk one-quarter of a mile, climb stairs, do housework, or use a mobility aid compared with persons without diabetes in the same age group.

KEEP MOVING WITH DIABETES

Activity is great medicine! Being active can help you to lower your blood glucose levels, your blood pressure, and also your cholesterol levels. Plus, exercise aids in losing weight, and it just helps you feel better in general. You can even lower your risk of certain diseases, such as heart disease, just by staying active. Try to include some type of activity in your daily routine. Sure, you're busy, but who isn't?

Make exercise a priority, and you'll find ways to make it happen.

WHAT IS THE BEST KIND OF ACTIVITY?

The three kinds of activity described below are helpful for diabetes.

- *Aerobic exercise* such as brisk walking, swimming, dancing, and mowing the lawn is the best type to lower blood glucose.
- *Resistance training* helps tone and strengthen muscles. Weight lifting, leg lifts, and resistance bands help make muscles stronger. Start gradually.
- *Flexibility training* refers to the range of motion in your joints. Slow, easy stretches should be done once you've been active and have given your muscles a chance to warm up.

HOW OFTEN? HOW LONG?

If you've never had a regular activity or exercise program before, start off slowly to avoid injury. If you are already walking or doing some form of regular activity, you may be ready to move to the next level.

- **If your goal is to improve blood glucose control and your overall fitness level:** Aim to be active at least 3 to 4 days a week for 20 to 30 minutes per day.

- **If your goal is to lose weight:** Aim to be active at least 4 to 5 days a week, for 45 to 60 minutes per day.

HERE'S WHAT YOU CAN DO.

- Check with your healthcare provider to make sure it is safe to start being more active.
- If you take insulin or certain types of diabetes pills, you have a higher risk for a low blood glucose level. Find out if the medicine you take puts you at risk and learn what to do to prevent your glucose from going too low, and how to treat low glucose.
- You may need to take a treadmill stress test or have some blood work before you start an activity program.
- Learn how activity affects your blood glucose. Check your blood glucose using your meter before and after you exercise.
- Make a list of three activities that you already enjoy and that you'll try to do more often. Remember that walking your dog, dancing, or hiking with a friend can be fun and good for you, too! Then, list three *new* things to try! Set a date to start and keep track of how well you do.
- Use a pedometer to measure your steps. The goal for most adults is to reach at least 10,000 steps each day.

CHAPTER

14

WALKING
Workouts for Everybody

Because walking is the easiest way to start exercising, here we offer three more plans designed for tender joints that will result in **maximum weight loss**—even for absolute beginners.

R eady to get in shape, but not sure where to begin? Start walking. You can do it anywhere, it doesn't require fancy equipment, and the results are amazing. Just ask Anita Keegan: In a little over a year, the 56-year-old went from feeling winded walking from her bed to the fridge to completing a marathon and losing 140 pounds! Anita isn't alone; walking is the exercise of choice for more than 2,300 members of the National Weight Control Registry database who've successfully lost an average of 66 pounds and kept the weight off for more than 5 years. Whether you've never walked for exercise or are trying to get back into a routine, our three tailored plans will put you on the path to a slimmer, healthier you in just 2 weeks.

Walk Off Weight

Best if: You're more than 30 pounds overweight

Mini sessions build up gradually, burning more calories as you progress while keeping joints pain free. Extra weight puts more impact on your hips and knees, but every pound you drop takes 4 pounds of pressure off joints!

Here's how to ensure success.

Divvy it up. Short workouts can add up to the same weight loss and health benefits as one long one, but they feel more manageable, helping you stick with it.

Choose softer surfaces. In low-traffic areas, opt for the road rather than the sidewalk. Concrete is ten times harder than asphalt, delivering the most shock to your legs. A smooth dirt trail, a treadmill, or rubber tracks is better.

Use good form. Squeeze your butt with every step to reduce bouncing and jarring.

Workout at a Glance

WEEK 1
Walk for 10 minutes, twice a day, 5 times a week

WEEK 2
Walk for 15 minutes, twice a day, 5 times a week

WEEK 3 AND BEYOND
Keep on building. Increase the duration of your walks to 20 minutes, twice daily, 5 times a week.

Go a little faster. After 3 minutes of easy walking, pick it up to a brisk pace (like you're late for an appointment) for as long as possible.

Inch up your endurance. Once a week, do one longer walk, adding 5 minutes each time, until you reach 60 to 90 minutes.

Maximize Your Metabolism

Best if: You notice weight creeping up with age

Walking combined with toning fuels calorie burn and fortifies bones. After age 30, women lose about 5 pounds of muscle a decade, causing them to burn about 70 fewer calories a day—enough to add 7 pounds of fat a year.

Here's how to ensure success.

Don't baby yourself. Research shows midlife exercisers are no more injury prone than college-age women. In fact, they may naturally progress more quickly. Maintain a moderate to brisk pace for these workouts.

Add impact. Short bursts of skipping or jumping strengthen bones, lowering your risk of osteoporosis.

THE EXPERT

Lee Scott, a Toronto-based walking coach and creator of the DVD Simple Secrets for a Great Walking Workout, *designed these routines.*

Workout at a Glance

WEEK 1
Monday: Walk for 5 minutes.
Do Upper Body exercises (See page 136.)
Walk for 5 more minutes.

Tuesday: 10-minute walk

Wednesday: Walk for 5 minutes.
Do Lower Body exercises (page 137).
Walk for 5 more minutes.

Thursday: 15-minute walk

Friday: Walk for 7 minutes.
Do Upper and Lower Body exercises.
Walk for 8 more minutes.

Saturday: 20-minute walk

Sunday: Rest

WEEK 2
Monday: Walk for 10 minutes.
Do Upper and Lower Body exercises.
Walk for 10 more minutes.

Tuesday: 20-minute walk

Wednesday: Walk for 10 minutes.
Do Upper and Lower Body exercises.
Walk for 10 more minutes.

Thursday: 25-minute walk

Friday: Walk for 10 minutes.
Do Upper and Lower Body exercises.
Walk for 10 more minutes.

Saturday: 30-minute walk

Sunday: Rest

WEEK 3 AND BEYOND
Build your distance. Add 5 minutes a week to each walk. Cool: 30 to 60 mins/session.
Add a hill day. When you're not doing the toning moves, climb some hills in your neighborhood or use the incline on a treadmill to ramp up intensity.

Challenge your muscles. Once you've mastered 12 reps for a move, do the "Make It Harder" version.

Percentage of adults who say walking is their favorite spring-time exercise, according to *Medicine & Science in Sports & Exercise:*

51

UPPER BODY EXERCISES

Bench Dips

> Sit on a low wall or the back of a bench with your hands next to your hips.

> Slide your butt just off the wall, keeping your knees over your ankles.

> Bend your elbows back to 90 degrees, lowering your butt toward the ground.

> Hold for 1 count; straighten your arms, lifting back to the starting position.

> Do 10 to 12 reps.

> **Make it harder:** Extend your right leg to do one-legged dips.

> Switch legs halfway through.

Standing Press

> Place your hands at chest level against a tree or wall; walk your feet back until your arms are fully extended.

> Bend your elbows and bring your chest toward the tree, keeping your body in line from head to heels.

> Straighten your arms, returning to the starting position.

> Do 8 to 12 reps.

> **Make it harder:** After bending your elbows, hold for 10 seconds before pressing back to the starting position.

LOWER BODY EXERCISES

Side Lunge

> Stand with your feet together, with your hands on your hips.
> Step your left leg 2 to 3 feet out to the side, bend your left knee and lower, keeping your left knee over your ankle and your right leg straight.
> Stand back up, tap your left foot in the starting position, then lunge again.
> Do 10 to 12 reps with each leg.
> **Make it harder:** Don't tap your foot as you stand.
> Instead balance on your other leg between lunges.

NOTES FROM JOSLIN | Elliott P. Joslin, MD, founder of the Joslin Diabetes Center in Boston, was a firm believer in exercise. One of his most well-known quotes is, "It is better to discuss how far you have walked than how little you have eaten."

LOWER BODY EXERCISES

Skipping

> Do it just like when you were a kid.

> Skip for 15 to 30 seconds.

> If you are indoors or have limited space, skip or jump in place; if your joints are especially sensitive, simply lift up onto your toes without leaving the ground.

> **Make it harder:** Do 2 or 3 skipping intervals, leaping as high as you can. (Don't do this on a treadmill!)

Single Leg Squat

> Stand with your weight on your right foot with your left toes lightly resting on the ground. (Hold on to a wall or the back of a bench for balance if needed.)

> Bend your right knee and hips to sit back, as though you're lowering halfway into a chair.

> Pause; straighten to stand.

> Do 10 to 12 reps with each leg.

> **Make it harder:** Sit lower—up to 90 degrees—and raise your left foot off the ground.

Shape Up Fast

Best if: You used to be active but have been off the wagon for several months

Speed bursts boost fitness and slim you down quickly. An active past means that you can build intensity quicker than a novice, and intervals (short bouts of fast walking) are the easiest way to do that.

Here's how to ensure success.

Ease in and out. Begin each workout with 3 to 5 minutes at an easy stroll to prep your muscles and reduce your risk of injury. Slow it down for the last 3 minutes.

Take smaller steps. You'll move faster than if you take longer strides.

Bend your arms. You'll pump them faster, helping you to cover more ground and burn up to 15 percent more calories.

Workout at a Glance

WEEK 1
Monday: Basic Workout 1 (See page 140.)
Tuesday: Interval Routine 1
Wednesday: Basic Workout 1
Thursday: Interval Routine 1
Friday: Basic Workout 1
Saturday: Basic Workout 1
Sunday: Rest

WEEK 2
Monday: Basic Workout 2 (See page 140.)
Tuesday: Interval Routine 2
Wednesday: Basic Workout 2
Thursday: Interval Routine 2
Friday: Basic Workout 2
Saturday: Basic Workout 2
Sunday: Rest

WEEK 3 AND BEYOND
Walk longer. Add 5 minutes to the brisk portion of the Basic Workouts each week up to 60 minutes.

Increase your intervals. Extend the power portion of your Interval Routines by 30 seconds each week until you hit 2 minutes. Then return to 30 seconds and ramp it up to a level in which you don't want to talk.

Add another intensity day. Do the Interval Routine three nonconsecutive times a week instead of twice. (You can cut the Basic Workout to 3 days if needed.)

Incorporate toning. Do the Upper and Lower Body moves from the Maximize Your Metabolism Workout two or three times a week on non-Interval days, allowing at least 24 hours between sessions.

5 MORE REASONS TO WALK

Studies show that even small amounts of brisk walking can keep you healthy. Here's the amount you need daily to lower your risk of five diseases.

17 MINUTES reduces depression symptoms 41%

17 MINUTES reduces colon cancer 31%

18 MINUTES reduces coronary heart disease 36%

21 MINUTES reduces stroke 43%

30 MINUTES reduces type 2 diabetes 30%

BASIC WORKOUT 1
30 minutes total

10 minutes Moderate walk (4–5)*

10 minutes Brisk walk (6–7)*

10 minutes Moderate walk

INTERVAL ROUTINE 1
25 minutes total

10 minutes Moderate walk

4 sets alternating 30-second Power walk (7–8)* with 2 minutes Brisk walk

5 minutes Moderate walk

BASIC WORKOUT 2
35 minutes total

10 minutes Moderate walk

15 minutes Brisk walk

10 minutes Moderate walk

INTERVAL ROUTINE 2
30 minutes total

10 minutes Moderate walk

5 sets alternating 60-second Power walk with 2 minutes Brisk walk

5 minutes Moderate walk

*On a scale of 1 to 10 where 1 is strolling and 10 is sprinting as fast as you can

15

Joint-Friendly

WORKOUTS

More commonly than many people realize, **people with diabetes are at increased risk of bone and joint disorders.** If that's a concern for you, try these exercises and machines to help you blast calories, slim down, and increase energy—without causing you pain in the neck, or anywhere else for that matter.

If you want to shed pounds fast and beat a slowing metabolism, vigorous activities like running burn the most calories but are often the hardest on your joints. So what's a 40-pluser to do? Try our three fat-blasting routines designed for cardio machines. Ellipticals and stationary bikes erase pounding altogether, and treadmills offer a more forgiving surface than city streets, as well as at-your-fingertips incline control that can nearly triple your calorie burn. Combine these joint-friendly features with our high-energy interval workouts, and you're guaranteed to torch some mega-calories and slim down really quickly—up to 6 $\frac{1}{2}$ pounds this month—without wreaking havoc on your knees, hips, or lower back. To make it even easier, flip to page 147 for *Prevention*-tested cardio machines. In a Brown University study, home treadmill walkers lost twice the weight of those who sweated off-machine.

Workout at a Glance

What you need: Any type of cardio machine, such as a treadmill and supportive athletic shoes.

When to do it: Aim to complete each of the 3 workouts once a week on alternate days. To avoid injury, we don't recommend doing these high-intensity workouts on back-to-back days.

How to do it: Use the pacing guide shown opposite to find the right effort level for each interval.

For quicker results: Do the 60-minute Weight Loss Workout 3 times a week, plus 30 to 60 minutes of moderate cardio such as walking or biking on the in-between days. Also, shave off 200 calories a day from your diet.

Find Your Calorie-Burning Level
Follow these degrees of effort for a challenging workout precisely tailored to your ability. Experiment with speed, resistance, and incline options on your cardio machine to push yourself without pain.

Interval: Warm-Up, Cooldown
How it feels: Gentle effort
Level*: 3–4

Interval: Easy
How it feels: You can sing without strain
Level*: 4–5

Interval: Moderate
How it feels: You can carry on a conversation
Level*: 5–6

Interval: Brisk
How it feels: You're slightly breathless
Level*: 6–7

Interval: Power
How it feels: You can say only a few words at a time
Level*: 7–8

Interval: Peak
How it feels: No breath for talking
Level*: 8–9

30-MINUTE ENERGY-REVVING ROUTINE

Burns: 250 Calories**

Regularly alternating 1-minute high-intensity bouts with 1 minute of recovery ensures that you maximize your calorie burn even when you have limited time to work out.

Time	Interval	Level*
Start	Warm-Up	3–4
3:00	Moderate	5–6
4:00	Power	7–8
5:00	Repeat, alternating Moderate and Power intervals 11 more times	
27:00	Cooldown	3–4
30:00	Finish	

*Based on a 1-to-10 scale where 1 is sitting on the couch and 10 is all-out sprinting.
**Based on a 150-pound person.

45-MINUTE FAT-BURNING PLAN

Burns: 370 calories**

Each high-intensity interval in this workout is shorter than the last, making it easier for you to give it your all right up to the finish and incinerate more calories.

Time	Interval	Level*
Start	Warm-Up	3-4
3:00	Brisk	6-7
11:00	Moderate	5-6
15:00	Brisk	6-7
22:00	Moderate	5-6
26:00	Brisk	6-7
32:00	Moderate	5-6
36:00	Brisk	6-7
41:00	Cooldown	3-4
45:00	Finish	

*Based on a 1-to-10 scale where 1 is sitting on the couch and 10 is all-out sprinting.
**Based on a 150-pound person.

NOTES FROM JOSLIN

Physical activity lowers blood glucose, sometimes within minutes! Glucose is a quick, easy-to-burn fuel the body uses when it needs energy in a hurry. The more you move, the more glucose is used. See for yourself. The next time you exercise for more than 20 minutes, check your blood glucose before and after. Exercise really is good medicine!

60-MINUTE WEIGHT LOSS WORKOUT

Burns: 450 calories**

This pyramid-style routine gradually inches up the intensity. You'll hit your peak effort midway to keep your energy high so you can go longer and see results sooner.

Time	Interval	Level*
Start	Warm-Up	3-4
5:00	Easy	4-5
7:00	Moderate	5-6
9:00	Easy	4-5
13:00	Brisk	6-7
15:00	Moderate	5-6
19:00	Power	7-8
21:00	Moderate	5-6
25:00	Peak	8-9
26:00	Easy	4-5
31:00	Peak	8-9
32:00	Easy	4-5
37:00	Power	7-8
39:00	Moderate	5-6
43:00	Brisk	6-7
45:00	Moderate	5-6
49:00	Brisk	6-7
51:00	Moderate	5-6
55:00	Cooldown	3-4
60:00	Finish	

The Top Joint-Friendly Machines

We tested the machines, and here are our favorite new home models.

THE BEST ELLIPTICAL

SportsArt E83 ($2,600; www.sportsart fitness.com) This machine allows you to custom-fit the stride length, since a 5-foot-4 woman takes shorter steps than a 6-foot man. Too short a stride will be bouncy, increasing impact, while one that's too long will overextend your hip and back region.

Tip: Lift your knees as you stride—rather than simply gliding forward—to target more muscles and minimize pressure on hips.

THE BEST TREADMILL

NordicTrack C2155 ($1,200; www.nordic track.com) You can adjust the surface cushioning from hard (similar to asphalt) to softer (like dirt), reducing impact by up to 33 percent. We loved the one-touch controls for quickly changing speed or incline, making interval workouts a snap.

Tip: Instead of speeding up for harder

intervals, increase the incline to a 5 percent grade to melt more calories with less impact on joints.

THE BEST STATIONARY BIKE

Vision Fitness R2050 ($900; www.vision fitness.com) There's no hunching over with this recumbent design. The large seat is easy to get into and out of and provides lumbar support so you can work out longer without aggravating back pain.

Tip: Set the resistance so you pedal 70 to 90 rpm to burn the most calories with the least stress on your knees.

For additional tips and more cardio machines, check out www.prevention.com/cardiomachines.

THE EXPERT

Jay Blahnik, a certified personal trainer, spokesperson for IDEA Health and Fitness Association, and consultant to exercise equipment manufacturers such as Nautilus, created these workouts.

Warm Up to a Better Workout

Trading stationary stretches for more active moves is a better way to lubricate joints, reduce risk of injury, and get blood flowing to your walking muscles, studies find. Try these four moves, courtesy of Tom Dooley, national walking coach for the Leukemia and Lymphoma Society's Team in Training, before your next workout for a smoother, easier stride.

Hurdles

(loosens tight hips): Balance on your right leg (holding a chair or wall for support) with your left leg bent so your heel is behind you. Rotate your left leg out to the left side (shown bottom right) and forward as if you're drawing a circle with your knee. Do 15 times, then switch legs.

Windmills

(relaxes shoulders and neck): Stand with your arms at your sides. Circle your right arm up in front of you overhead (shown top right), and then down behind you (like you're swimming the backstroke). Do 15 circles, then switch arms and repeat.

Foot Rock-Overs

(stretches arches): Stand with your feet staggered, with your right foot flat about 12 inches behind your left foot and your left toes lifted off the floor

(shown below). Shift your weight forward, simultaneously lowering your left toes and rolling onto the ball of your right foot, lifting your right heel. Reverse to the starting position. Do 15 times, switch feet, and repeat.

Heel Raises

(strengthens calves): Stand with your feet parallel, hip-width apart, with your hands on a chair or wall for support, if needed. Lift your heels and raise onto your toes for 2 seconds, then lower. Do 15 times. Repeat with your heels together and your toes pointing out, then with your toes together and your heels out.

Watch
AND LOSE

Try these workouts when you're simply too busy—or too broke—to get to a gym. **You can get slim and strong at home!** We picked the top DVD workouts for weight loss, energy, and allover toning.

he right exercise DVD can help you shape up faster and for less money than a gym membership. One University of Florida study found that over 15 months, home exercisers were more consistent and lost 10 extra pounds compared with gym goers.

At *Prevention*, we've been working our DVD players—and our bodies—overtime to screen more than 40 new releases and classic workouts to find the all-time best ones to help you lose weight, get toned, boost your energy, or simply get started.

DVDs for Beginners

Our picks provide simple moves and easy-to-follow routines to help you build a solid foundation of strength and cardio fitness.

STRONG BODY, AGELESS BODY

Instructor: Erin O'Brien

Price: $14.99

Why we love it: Short, snappy segments keep this weight workout upbeat, while O'Brien provides tips on proper form and technique for maximum firming without injuring yourself.

Bonus: The program combines upper- and lower-body moves for head-to-toe toning.

What you'll need: 3- to 5-pound dumbbells, and exercise mat

WALK YOURSELF FIT

Instructor: Chris Freytag

Price: $19.98

Why we love it: It's not just because we developed it, we swear! The moves in this indoor workout are simple to learn because they're based on walking; steps like the "salsa walk" and "curb hops" keep it fun and interesting.

Bonus: Three walking workouts improve stamina, burn calories, and tone muscles, especially in your butt and thighs.

What you'll need: 3- to 5-pound dumbbells for the Body Shaping Walk

DVDs for Weight Loss

These high-intensity workouts hit multiple muscle groups at once to maximize calorie burn and drop pounds fast.

STRENGTH IN MOVEMENT

Instructor: Jen Carman

Price: $14.95

Why we love it: Nonstop weight-and-cardio segments are packed with uncomplicated moves. Our favorite feature is swinging a medicine ball during cardio, which really revs your metabolism.

Your 7-Day Routine for Beginners

Day	DVD	What sections to play	Total time
Mon	*Walk Yourself Fit*	Cardio Workout (warm-up and cooldown included)	28 minutes
Tue	*Strong Body, Ageless Body*	Warm-Up, Standing Exercises, Stretch	26 minutes
Wed	*Walk Yourself Fit*	Cardio Workout (warm-up and cooldown included)	28 minutes
Thu	Rest		
Fri	*Strong Body, Ageless Body*	Warm-Up, Floor Work, Stretch	25 minutes
Sat	*Walk Yourself Fit*	Body-Shaping Workout (warm-up and cooldown included)	23 minutes
Sun	Rest		

Your 7-Day Routine for Weight Loss

Day	DVD	What sections to play	Total time
Mon	*Strength in Movement*	Just hit wide- or full screen	55 minutes
Tue	*Dance Off the Inches*	Fat Burning Jam	36 minutes
Wed	*Strength in Movement*	Just hit wide- or full screen	55 minutes
Thu	*Dance Off the Inches*	Fat Burning Jam	36 minutes
Fri	*Strength in Movement*	Just hit wide- or full screen	55 minutes
Sat	*Crunch: Belly, Butt & Thighs Boot Camp*	Just hit play	40 minutes
Sun	Rest		

Bonus: No downtime pumps up intensity to torch calories even after your workout is over.

What you'll need: 2- to 6-pound medicine ball; 3-, 5-, and 8-pound dumbbells; and mat

DANCE OFF THE INCHES
FAT BURNING JAM

Instructor: Michelle Dozois

Price: $14.95

Why we love it: Anyone can learn the 10 simple dance steps (thanks to an easy-to-follow instructional segment) that make up this high-energy routine. It's so much fun, it doesn't feel like exercise.

Bonus: The workout simultaneously burns fat, loosens up hips and shoulders, and boosts cardio fitness.

What you'll need: Nothing

CRUNCH: BELLY, BUTT & THIGHS
BOOT CAMP

Instructor: Teri Ann Krefting

Price: $14.95

Why we love it: This fat-busting program has aerobic/toning intervals that are demonstrated at progressively more challenging levels. Work up to the hardest ones to slim down and tone up faster.

Bonus: Beyond serious firming, the three standing segments blast fat, and the 7-minute ab routine tightens your midsection.

What you'll need: Mat

DVDs for Allover Toning

By using different body-firming tools—dumbbells, bands, and your own body weight—you'll challenge your muscles in new ways for faster results.

TIGHT ON TIME HOT SPOTS

Instructor: Tamilee Webb

Price: $14.95

Why we love it: A new spin on supereffective old standards such as squats, lunges, and crunches makes this workout fresh.

Bonus: These 10-minute segments tone up common trouble spots, such as belly, arms, butt, and legs.

What you'll need: 2- to 5-pound dumbbells, band, and mat

SLIM & SCULPT PILATES

Instructor: Suzanne Bowen

Price: $16.95

Why we love it: The exercise band simulates Pilates gym machines to get you stronger and firmer in less time.

Bonus: Although Pilates offers the most effective workout for your abs, these routines also tone your arms and legs.

What you'll need: Mat and exercise band that's included

BALOCITY

Instructor: Deanna McBrearty

Price: $19.95

Why we love it: Dance-inspired moves make this the perfect cardio routine to complement a total-body toning program.

Bonus: Burn calories as you target often-neglected areas such as the inner and outer thighs.

What you'll need: Mat

Your 7-Day Routine for Allover Toning

Day	DVD	What sections to play	Total time
Mon	*Tight on Time Hot Spots*	Warm-Up, Arms & Shoulders, Super Abs, Cooldown	28 minutes
Tue	*Balocity*	Workout	50 minutes
Wed	*Slim & Sculpt Pilates*	Pilates for Lower Body, Pilates for Abs	20 minutes
Thu	*Balocity*	Workout	50 minutes
Fri	*Tight on Time Hot Spots*	Warm-Up, Total Body Rocks, Total Body Tubing (under Bonus Workout), Cooldown	28 minutes
Sat	*Slim & Sculpt Pilates*	Pilates for Abs, Pilates for Upper Body	20 minutes
Sun	Rest		

No-Sweat Home Workouts

Here's a novel way to think about exercise: It's something you can do all day, whether you're cooking in the kitchen, relaxing in the bedroom, or lugging a laundry basket down the hall. Fitting in hour-long workouts just isn't realistic for most of us; fortunately, research shows that mini-bouts of activity—a few squats here, some quick crunches there—can have as big an impact on your fitness level and health as longer routines can.

An 18-month study at the University of Pittsburgh found that doing three 10-minute bursts of exercise daily was as beneficial for weight loss and heart health as a single 30-minute workout. The trick is to figure out what to do in those 10 minutes. A brisk walk is always a smart option, but mixing things up keeps you motivated and your body challenged. Here, top trainers share their favorite ways to fit fitness into every room in the house (bathroom included!).

Living/Family Room

■ I have a BOSU—a half-dome squishy balance gadget—in my family room. One of my kids is always sitting or standing on it while watching TV. My youngest is constantly balancing—working his core without realizing it!

—*Chris Freytag, star of the DVD* Prevention Fitness Systems: Short Cuts to Big Weight Loss

■ Tuck a resistance band behind a pillow or under a couch cushion. You can get an entire-body workout while watching *Dancing with the Stars*. Stand on the middle and pull the ends to the front, back, and sides for an upper-body sculpting session; tie it in a loop around your legs and do leg lifts in every direction to tone your thighs and butt.

—*Jennifer Mrozek Sukalo, owner of Healthy Lifestyle Solutions in Scottsdale, Arizona*

■ Keep a workout DVD in your player at all times. Just push play and go.

—*Stella Sandoval, star of the DVD* 10 Minute Solution: Latin Dance Mix

Kitchen/Dining Area

■ I clean the floor by "foot." Instead of using a mop, I step on a damp cloth and scrub with my right foot; my left foot dries with a second towel. For the final shine, I use two clean towels and glide to polish. My heart rate goes up and my hips get a workout, and it makes me giggle! It burns as many calories as a brisk walk.

—*Patricia Moreno, creator of the DVD* intenSati: Great Body Great Life

■ Put a mini-trampoline in your kitchen, and march and bounce on it for 5 to 10 minutes while you're waiting for your coffee to brew.

—*Tamilee Webb, star of the DVD* The Best of Tamilee: Buns, Abs & Arms

Bedroom

■ I store a yoga mat under my bed and pull it out when I watch the news so I can stretch. I try to get in 10 minutes every night.

—*Chris Freytag*

■ Slip a set of wrist weights around the handle of your vacuum cleaner, and then clean your way to stronger muscles and bones (or strap them on your wrists before you vacuum). The extra weight ups resistance, so you're sneaking in light strength-training.

—*Lynn Anderson, MD, star of the DVD series* Anti-Aging Workout for Every Body

■ Don't sit down when you're getting dressed. Stand on one foot and lift the other up to put on your shoes or pants. This helps with balance and also firms your core.

—*Patricia Moreno*

■ Do 10 triceps dips and 10 incline push-ups on the edge of the bed the minute you get up.

—*Tamilee Webb*

Bathroom

■ There's a small balance tool called a Dyna Disc (www. lifestylesport.com)—a wobbly plastic pillow that I put under the sink in the bathroom. I stand on it while I wash my face. I also balance on one leg while putting on makeup, and do squats while drying my hair.

—*Jennifer Mrozek Sukalo*

■ Get a nonskid plastic step stool for the bathroom. Stand on top and lunge back and tap a toe on the floor while brushing your teeth. Do a minute on each side.

—*Patricia Moreno*

■ Sandwich your shower with a mini-workout: As the water is heating up, whip off a set of crunches on the bath mat. After you loosen your muscles in the warm water, towel off, then do some stretches.

—*Ellen Barrett, star of the DVD series* Prevention Fitness Systems: Flat Belly Workout

Hallways

■ Leave a pair of dumbbells by the bedroom door. Grab them on your way out and do walking lunges for great butt and thigh toning. Put the dumbbells down in another high-traffic spot so they're ready for the next round.

—*Stella Sandoval*

■ Clear clutter from staircases so that you can use every trip to firm your thighs: Head upstairs two steps at a time, or one at a time as fast as you can, or go up backward to increase balance and coordination (hold the rail for safety). Or try going up sideways, crisscrossing as you step.

—*Minna Lessig, star of the DVD* Tank Top Arms, Bikini Belly, Boy Shorts Bottom

■ Stash a basket by the front door with everything you need for a walk: dog leash and toys; shoes, sweatshirt, and hat; fanny pack for ID, keys, money, cell phone, and iPod.

—*Stella Sandova*

Your 7-Day Routine for an Energy Burst

Day	DVD	What sections to play	Total time
Mon	*intenSati*	Warm-Up, Upper Body	28 minutes
Tue	*Hot Body Cool Mind*	Under Waking Energy Workout Segments: Waking Energy Sitting	50 minutes
Wed	*intenSati*	Warm-Up, Lower Body	20 minutes
Thu	*Hot Body Cool Mind*	Under Waking Energy Workout Segments: Waking Energy Standing	50 minutes
Fri	*intenSati*	Warm-Up, Yoga Stretch	28 minutes
Sat	*Hot Body Cool Mind*	Under Waking Energy Workout Segments: The Five Tibetans, Yin Yoga, and Meditation (short)	20 minutes
Sun	Rest		

DVDs for an Energy Boost

These inspiring DVDs rev you up physically, mentally, and emotionally, so you'll feel fitter and more confident.

INTENSATI GREAT BODY GREAT LIFE

Instructor: Patricia Moreno
Price: $14.99

Why we love it: Motivational chants while you're kicking and punching boost self-esteem and distract you from how hard you're working, so you feel refreshed, not worn out.

Bonus: You'll burn calories, sculpt shapely muscles, and have a more positive attitude.
What you'll need: Mat

HOT BODY COOL MIND: WAKING ENERGY

Instructor: Jennifer Kries
Price: $19.95

Why we love it: The flowing series of qigong- and yoga-based moves found on this DVD invigorates your whole body.
Bonus: Stretches muscles, lubricates joints, and reduces stress. It's also gentle enough to do first thing in the morning.
What you'll need: Chair and mat

CHAPTER 1

The Belly-Slimming
WORKOUT

Here's the ultimate shape-up plan to flatten your belly, which is key to controlling your diabetes. Along the way, you'll firm your thighs and sculpt your butt.

See results in 4 weeks!

Are you an apple or a pear? In other words, does your extra weight tend to concentrate around your belly or your thighs?

Being shaped like an apple, with a lot of extra weight around your waist, unfortunately increases your chance of developing insulin resistance, diabetes, and cardiovascular disease. On the flip side, losing weight can help you better control your diabetes, and avoid complications such as heart attacks and stroke.

Our workout will flatten your belly, and along the way tone your arms, firm your butt and thighs, and burn off fat. The core of the plan is a 30-minute sculpting routine combining trouble-spot toners and cardio-based moves, such as side hops and push-up jumps. These rev your metabolism and keep it elevated even after the workout, so you slim down and firm up fast.

In a study from Anderson University, exercisers who did this type of high-energy strength-training boosted their calorie burn 11 percent more than those who did a traditional routine—and kept their metabolism 6 percent higher for an hour afterward. It's supereffective at flattening your belly, too, because all the moves target your midsection. We've also included a series of 30-minute cardio routines that burn up to 260 calories per session. Start today, and you can drop about 15 pounds in just a few months.

THE EXPERT

Certified fitness instructor Violet Zaki, who has gotten hundreds of women swimsuit ready through her SummerBody Zone classes at Equinox in New York City, designed this plan.

Program at a Glance

THE WORKOUT

What you'll need: 5- to 10-pound dumbbells. The weight should be hard to lift by the end of each set. When the exercise starts to feel too easy, increase the amount.

What to do: 3 days a week: Do the Body Shape-Up (see page 159). Perform the exercises in a circuit, moving immediately from one move to the next until you've completed the routine three times.

6 days a week: Do Fat-Burning Cardio (see page 165). Rotate through these three high-energy aerobic workouts, doing a different one each day, to blast fat fast. Each 30-minute routine burns about 200 calories and turns up your metabolism, so you melt extra calories for hours after you're done.

BODY SHAPE-UP

Plié with Kick

Firms your shoulders, abs, hips, butt, and inner and outer thighs and boosts your heart rate

> Stand with your feet in a wide straddle stance with your toes angled outward.
> Hold the weights at your shoulders with your palms facing in.
> Bend your knees until your thighs are almost parallel with the ground with your knees over your ankles.
> At the same time, extend your arms overhead. (A)

> As you straighten your legs and lower the weights, raise your right leg and kick it around in a half circle, from left to right, keeping your foot flexed and your toes forward. (B)
> Repeat the move, this time kicking your left leg.
> That's 1 rep.
> Do 15 times at a brisk but controlled pace.

Dead Lift and Row

Firms your back, abs, butt, and backs of thighs (hamstrings)

> Stand with your feet together with your arms by your sides holding the weights and your palms in.
> With your abs tight, slowly raise your left leg behind you as you lower your upper body forward until it's parallel to the ground with your arms hanging beneath your shoulders.
> Keep your shoulders and hips squared toward the floor and point your left toes down.
> Bend your elbows and pull the weights toward your chest as pictured here.
> Hold for a second.
> Lower your arms and then your left leg, as you rise to the starting position.
> Do 10 times with each leg.

Push-Up Jumps

Firms your arms, chest, abs, butt, and fronts of
thighs and boosts your heart rate

> Stand with your feet together.
> Extend your arms in front of your chest at
  shoulder level with your palms in.
> Bend your knees and hips and sit back
  45 to 90 degrees into chair pose, keeping
  your knees behind your toes (A).
> Step your left leg back into a lunge and
  place your hands on the ground on either
  side of your right foot, with your right
  knee directly over your ankle (B).
> Bring your right foot back by your left and
  lower your knees to the ground, with your
  feet in the air. Perform a push-up (C).
> For a challenge, do a full push-up: legs ex-
  tended, balancing on toes.
> Jump or walk feet forward toward your
  hands and rise up into chair pose (A).
> Repeat, lunging with your right leg back.
> Do five times with each leg, moving at a
  brisk but controlled pace.

A

B

C

BODY SHAPE-UP (CONT.)

Dip and Bridge

Firms your triceps, abs, and butt

> Sit on the floor with your knees bent and your feet flat.
> Place your hands behind your butt with your fingers pointing forward.
> If your wrists hurt, make fists and balance on your knuckles or hold dumbbells to keep your wrists in line with your arms.
> Squeeze your glutes and lift your butt off the ground so that your body forms a table.
> Keeping your abs and butt tight, bend your elbows back to lower your body about 4 inches.
> Straighten your arms, raise your body, and extend your right leg as pictured; hold for a few seconds and then lower your leg.
> Do 10 times with each leg.

Side-to-Side Hops

Firms your abs, butt, and thighs and boosts your heart rate

> Place dumbbells on the ground about 2 feet apart to serve as markers.
> Stand with your feet together behind the left dumbbell and lower into a partial squat with your hands on your thighs.
> Spring up and hop sideways toward the other dumbbell with your right leg leading and left leg following.
> Land one foot at a time with your knees soft, and lower into a partial squat.
> The lower you squat, the more challenging the move.
> Hop back again quickly.
> Do 5 to 10 jumps per side.

Sit-Up Fly Bridge

Firms your chest, abs, and butt

> Lie faceup with your knees bent and feet flat on the ground.
> Hold the weights in your hands with your arms open out to the sides, your elbows slightly bent, and your palms facing up.
> Squeeze your chest and bring the weights together above your chest.
> Contract your abs and lift your head, shoulders, and upper back off the ground into a crunch as pictured and hold for a second.
> Lower your upper body, bringing your arms out to the sides, and then contract your abs and butt and lift your hips a few inches off the ground.
> Hold for 5 seconds and lower.
> Do 20 times.

BODY SHAPE-UP (CONT.)

Reverse Reach

Firms the sides of your abs

> Sit with your legs extended and about shoulder-width apart with your toes pointed and your arms out to the sides at shoulder height.
> Twist to the left, lean back slightly, and bring your hands around to touch the ground behind you, as pictured.
> Keep your hips on the ground.
> Return to the starting position and repeat to the right.
> That's 1 rep.
> Do 10 times.

NOTES FROM JOSLIN | Check your blood glucose before and after exercising to reduce your risk of lows (hypoglycemia). If you take diabetes pills, look for a reading greater than 90 mg/dl after exercising, and if you take insulin, look for a reading greater than 110 mg/dl. It's also possible for your glucose to drop 12 hours or more after doing an activity, so more frequent monitoring is helpful. Feeling sweaty, shaky, hungry, tired, and/or headachy are some low blood glucose symptoms to watch for.

3 Fat-Burning Cardio Routines

High-intensity workouts burn more calories per minute than easy exercise; so to lose fat fast, you have to move fast. The good news is that even brief bursts are enough to get the job done.

In a Canadian study, exercisers who did 30-minute workouts that included some short but hard efforts lost three times as much fat after 15 weeks as their peers who did similar 45-minute workouts without vigorous bouts.

Here are three 30-minute cardio workouts you can do while walking, running, cycling, swimming, using any cardio machine, or even just dancing in your living room. Each workout is based on an effort level of 1 to 10.

1 to 2: No effort; barely moving

3 to 4: Easy effort; can sing

5 to 6: Moderate effort; can talk in sentences

7 to 8: Hard effort; can say only a few words at a time

9 to 10: Very hard effort; no talking, just breathing!

Chutes and Ladders

Burns 155 to 245 calories*

Work as if you're climbing a ladder, then slide down to an easy pace for equal amounts of time. Because you get plenty of recovery, really push it during the intervals to maximize your cardio fitness level and fat-burning ability.

Minutes		Effort level
0–4	Warm-Up	3–4
4–5	Ladder	9
5–6	Chute	5–6
6–8	Ladder	9
8–10	Chute	5–6
10–13	Ladder	9
13–16	Chute	5–6
16–19	Ladder	9
19–22	Chute	5–6
22–24	Ladder	9
24–26	Chute	5–6
26–27	Ladder	9
27–30	Cool down	3–4

*Calorie-burn ranges based on a 150-pound person doing activities such as walking (low end), cycling (mid), and jogging (high end)

Roller Coaster

Burns 165 to 260 calories*

Like the carnival ride, this routine builds and builds until you hit your peak effort; then it goes back down for an easy recovery. These types of vigorous intervals give your endurance and metabolism a huge boost—even after your workout is over.

Minutes		Effort level
0–4	Warm-Up	3–4
4–7	Build	7–8
7–9	Build	8–9
9–10	Peak	10
10–13	Recover	5
13–16	Build	7–8
16–18	Build	8–9
18–19	Peak	10
19–22	Recover	5
22–25	Build	7–8
25–27	Build	8–9
27–28	Peak	10
28–31	Cool down	3–4

*Calorie-burn ranges based on a 150-pound person doing activities such as walking (low end), cycling (mid), and jogging (high end)

Pyramids

Burns 145 to 240 calories*

Push for increasingly longer intervals with little recovery to go up the pyramid; then shorten the intervals on the way down. You'll keep your heart rate high to use more calories and improve overall fitness.

Minutes		Effort level
0–4	Warm-Up	3–4
4–5	Push	8
5–6	Recover	5–6
6–8	Push	8
8–9	Recover	5–6
9–12	Push	8
12–13	Recover	5–6
13–17	Push	8
17–18	Recover	5–6
18–21	Push	8
21–22	Recover	5–6
22–24	Push	8
24–25	Recover	5–6
25–26	Push	8
26–30	Cool down	3–4

*Calorie-burn ranges based on a 150-pound person doing activities such as walking (low end), cycling (mid), and jogging (high end)

The Trouble-Spot
TAMERS

Here's the final step in your exercise—and body—makeover: taking on your trouble spots. These four moves will **slim, sculpt, and lift your top trouble spots fast.**

What are your trickiest trouble zones? If you said belly, butt, and thighs, you're in good company: 84 percent of women cite these as their biggest problem areas. To the rescue: a multitasking routine combining principles of Pilates, yoga, and ballet to target multiple muscle groups and slim you down from every angle. In 3 to 4 weeks, you'll be leaner and stronger. Bonus: Since new muscle revs your metabolism, you'll burn more fat all day long. Plus, you'll have extra energy for brisk cardio workouts—to flatten your belly even faster.

THE EXPERT

Tracey Mallett, certified Pilates instructor in L.A. and creator of the Renew You Sleek and Lean *DVD, designed this workout.*

The percentage of women in a *Prevention* poll who say their belly is their toughest trouble spot to tone:

67

Workout at a Glance

What you need: A sturdy chair and a resistance band (optional)

How to do it: Do this routine three to six times a week. Start with the Main Move. If that's too challenging, try the Make It Easier option. Once you've mastered the Main Move, progress to the Make It Harder version. Short on time? Squeeze in just one move, choosing the exercise labeled as best for your toughest trouble spot.

For quicker results: Do 30 minutes of moderate cardio at least three or four times a week. Vary your workouts to target different muscles and melt more calories.

Dipping Toes

Best for abs; also tones thighs

> Sitting on a bench or chair, lean back and lift your knees toward your chest with your hands lightly on the seat for balance.
> With your abs pulled in and your torso lifted, slowly lower both of your feet together as close as you can to the ground without touching.
> Pause, then use your abs to pull your knees back up to the starting position.
> Repeat 20 times.
> **Make it easier:** Alternate lowering just one foot at a time.
> **Make it harder:** Extend your arms in front of you while lowering one leg or both legs at the same time.

Standing Side-Overs

Best for the sides of your abs

> Stand with your hands behind your head with your feet together.
> Lift your left leg to the side about a foot as you simultaneously bend your upper body to the left.
> Pause and return to the starting position.
> Do 8 to 10 reps.
> Switch sides and repeat.
> **Make it easier:** Rest your right hand on a bench or chair for support and place your left hand behind your head.
> **Make it harder:** Tie an exercise band in a loop and place it around both of your ankles to provide resistance as you lift your leg.

Plank Extension

Best for your butt; also tones your abs

> Place your hands on the seat of a bench or chair and walk your legs back until your body forms a straight line from your head to your heels with your wrists beneath your shoulders.
> Using your abs to prevent your back from sagging, raise your right leg 6 to 12 inches.
> Pause and lower.
> Do five times, then switch sides.
> **Make it easier:** Get down on your hands and knees, and then extend your right leg behind you.
> Lift and lower five times, then switch legs.
> **Make it harder:** Do the move on the ground in a full push-up position, balancing on your hands and toes.

NOTES FROM JOSLIN | Research has shown that resistance training can improve blood glucose, help with weight loss, and lower high blood pressure. It can make your muscles and bones stronger. In older adults, it helps to improve balance and coordination needed to prevent falls. To get results, resistance training needs to be performed at least twice a week.

Warrior 3 to Stork

Best for your thighs; also tones your butt and abs

> Begin with your arms overhead with your palms facing in, your right knee bent slightly, and your left foot behind you so only your toes touch the ground.
> Raise your left leg to about hip height and lower your torso and arms until they're about parallel with the ground (warrior).
> Then use your abs to stand up, raising your left knee in front of you without touching the ground.
> Return to the warrior pose without your left foot touching the ground.
> Do 8 to 10 reps; then switch sides.

> **Make it easier:** Don't hinge forward as far and lift your back leg only halfway up to hip level.
> You can also rest one hand on the back of a bench or chair for balance.
> **Make it harder:** With your body hinged forward, do eight tiny pulses, lifting and lowering your back leg just an inch.

5

STRESS

Stress isn't good for anyone, least of all if you

Medical Breakthroughs		**176**
CHAPTER 19:	The Om Workout	**182**
CHAPTER 20:	Beauty Sleep	**190**
CHAPTER 21:	The Slumber Diaries	**197**
CHAPTER 22:	Laugh Away Stress	**205**
CHAPTER 23:	Super-Simple Memory Fix	**209**

LESS

have diabetes. Here's how to lessen yours.

STRESS
Medical Breakthroughs

Stress stinks. Besides making people crabby and encouraging us to reach for the Häagen-Dazs, for people with diabetes stress can alter blood sugar levels. First, people under stress might not eat right, monitor their blood sugar, exercise, or limit drinking, all of which can send sugar skyrocketing. Second, stress hormones actually alter blood sugar levels directly. That's why reducing stress is especially important for people with diabetes.

Here's how to lessen your stress.

FIND CALM IN MINUTES

We already know that regular workouts can fight depression. Now, new research shows a single 20-minute exercise session per week is enough to reduce stress, ease anxiety, and boost happiness and energy levels, according to a new Scottish study of about 20,000 adults. Even better, the researchers discovered that almost any type of physical activity—including house or yard work, or even a brisk walk—helped lower levels of mental distress.

MEND YOUR MIND

Feeling tense? Try some tree therapy: A stroll through a forest or park can lower levels of the stress hormone cortisol better than an urban outing, say Japanese researchers. In a separate study at Japan's Nippon Medical School, the number of cancer-fighting blood proteins rose among adults who wandered through a forest; the high levels lasted at least a week.

No time for a walk? Even staring out a window at a natural setting lowers stress levels, found scientists at the University of Washington.

DON'T WORRY; BE PERFECT

A little old-fashioned fastidiousness isn't necessarily unhealthy behavior, say new cognitive studies of adults by Gordon Flett, PhD, of Toronto's York University and Patricia DiBartolo, PhD, of Smith College. Be sure to take note of the following subtle differences.

Perfectly healthy: You want your pantry shelves to be organized.

Perfectly unhealthy: You want every room and closet to always be in order.

Perfectly healthy: When you make a mistake at work, you accept it as inevitable and learn from it.

Perfectly unhealthy: Missing a deadline drives you to tears and leads you to believe you'll never be promoted.

Perfectly healthy: You try hard to exercise five times a week, but sleep and family time always take priority.

Perfectly unhealthy: You work out every day—even if it means always being exhausted and never seeing your husband.

LAUGH FOR YOUR LIFE

Laughter is indeed the best medicine, says Steven Sultanoff, PhD, a past president of the Association for Applied and Therapeutic Humor (www.aath.org).

The percentage of Americans who take walks or exercise to relieve stress, according to a 2007 American Psychological Association survey:

50

"The bottom line: A hearty chuckle feels good," he says, and is shown in studies to:

Boost immunity: "T-cell antibodies, which fight infection, appear to increase with laughter, the physical response to humor."

Improve your mood: "Wit and distressing emotions can't occupy the same mental space. Laughter can actually block out bad feelings."

Ease aches: "Researchers have repeatedly found that humor might increase pain tolerance."

Relieve stress: "Several studies show that levels of cortisol [also known as the stress hormone] drop substantially in response to laughter."

Change your outlook: "Humor relieves negative thoughts associated with physical and emotional health problems."

■ CLICK YOUR WAY TO BETTER MENTAL HEALTH

Playing Bejeweled 2, Peggle, or Bookworm Adventures—games available free at www.popcap.com—produced brain benefits after just 15 minutes, found East Carolina University researchers. Among 143 adults connected to brain monitors, Bejeweled 2 players reduced stress levels by 54 percent more than subjects who searched for online articles; Peggle players lowered psychological tension by 66 percent more; and Bookworm Adventures players reported a 43 percent greater reduction in depression symptoms. After trying these, achieve more mental mastery at www.prevention.com/braingames.

■ STRESS LESS

Having trouble balancing work and family life? Stressing about your workload is more likely to cause problems at home than the amount of time you're putting into your job, according to research by Remus Ilies, PhD, of Michigan State University's Eli Broad Graduate School of Management. To make sure you leave your work at the office, set a daily limit (5 to 10 minutes maximum) for venting about your job to your family. Another idea: Keep a nightly log of good things that happened at work. It could put out any lingering emotional fires from earlier in the day and allow you to relax more at home.

■ TAKE A BITE OUT OF HEALTH

Stress doesn't just take a bite out of health; it can also weaken the health of your bite. According to a Brazilian analysis of 14 past studies, stressed-out people have a higher risk of periodontal disease. Chronically elevated levels of the stress hormone cortisol may impair the immune system and allow bacteria to invade the gums, say researchers. If you're working long hours and eating dinner at your desk, keep a toothbrush on hand. And "protect your mouth by exercising and sleeping more, which will help lower stress," says Preston Miller, DDS, president of the American Academy of Periodontology.

■ STOP STRESS EATING

Can't resist the office vending machine? Blame your boss. According to research-

ers at Emory University, when alpha female monkeys ordered around less dominant pack members, the inferior animals ate significantly more (and gained more weight) over a 2-month period than the "mean girls" in charge. The submissive monkeys also had higher levels of cortisol, which is the stress hormone linked with dangerous belly fat.

Here are a few work-friendly ways to prevent stress eating.

E-mail yourself every time you eat. Include circumstances—a tense conversation with your manager, a sudden deadline—and note how you were feeling (sad, stressed, panicked). Review the messages every Friday and look for emotional eating patterns. Create a plan for what you'll do differently next time.

Instead of turning to food, e-mail a buddy and tell her how you're feeling. Wait for a response before you head to the kitchen.

Sip green or black tea before you reach for a snack. The drink contains theanine, which is an amino acid that increases levels of relaxing chemicals in the brain.

■ HANG UP ON RINGXIETY

Sixty-seven percent of US adults say they've heard their cell phone ring or felt it vibrate when it actually hadn't, which experts are now calling "ringxiety." People who hear phantom rings use more monthly minutes (839 versus 448) than other cell-phone users, says study author David J. Laramie, PhD, who performed the research at Alliant International University, so they might be in a state of constant expectation that their phone will ring.

■ TALK AWAY DEPRESSION

If you're prescribed antidepressants to combat an episode of depression, staying on them for years after symptoms ease may not be worthwhile, according to a new study. Although guidelines recommend that patients continue using the drugs for up to 2 years after symptoms disappear—in theory, to prevent a relapse—Dutch researchers say about 60 percent of patients suffer a recurrence during that time despite still taking medication.

A better way to keep depression away: If symptoms have been relieved by meds, then switch to cognitive therapy (CT), suggest the researchers. Among patients who stopped meds and tried CT, only 8 percent suffered depression again within 2 years. Also, consider using both tactics simultaneously; past studies have shown success with a combo regimen. Don't stop any antidepressant drug without asking your doctor first.

EASING UP ON STRESS

Did you know that stress can affect blood glucose levels? If you have diabetes, some kinds of physical stress (illness or surgery) or mental stress, such as a demanding boss or marital problems, can raise your glucose levels. This is because stress hormones (e.g., adrenaline) trigger the release of stored energy, such as glucose, as part of the "fight or flight" response. Stress can also affect blood glucose levels if you respond to a stressful situation by eating more or less than usual.

Everyone has some stress in their lives, but adding diabetes to the mix can make managing that stress challenging, especially if high or low blood glucose levels are causing fatigue or irritability.

Know your stress signals. They are not the same for everyone.

- Do you get sweaty, short of breath, have a headache or a stomachache?
- Are you cranky or irritable?
- Do you stay in bed or have trouble sleeping?
- Do you overeat or lose your appetite?

WHAT YOU CAN DO TO DECREASE STRESS

- Breathe deeply and slowly. How we breathe can make us feel better or worse.
- Try to avoid being with negative people. Stick with people who make you feel good about yourself.
- Look for the humor in life. A good laugh physically relaxes tense muscles, making you feel better.
- Learn to say, "No." Ask yourself: Do you really want to do it, and do you have the time? Let yourself cancel plans if you should have said, "No" but you said, "Yes."

If stress becomes overwhelming, you may wish to consider counseling. Many diabetes centers have counselors who are trained to help people handle stresses that may be affecting their diabetes self-management.

DEPRESSION AND DIABETES

Did you know that people with diabetes are more likely to be depressed than people without diabetes? Taking care of diabetes is often complex, demanding, and frustrating. And if your diabetes is not well controlled, or if you have diabetes complications, it's not uncommon to feel depressed. If you have any of the following symptoms make sure you talk with your healthcare provider.

- Feelings of hopelessness and sadness
- Loss of interest in activities that were once pleasurable
- Loss of appetite or weight loss
- Difficulty sleeping
- Fatigue or decreased energy
- Difficulty concentrating

Depression is treatable, and you can feel better!

WHAT YOU CAN DO TO AVOID DEPRESSION:

Check your blood glucose often and stick with your diabetes treatment plan. If your blood glucose stays elevated, talk with your healthcare provider. If you are feeling ill or just sad and you don't feel like eating, follow your "sick day plan" to make sure you get some carbohydrate so that your blood glucose levels don't go too low.

Over time, most people with diabetes, are remarkably resilient and able to deal effectively with their diabetes. Remember, you are not alone! Don't isolate yourself. Seek support from family and friends. Include family members in your healthcare visits so they will have a better understanding of diabetes management. Join a local diabetes support group and learn how others with diabetes handle life's challenges. Ask your healthcare provider or your local American Diabetes Association for the locations of groups in your area.

CHAPTER
19

The Om
WORKOUT

Yoga is a terrific, gentle, easy way for people with diabetes to battle stress. Here, our **fast yoga routine** de-stresses, firms, and even banishes cravings.

During stressful times, it's hard to find time to exercise and even harder to resist the call of the drive-through. To make matters worse, stress can trigger the body to release excessive amounts of cortisol, the "cravings" hormone that makes you reach for comfort foods high in fat and sugar.

To keep your stress level, and pants size, in check, try our quick and easy yoga routine. "Yoga not only reduces stress, but it may also help lessen emotional eating," says Bruce W. Smith, PhD, assistant professor of psychology at the University of New Mexico. His preliminary study found that yoga diminished binge eating by 51 percent, with participants losing an average of 6 pounds in 8 weeks. It might also help on a biochemical level. Researchers at Jefferson Medical College drew blood samples from 16 yoga novices and found that cortisol levels dropped by about 15 to 20 percent as early as day one.

Start today and you'll be calmer, happier, and stronger, and keep the pounds at bay to boot.

THE EXPERT
_____

Tom Larkin, owner of Sanctuary for Yoga, Body and Spirit in Nashville, created this workout. He teaches Vinyasa yoga, which focuses on the integration of breath and movement to help reduce stress.

Workout at a Glance

What you need: A yoga mat or carpeted space

How to do it: This 30-minute plan is designed to flow from one pose to another, so do the moves in the order given, taking time to breathe evenly and fully. When Downward Facing Dog is used as a transition, hold the pose for just a few breaths, then ease into the next move. Repeat the routine three times through. You can do this practice daily, but try to do it at least three times a week. (In a pinch, do our "10-Minute Stress Buster" on page 189.) Begin with the Main Move. If it's too tough, start with the Make It Easier option.

Active Cat

Firms your arms, chest, back, abs, butt, and legs

> Kneel on all fours with your arms straight, your wrists beneath your shoulders, and your knees under your hips.
> Inhale and extend your right leg behind you parallel to the floor.
> Exhale, bend your elbows, keeping them close to your body, and draw your torso forward, lowering your upper body toward the floor.
> Inhale, and in one motion with your abs tight, press your torso back, rounding your spine while bringing your right knee to your chest.
> Repeat six more times; switch sides.
> **Make it easier:** Don't raise your leg at the beginning of the move; keep both of your knees on the floor while drawing your torso forward.

Lose Weight with Yoga!

For more tips, poses, and belly-flattening workouts, go to www.prevention.com/yoga.

Downward Facing Dog

Stretches and firms your shoulders, torso, and legs

> Kneel on all fours with your knees beneath your hips, your hands 3 to 5 inches in front of your shoulders, and your toes tucked.
> Keeping your abs tight, tuck your pelvis, inhale, and straighten your legs by lifting your hips until your body forms an upside-down V.
> Exhale and lift your hips higher by pressing back from your hands; lower your heels toward the mat.
> Hold for five breaths.
> Inhale, look forward, and walk your feet up to your hands.
> Exhale and roll up to stand.
> **Make it easier:** Keep your heels lifted and your knees bent while in the upside-down V position.

| NOTES FROM JOSLIN | Make the most of your day by being more active, even if you think you have no time. Remember that small changes add up. Try walking, biking, or taking the bus instead of driving. Park your car farther away from the store. Take the stairs instead of the elevator. Go for a walk or bike ride after dinner instead of watching television. Every little bit counts. Aim for 150 minutes of physical activity per week as a goal. |

Extended Side-Angle

Stretches and firms your shoulders, chest, back, abs, butt, and legs

> Stand with your feet about 3½ feet apart, with your right foot pointing out and your left one turned in slightly.
> Inhale and lift your arms out to the sides at shoulder level.
> On an exhale, bend your right knee 90 degrees and hinge to the right with your hips, extending your torso over your right thigh.
> Inhale and place your right hand on the floor behind your right foot, also extend your left arm overhead with your palm facing down.
> Look toward your left hand; hold for five breaths.
> Inhale and return to center, straightening your right leg.
> Repeat on the opposite side, without standing back up.
> **Transition:** Place both hands on the floor on either side of your left foot.
> Step your left foot back toward your right.
> Exhale and press your hips up to Downward Facing Dog (opposite page).
> Move to Side Plank from here.
> **Make it easier:** Place your elbow on your knee instead of bringing your hand to the floor.

THE SECRET TO CALM

Why is yoga such an effective stress buster? It's all in the breathing. "Long, slow exhalations can quiet the sympathetic nervous system, which is part of the flight-or-fight system, and activate the parasympathetic one, an important part of your body's relaxation response," explains Roger Cole, PhD, a scientist based in Del Mar, California, and a yoga instructor at Yoga Del Mar.

Side Plank

Stretches and firms your arms, chest, back, waist, abs, and legs

> From Downward Facing Dog, inhale and lower your hips into plank (forearms on floor, elbows under shoulders).
> Exhale as you rotate to the right, turn your left arm forward, stack your legs, and extend your right arm.
> Hold for five breaths, then rotate back to plank.
> Repeat, rotating to the left.
> Transition: From plank, exhale, lift your hips, and straighten your arms into Downward Facing Dog. (See page 186.)
> **Make it easier:** Bend your bottom leg and rest your foot on the floor behind you.

Warrior 3

Stretches and firms your arms, chest, lower back, butt, and legs

> From Downward Facing Dog, inhale, look forward, and walk your feet up to your hands.
> Exhale and roll up to stand with your feet together.
> Bend forward and place your fingertips on the floor.
> Inhale and lift your right leg behind you, keeping your abs tight.
> Inhale and lift your chest and arms.
> Hold for five breaths, trying to lift your leg and chest higher.
> Switch sides.
> **Make it easier:** Keep your fingertips on the floor and slightly bend your standing leg.

Yogic Bicycles

Firms your arms, chest, back, abs, butt, and legs

> Lie faceup on the floor with your hands behind your head, your knees bent 90 degrees, and your head and shoulders off the floor.
> Exhale, twist your right shoulder toward your left knee, and extend your right leg. (Be careful not to pull on your neck.)
> Inhale and return to the starting position; repeat, twisting to the right, for 1 rep.
> Do 10 times.
> **Make it easier:** Keep your knees bent.

10-Minute Stress Buster

No time for a full workout? That's just when you need it most. Our mini routine will help you recharge and unwind—without having to slip into workout clothes.

Head-to-Knee Pose: Sit on the floor with your right leg extended in front of you, your foot flexed, your left leg bent so the sole of your foot gently presses into your right thigh, and your arms at sides, palms down. Inhale, lift your chest, and lengthen your torso. Exhale, twist your torso slightly to the right, and fold forward over your leg. Hold and breathe for about 1½ minutes. Inhale and sit up. Repeat on the other side.

Cobbler's Pose: Sit with the soles of your feet together with your hands on the floor behind your hips. Inhale and lift your chest without arching your back. Take 10 breaths, then relax, hugging your knees to your chest. Do four times.

Child's Pose: Begin on all fours, then sit back on your heels. Lower your forehead to the floor, bringing your hands next to your feet with your palms facing up. Rest for 10 breaths.

Corpse Pose: Lie faceup with your legs extended, your arms at your sides, and your palms up. Breathe deeply as you focus on and relax one body part at a time, from your legs to your head. Relax in this pose for at least 3 to 5 minutes.

CHAPTER

20

Beauty
SLEEP

A recent study shows that people who get fewer than 6 hours of sleep per night are more prone to abnormal blood sugar levels. **Rest assured: You can sleep soundly tonight—**and wake up slimmer, happier, and healthier. Here's how.

Is a good night's sleep the first thing you sacrifice when life gets too full and busy? If so, this is your wake-up call: You're not just sabotaging your next day's performance (news to none of us), but you're actually harming your health.

"Sleep deprivation is a serious medical risk, but few people are aware of that," says Joyce Walsleben, PhD, an associate professor of medicine at NYU School of Medicine. "You have to pay as much attention to your sleep as you do to eating a nutritious diet."

A spate of studies is turning up clear links between inadequate sleep and obesity, as well as several related conditions: type 2 diabetes, heart disease, and hypertension. For example, people who typically get fewer than 7 hours of shut-eye per night are more likely to be obese than their well-rested peers, according to an analysis of almost 7,000 people enrolled in the National Health and Nutrition Examination Survey.

"Sleeping less and weighing more are two of the most obvious social trends over the past century," says Eric Olson, MD, codirector of the Sleep Disorders Center at the Mayo Clinic in Rochester, Minnesota. "The less you sleep, the more likely you are to be overweight."

The good news is that with adequate shut-eye, these conditions may be reversible, our experts say. Drawing on studies about what robs us of quality sleep, they have devised strategies that can help you get the rest you need. Here's a lineup of the most insidious sleep thieves—and the latest recommendations on how to bar them from your bedroom forever.

Sleep Thief #1: An Overactive Mind

The reason you sometimes obsess over a tricky work project or an argument with your best friend when you're trying to fall asleep: You can't refocus your thinking at

Three New Ways to Sleep Deeply

Slip on some socks. The instant warm-up widens blood vessels in your feet, allowing your body to transfer heat from its core to the extremities, cooling you slightly, which induces sleep, says Phyllis Zee, PhD, director of sleep disorders at Northwestern University's Feinberg School of Medicine. Wearing an old-fashioned nightcap achieves the same result.

Stay on schedule. People who follow regular daily routines—bedtimes and wake-up times, work hours and meals—report fewer sleep problems than those with more unpredictable lives, according to a study from the University of Pittsburgh Medical Center. Recurring time cues synchronize your body rhythms and sleep-wake cycles, says Lawrence Epstein, MD.

Go dark. Any light signals the brain to wake up, but "blue light" from your cell phone and your clock's digital display are the worst offenders. For a sound sleep, turn your clock around and banish lighted devices from the bedroom.

---

the edge of slumber the same way you can when you're alert, says Colleen E. Carney, PhD, an assistant professor of psychiatry at the Insomnia and Sleep Research Program at Duke University Medical Center. "People have little control over their thoughts, because they may be going in and out of a light stage of sleep, even though they think they're awake," Dr. Carney says.

REST EASY

When fretful, get up and go to another part of the house, but leave the lights off. "Your anxious thoughts will usually stop right away. Then you can go back to bed and fall asleep," Dr. Carney says. This well-studied strategy, called stimulus control, also prevents you from associating your bed with anxiety.

Another tip: Set aside time early in the evening to problem solve. Think about and write down your pressing concerns, along with a possible solution for each, a few hours before retiring.

Sleep Thief #2: Weekend Sleep-Ins

Late nights followed by extra sack time the next morning throw off your internal clock, which is controlled by a cluster of nerve cells in the brain that also regulate appetite and body temperature, says

Lawrence Epstein, MD, medical director of Sleep HealthCenters in Brighton, Massachusetts. When Sunday rolls around, you're reprogrammed to stay up past your bedtime, and you feel like a zombie on Monday morning.

REST EASY

Even if you've been up late, don't sleep in more than an hour longer than usual, Dr. Epstein says. To make up for lost slumber, take an afternoon catnap (no more than 30 minutes, though, because an extended daytime snooze can keep you awake at night).

Sleep Thief #3:
A Bedmate

A snorer's sawing can reach 90 decibels—as loud as a blender. Even if you can get to sleep, your partner's snoring will likely wax and wane through the night and wake you up during REM sleep, the most restful phase.

REST EASY

Encourage the snorer to side sleep rather than back sleep. If that doesn't work, earplugs will, but only if they stay in, says Meir Kryger, MD, director of research and education at Gaylord Sleep Center at Gaylord Hospital in Wallingford, Connecticut. Try Hearos Ultimate Softness ($1) or Howard Leight MAX ($1); both are made of flexible, washable polyurethane.

Sleep Thief #4:
Your Hormones

Fluctuating levels of estrogen and progesterone before or during your period or throughout perimenopause can sabotage sleep, says Dr. Walsleben. You may notice problems—mainly waking up during the night—long before you start having hot flashes, she says.

REST EASY

A hot bath a couple of hours before turning in and, if you're often awakened by cramps, an over-the-counter pain reliever

THIS IS YOUR BODY WITHOUT SLEEP

YOU CRAVE JUNK FOOD. Sleep loss may cause you to want more calories than your body needs, especially in the form of sugary snacks and starches. After going without enough sleep for 2 nights, people in one study had more of the hunger-inducing hormone ghrelin and less of the appetite-suppressing hormone leptin.
Long-term risk: Obesity

YOU'RE LESS ABLE TO PROCESS GLUCOSE. It's the fuel that every cell in your body needs to function. After just 6 days of sleep restriction, people develop resistance to insulin, the hormone that helps transport glucose from the blood-stream into the cells, say University of Chicago researchers. In another study, tests showed that participants who slept fewer than 6 hours a night and claimed to be "natural short sleepers" couldn't metab-olize sugar properly.
Long-term risk: Type 2 diabetes

YOU'RE ALWAYS IN FIGHT-OR-FLIGHT MODE. The University of Chicago study also found that inadequate shut-eye caused levels of cortisol, the stress hormone, to spike in the afternoon and evening—increasing heart rate, blood pressure, and blood glucose. Aside from posing future health problems, the cortisol-induced alertness comes at an inopportune time—when you should be winding down your day or sleeping.
Long-term risks: Hypertension, heart disease, and type 2 diabetes

YOUR IMMUNE SYSTEM WEAKENS. People who got insufficient sleep for 10 days had elevated levels of C-reactive protein, which is an inflammation marker that's been linked to heart disease and some autoimmune diseases, according to one study. Other research revealed that sleep-deprived men failed to mount the normal immune response after receiving flu shots. They had only half as many disease-fighting antibodies 10 days after the vaccination, compared with other men who were well rested.
Long-term risk: Inflammation, which can lead to heart disease, stroke, and type 2 diabetes

YOU'RE NOT MENTALLY SHARP, AND YOUR MOOD TAKES A NOSEDIVE. After a restless night, reaction time is decreased, making driving (among other activities) dangerous. Chronically tired people are also less happy. "Sleep and mood are regulated by the same brain chemicals," says Joyce Walsleben, PhD.
Long-term risk: Depression, but probably only for those who are already susceptible to the illness

at bedtime may be all you need to counter premenstrual insomnia. For a stubborn case, ask your physician whether a short-acting sleep medication, taken two or three nights a month, would make sense.

During perimenopause, stay on a consistent sleep-wake schedule, exercise at least 20 to 30 minutes a day, and avoid caffeine after lunch and alcohol within 3 hours of bedtime. A cocktail helps you nod off, but its rebound effect will wake you up, Dr. Epstein says. For hot flashes and night sweats, try sleeping in a cool room and wearing light clothing. (Several companies make pajamas that wick away moisture.) If you're still tossing and turning, consider hormone therapy, Dr. Walsleben says. Recent research suggests that it may be safe for many women in their fifties (particularly the new low doses) when used for fewer than 5 years.

Sleep Thief #5: Eating too Little

Going to bed hungry interferes with sleep—hunger pangs simply wake you up—and

some evidence suggests that people trying to lose weight may wake up frequently, says Peter Hauri, PhD, a professor emeritus at the Mayo Clinic.

REST EASY

Dr. Hauri suggests saving some of your calories for a high-protein bedtime snack, such as a small serving of cheese or a hard-boiled egg. Protein produces greater satiety than carbohydrates and fat.

NOTES FROM JOSLIN	Recent research suggest that tai chi, a Chinese martial art, can lower A1C and improve immune function in people with type 2 diabetes. Tai chi also improves respiratory and cardiovascular function and flexibility, and it reduces stress.

The
SLUMBER DIARIES

In the shadowy world of sleep research, the most trusted experts are those who have tried everything. Enter Gayle Greene, bona fide insomniac and **your personal guide to the Land of Nod.**

I f you have an occasional bout of sleeplessness, there's no shortage of tips to follow. Avoid caffeine, late-night eating, and—ha, my favorite—stress. If a cure really were as simple as switching to decaf or attending more yoga classes, we wouldn't be a nation plagued by sleeplessness. Some 58 percent of American adults complain of insomnia, according to the National Sleep Foundation, and among women and the elderly, the rate jumps to more than two-thirds.

As someone who's lived with insomnia for half a century and written a book called, aptly, *Insomniac*, I've learned that what helps me doesn't always square with what experts say. For some problem sleepers, medication might be the best option, but on the other hand if you're looking for natural solutions, it might help to learn from someone who's been there, done that. Here's what experts advise, and the trial and error that led to my perfect sleep formula. Consider these options your first step to a better night's rest.

Skip the Nightcap

The Science: Alcohol is probably the substance used most often for sleep, reports a study in *Principles and Practice of Sleep Medicine*, one of the most authoritative texts on the subject. (It is also a major ingredient in many over-the-counter cold medications.) However, when you fall asleep under the influence, both the quantity and the quality of your sleep are adversely affected. Even small to moderate intakes of alcohol can suppress melatonin (a hormone that helps regulate sleep), interfere with restorative N-REM cycles, and prevent dreaming, according to Rubin Naiman, PhD, a clinical assistant professor of medicine at the Arizona Center for Integrative Medicine at the University of Arizona and coauthor of *Healthy Sleep*.

What works for me: I enjoy light social drinking too much to cut out alcohol completely, but I would never use it for sleep, because even a half glass of wine perks me up. I can usually get away with one or two glasses of white wine (not red) if I drink early in the evening and then switch to sparkling water, putting some hours between my last glass of wine and bedtime. My sleep may occasionally be the worse for it, but I can live with it; the greater relaxation of a pleasurable evening with friends outweighs the physiological damage it does.

Eliminate Caffeine

The Science: Caffeine boosts alertness, activates stress hormones, and elevates heart rate and blood pressure—none of which are very helpful when you're trying to get shut-eye. Some people are more sensitive than others to caffeine's effects, and one's sensitivity may be hereditary. And even if you've never had a problem with coffee, you may develop one over time; age-related changes in body composition can affect the speed at which caffeine is metabolized.

If you are sensitive to caffeine, take note that its half-life—the time required by your body to break down half of it—can be as long as 7 hours. In other words, if you were to have your last cup of coffee at 1 pm, a quarter of the caffeine it contained could still remain in your system as late as 3 am. In women, estrogen may delay caffeine metabolism even further. Between ovulation and menstruation, you take about 25 percent longer to eliminate it, and if you're on birth control pills, you take about twice the normal time. (Newer, low-estrogen pills may have less of an impact.)

Should Insomniacs Stay in Bed?

"If you can't sleep, get out of bed and do something else"—we hear this all the time. Experts are quite divided on this point: Some say yes, some no. We say, maybe. A series of studies done in the 1990s by National Institutes of Health researcher Thomas Wehr, MD, found that levels of melatonin and prolactin, a tranquility-promoting hormone, are both elevated when subjects doze. Sometimes you may drift off to sleep, and even if it's a wakeful kind of sleep, it's better than nothing.

"If you wake up in the middle of the night and your mind is agitated, it's probably a good idea to get out of bed," says Rubin Naiman, PhD, director of sleep programs for Miraval Resort in Tuscon. "But when people wake up and are at peace with it, it's fine to stay in bed. Occasional wakefulness is a normal part of the sleep cycle."

What works for me: It took me until my fifties to finally admit that when I woke in the middle of the night, heart pounding, it may have had something to do with the mocha java that jump-started my day— only a few cups, I told myself, and never after 3 pm. So I cut out coffee, and slept blissfully—for a week or so. Then my same old broken sleep pattern reasserted itself, only I was doubly miserable, without sleep and without coffee to perk me up. So I tried tea. It has about half the caffeine content of coffee and contains an as-yet-unnamed substance that may help calm the stress system, according to a 2007 study published in *Psychopharmacology*. Black tea was too strong for me, so I turned to green, which has about one-third the caffeine content of black. These days I drink 2 to 3 cups of green tea just after I get up. I don't love it the way I did coffee, but I like that it perks me up in the morning without keeping me up at night. So if you find life with decaf coffee just too bleak, there are options.

Turn Down the Thermostat

The Science: Most sleep researchers advise keeping your bedroom cool, but not cold. The National Sleep Foundation recommends between 54 and 75°F. This is because a cool room makes it easier for your core body temperature to drop, which must occur for you to fall asleep. (Body temp reaches its lowest point about 4 hours after you nod off.) However, the

thermostat is only part of the story: Proper air circulation and blankets that aren't too heavy—a big problem in hotel rooms—can also facilitate a drop in body temperature. A series of fascinating studies done in the past decade and a half by Swiss researchers Kurt Kräuchi and Anna Wirz-Justice, PhD, found an inverse relation between warm feet and cool body temp: When your feet and hands are warm, the blood vessels dilate, allowing heat to escape and body temperature to fall, initiating sleep. Conversely, when hands and feet are cold, the vessels constrict, retaining heat, which may keep you awake.

What works for me: I sleep in a cool room—much cooler than 75°F!—but I make sure my feet are warm. Wearing light socks makes it easier to resist the temptation to pile on too many blankets

in the winter. A hot bath seems an odd way of cooling down, but it works for me; afterward, body temperature falls off rapidly, "guiding the brain into sleep mode," explains Stanley Coren, PhD, author of *Sleep Thieves*. He recommends going directly from bath to bed, while other experts recommend waiting up to 45 minutes. I find I need twice that. Because temperature decline signals the body that it's time for sleep, turning on an electric blanket for 10 to 15 minutes and then turning it off may have the same effect.

Load Up on Carbs

The Science: Carbohydrates boost the availability of the sleep-inducing amino acid tryptophan in the blood, which in turn boosts serotonin. But don't assume that a big plate of pasta will put you to sleep. In fact, as a general rule, anything that raises body temperature, including the consumption of calories, wrecks sleep. Plus, if you have any digestive problems such as heartburn or gastroesophageal reflux disease (GERD), eating before bedtime is just asking for trouble.

What works for me: I avoid big meals within 5 hours of bedtime, and especially

NOTES FROM JOSLIN | Smoking before bed can cause sleep problems, as well as nightmares and difficulty waking in the morning. In addition to causing cancer, smoking increases blood glucose and blood pressure. If you smoke, quitting can help you sleep better and improve your health.

anything that's highly seasoned. (Spices raise body temperature.) But I also try not to go to bed hungry. That, too, can interfere with my sleep.

Don't Exercise within 3 Hours of Bedtime

The Science: Exercise, of course, raises core body temperature, which is why we're advised to skip it in the evening. However, I have found no studies actually showing that evening exercise is bad for sleep. In fact, some studies suggest that it might help.

What works for me: Sometimes, when I swim a mile or so in the early evening, I get a lovely wave of drowsiness—probably because the post-workout drop in body temperature signals my body it's time for

sleep. But my swimming is relatively relaxed, the equivalent of an after-dinner stroll; a strenuous aerobic workout might have the opposite effect. Some of the insomniacs I interviewed for my book told me that any evening exercise disrupts their sleep; some said that even daytime activity has a negative effect; some, like me, can swim or take long walks within an hour or two of bedtime. You need to find what works for you. I know that if I didn't exercise, I'd feel worse and my health would suffer, and that would ultimately undermine my sleep.

Develop a Sleep Ritual

The Science: Experts advise us to find relaxing activities in the evening to prepare us for slumber. "It should be something you do every night to signal to the body that it's time to unwind," explains clinical psychologist Michael Breus, PhD, clinical director of the sleep division for Southwest Sport and Spine in Scottsdale, Arizona, with board certification in clinical sleep disorders.

What works for me: I need a buffer zone between the day and sleep. When I plop into bed straight from an overscheduled day, when I work or socialize right up to the time I turn off the light, sleep doesn't come, or if it comes, it's light and patchy. Sometimes just stepping outside, onto a porch or balcony, helps me unwind. The sound of the wind in the trees and the clean, fresh smell of night air clear my

SIX REASONS YOU NEED A GOOD NIGHT'S REST

IT PREVENTS DIABETES. Sleeplessness increases insulin resistance, which is a precursor to type 2 diabetes.

IT MAINTAINS A STRONG IMMUNE SYSTEM. Sleep deprivation compromises immune function and makes you more vulnerable to disease.

IT SLOWS AGING. Too little sleep elevates levels of stress hormones and lowers levels of growth hormone, which is necessary for cell repair. In one study, young, healthy sleep-deprived subjects had the hormonal profiles of much older people.

IT KEEPS YOU SLIM. When you're sleep deprived, you have more of the appetite-stimulating hormone ghrelin in your blood and less appetite-curbing leptin, a combo that leaves you longing for junk food.

IT HELPS MAINTAIN A SHARP MEMORY. Even one sleepless night impairs concentration and memory and can affect job performance.

IT CAN MAKE YOU HAPPIER. Insomniacs face a higher risk of depression, alcoholism, and suicide.

head and shift my perspective. Even tidying up can be soothing: doing the dishes, putting away whatever I've been working on, anything that provides closure to one day and makes space for the next. A friend plays the piano just before he goes to bed. Nature programs work for some: "I have a tape about backyard bird-watching that I've never seen more than 5 minutes of," said one insomniac; another swore by the Golf Channel.

Dr. Breus recommends a "Power Down Hour": 20 minutes of doing things you have to finish, 20 minutes for personal hygiene, and 20 minutes for "relaxation"—however you define it. Because I work with words all day long, reading, writing, teaching, I'm often drawn to an activity that's more visually oriented. I enjoy a DVD, as long as it's not too action packed or adrenaline pumping. Then, if I get in bed and my mind keeps churning, I do a

form of visualization: I imagine a little man with a paintbrush (I picture him clearly, overalls and cap)—he paints a big black 100 on a billboard. I follow the brush strokes, slowly, carefully, as he paints 99, 98, and so on down, and often by the time I get to 80, it goes quiet inside.

Set a Regular Sleep-and-Wake Schedule

The Science: Most experts insist that we regularize our sleep. They point to evidence that our circadian rhythm—the natural ebb and flow of energy levels throughout the day—thrives on consistency. The more predictable our sleep schedule, the better our bodies work, they say. But even those who argue this most strongly admit that, while it helps to keep a regular sleep-wake schedule, it may not be the complete answer.

"Even if insomniacs keep regular sleep patterns, it doesn't necessarily mean they'll sleep well or long enough," says Kathryn Reid, PhD, a research assistant professor in the department of neurology at the Northwestern University Center for Sleep and Circadian Rhythm. Napping is an issue on which experts are divided.

What works for me: If I need a nap, I take one, with a few caveats. I don't take long naps and I don't nap most days. For me, even a few minutes has restorative effects. However, I try not to do it in the evening. Sara Mednick, PhD, an assistant professor at the University of California, San Diego, and author of *Take a Nap, Change Your Life*, advises leaving at least 3 hours between a nap and bedtime, but this is one of those rules where you have to find your own way. For me, any evening nap, even 5 or 6 hours before my bedtime, cuts into my nighttime sleep.

Always be careful about trying anything new the night before a day when you need a clear head, in case it backfires and keeps you awake. And it never hurts to make your doctor's office a first step, especially if your inability to sleep comes on suddenly. Sleeplessness can be a side effect of some medications or a sign of illness. And no matter what the experts say, listen to what your body tells you. Become a close observer of your sleep and the things that affect it—negatively and positively—and you'll likely chart your own path to the Land of Nod.

LAUGH

Away Stress

Diabetes can sure get you down. Here, Thomas Crook, PhD, explains how **clowning around improves your mood—** and also your memory and motivation.

A couple of years ago, my wife and I were visiting her mother, Mimi, who is now 90 years old. Mimi was demonstrating her remarkable memory for names by identifying everyone in her high school yearbook from many decades ago. When she was done, Mimi turned to my wife and said, "Well, that was fun, but I guess you and . . . what's his name . . . will have to be going now."

The story is now a comic standard in my family, and the first one I thought of when preparing this chapter. Like most funny anecdotes, the Mimi story has elements of surprise, tension, and resolution leading to laughter. But here's what you may not know: Humor is not just a silly diversion. It also yields important neuropsychological benefits—improving your mood, exercising your brain, masking pain, even strengthening your bonds with those who share a good chuckle with you.

What happens in your brain in response to a sidesplitting bon mot? Using functional magnetic resonance imaging (fMRI), researchers at the University College London Institute of Neurology

THE LAUGHTER-DIABETES CONNECTION

For someone with diabetes, a good chuckle can do even more than improve your memory, mood, and motivation. It can improve your blood sugar control.

Researchers in Japan studied 19 people with type 2 diabetes. Five people without

diabetes served as the control group. On two different days, the researchers gave the volunteers two identical 500-calorie meals.

On the first day, the people watched a 40-minute humorless lecture, but on the second day they watched 40 minutes of a Japanese comedy. The researchers tested the volunteers' blood sugar levels before and after the shows. They discovered that after watching the comedy, both the people with diabetes and the people without diabetes had lower blood sugar levels than they did after watching the lecture.

The researchers went so far as to say their study "suggests the importance of daily opportunities for laughter in patients with diabetes." That's certainly justification for catching the latest comedy.

found that as study subjects tried to understand verbal jokes, areas of their brains important to learning and understanding were activated. This means that as your brain wrestles with the meaning of a clever punch line, it's getting the same kind of workout that it would get from a brainteaser.

A good knee-slapper also produces a chemical reaction that instantly elevates your mood, reduces pain and stress, and boosts immunity (suppressed by both stress and pain). A recent fMRI study by Allan L. Reiss, MD, and colleagues at Stanford University traced this activity to a region called the nucleus accumbens (NAcc), which

rewards behaviors such as feeding and sex (and laughing) by releasing dopamine, a natural opiate.

Laughter promotes good health in another way, too—by strengthening connections. We use laughter to deflect anger and aggression and also to communicate goodwill. In fact, a good sense of humor is consistently rated by women as among the most desirable attributes of a potential partner.

Here are some ways you can reap the benefits of humor every day.

Keep an eye out for the unexpectedly silly side of daily life to combat negative thoughts. For example, at the end of a recent worry-filled day, I turned on a news channel that referred to its meteorologists as "the Weather Team That Tells the Truth." I thought the implication that other weather teams lie was hilarious. I laughed and immediately felt my worries melt away.

Make sure you don't go to bed stressed-out. Keep your evening entertainment light by reading a comic novel or watching a funny show. My wife and I were latecomers to *Seinfeld*, so we purchased DVDs of the early seasons, which we now watch at night.

Reframe unpleasant situations with humor. For example, I once heard a flight attendant deal with a surly, complaining passenger by saying: "You know, sir, on every flight I try to pick one passenger and ignore him or treat him poorly. Today, you are the passenger I chose." The result was laughter by both parties.

NOTES FROM JOSLIN | Did you know that 30 minutes of laughter a day, such as watching TV sitcoms or funny movies, can actually keep you healthy? A recent study showed that for adults with type 2 diabetes, laughter increased HDL (good cholesterol) by 26 percent and C-reactive protein (a marker of inflammation and cardiovascular disease) decreased by 66 percent at the end of 12 months. Laughter really is the best medicine!

Super-Simple

MEMORY FIX

It's not your imagination: Diabetes messes with your mind. Blood sugar swings can cause muddy thinking and memory problems. Strangely enough, one thing that might help is a little pressure. In the right dose, healthy stress can help you meet a deadline, ace a presentation, or solve a tough problem. Thomas Crook, PhD, shows you why.

My wife and I recently traveled to Arizona to visit our oldest daughter, our son, and their spouses. After trying to keep up with our four grandchildren for a few days, we left exhausted and with renewed appreciation for the stressful lives of young parents with demanding careers.

My daughter Carolyn is a trial lawyer, and I wondered how work and family pressures affect her ability to learn and recall the tremendous volume of information she needs to function well in court. After sifting through the latest neuroscience research, I was encouraged by what I learned: Certain kinds of stress can actually improve your mental performance.

When under stress, the body releases chemicals called glucocorticoids (GCs). Researchers have disagreed about how GCs affect learning and memory. Recently, Carmen Sandi, PhD, and a colleague of hers at the Brain Mind Institute in Lausanne, Switzerland, reviewed almost 200 studies in an attempt to resolve these differences. She found that medium to high GC (stress) levels facilitate some types of learning and memory, while very high and (surprisingly) very low GC levels impair them.

But for stress to give you a mental boost, it must relate to the task at hand—what she termed intrinsic stress. That's the kind of energizing pressure you feel when faced with a direct mental challenge, such as trying to meet a 5 pm. deadline. Extrinsic stress, on the other hand, does not directly relate to a specific mental task and can impair brain function.

So if you're stressed because your child is sick, it hurts your ability to deliver that report on time.

However, too much intrinsic pressure (a daily 5 pm deadline) can lead to very high GC levels and diminish the brain's ability to grow new neurons and neural connections. Yet aiming for zero stress is not the answer. Dr. Sandi's research shows that insufficiently challenging tasks (and very low GCs) can lead to poor results.

The key is balance. Here's some advice for manipulating the stress in your life to boost productivity.

Welcome the pressure. Tough deadlines, performance incentives, demanding supervisors—see them for what they really are: the structure and push you need to really excel.

Identify the source of your stress. Take a quick time-out to analyze its real cause. Knowing whether the pressure you're feeling is intrinsic or extrinsic is the first step to managing it.

Reduce the worst offenders. If you'll be working late on a project and you're most worried about the kids being home alone, hire a trustworthy babysitter. By addressing your biggest concerns, you'll gain a sense of control that will improve focus.

NOTES FROM JOSLIN | This just in: Recent studies indicate that eating 8 ounces of fatty fish, such as salmon, mackerel, sardines, halibut, or lake trout, twice a week may help prevent dementia. Fish oils are also important for heart health as they lower triglycerides, heart rate, and blood pressure.

Medical Breakthroughs   **214**

CHAPTER 24: Know Your Risk   **222**

CHAPTER 25: Diabetes Danger: Brain Attack   **233**

AVOID

Here's the latest research on

PART

COMPLICATIONS

diabetes-related complications.

COMPLICATIONS
Medical Breakthroughs

Diabetes wreaks havoc with your entire body. Uncontrolled diabetes can lead to serious medical complications, such as blindness, cardiovascular disease, kidney damage, and lower-limb amputations. But people with diabetes can avoid these life- and limb-threatening complications. **Here's the latest research on diabetes-related complications.**

People with diabetes can significantly lower their risk of heart disease and stroke simply by taking a daily statin. Researchers analyzed patients over 5 years and found that for every 1,000 diabetes patients given the cholesterol-lowering drugs, there were 42 fewer heart attacks and strokes than there would've been if they hadn't taken them. The statins even seemed to help those already diagnosed with vascular disease.

The one caveat: Avoid this regimen if you're pregnant.

■ NEVER HAVE A HEART ATTACK!

Here's some lifesaving advice: A huge study found that following five lifestyle guidelines slashes your heart attack risk by a whopping 92 percent. (And even incorporating just the first two into your routine cuts your risk by more than half.) Here's what researchers at Sweden's Karolinska Institutet and Boston University School of Medicine (who reviewed the histories of 24,444 women) say are the factors that count.

Moderate amount of alcohol: Drink no more than half a glass of wine daily.

Healthy diet: Base your diet on fruits, vegetables, whole grains, fish, and legumes.

Daily exercise: Move your body for more than 40 minutes of daily walking plus 1 hour a week of more strenuous activity.

Healthy body weight: It's best if your waist size is 85 percent or less of your hip size. Check yours by using a measuring tape.

Not smoking: Ideally you've never smoked, or you stopped at least 1 year ago.

■ ADOPT THE BEST ATTITUDE FOR YOUR HEART

Keep an optimistic outlook. It's proven to prevent a host of heart problems. According to a roundup by Harvard researchers,

a perennially sunny disposition will help you do the following.

Lower your blood pressure. Highly pessimistic adults are up to three times as likely to develop hypertension as happier ones, and people with the most positive emotions have the lowest blood pressure.

Ward off heart disease. Optimists have half the chance of developing cardiovascular disease compared with pessimists, according to one recent study.

Heal faster. Stay upbeat after bypass surgery, and you'll be 50 percent less likely to go back in the hospital.

Live longer. It's not just your heart: Multiple studies show that a cheerful outlook can ward off other health problems and add years to your life.

■ WALK OFF HARMFUL FATS

Brisk walkers may outpace joggers in lowering triglycerides, which is a blood fat that's linked with increased heart disease risk. Adults in a Duke University study who walked for 50 minutes four times a week decreased their triglyceride levels by 22 percent, which was nearly twice as much as those who ran for the same time.

Researchers think that lower intensity workouts might control triglycerides better because they use fats as their primary fuel, while high-intensity efforts draw on the quick energy of glucose.

■ AVOID THE WORST DIET FOR YOUR HEART

It might be a speedy way to slim down, but the Atkins diet can also raise your cholesterol and harm your heart just as quickly. When researchers at the University of Maryland School of Medicine put 18 adults on the Atkins, Ornish, or South Beach diet, those on Atkins increased their LDL (bad) cholesterol levels by 16 points and experienced hardening of the arteries in only 1 month.

The folks in the Ornish Diet group lowered bad cholesterol by 25 points, while those in the South Beach Diet group lowered it by 10 points. The people on the Ornish and South Beach diets experienced improved flexibility in their arteries.

Instead of cutting carbs to lose weight, reach for a balance of good carbs, lean protein, and healthy fats. (Of course, continue to monitor your carb intake if that's what your doctor has advised you to do.) Here's how.

Instead of: A cheese omelet for breakfast
Try: Scrambled egg whites and veggies wrapped in a whole-wheat tortilla
Instead of: A scoop of tuna salad for lunch

Heart Disease Danger

According to the American Diabetes Association, adults with diabetes have heart disease death rates about two to four times higher than adults without diabetes.

Try: Plain tuna mixed with pesto and veggies in a whole grain pita
Instead of: A bunless burger for dinner
Try: Lean beef and broccoli stir-fried in sesame oil with brown rice
Instead of: Turkey jerky as a snack
Try: Sliced apple wedges with 1 tablespoon almond butter

■ KNOW YOUR HEALTHY BRAIN NUMBER

198: Keep your total cholesterol under this level while in your forties, and you're 50 percent less likely to develop Alzheimer's disease than those with a score over 249, according to new research. Even a slight to moderate spike, between 221 and 248, raises risk by 30 percent.

Preventing Alzheimer's disease is especially critical for people with diabetes. Why? Because although experts aren't sure why, the two diseases are connected. People with type 2 diabetes have a higher risk of developing Alzheimer's, and also another form of dementia called vascular dementia. But fortunately some drugs prescribed for diabetes seem to slow the cognitive decline that's associated with Alzheimer's disease.

■ DOUBLE-TEAM HIGH BP

As many as two in three adults with diabetes have high blood pressure (BP), which is also sometimes called hypertension. Here's some promising new research to help.

Two-drugs-in-one combo pills gang up to reduce hypertension when other treatments fail, say University of Michigan researchers. Out of about 11,500 volunteers, a remarkable 73 percent of patients saw their BP drop to acceptable levels within 3 months using one of two dual therapies: an ACE inhibitor paired with either a calcium channel blocker or a diuretic. While both combo treatments zapped hypertension with equal effectiveness, the ACE inhibitor-calcium channel blocker pill (sold as Lotrel) reduced heart attacks and strokes by 20 percent more than the ACE-diuretic pill.

■ SET DOWN THE SALTSHAKER

You don't have to overhaul your diet to lower your blood pressure. Scientists at Shiraz University in Iran asked 60 adults

According to the American Diabetes Association, people with poorly controlled diabetes (A1C > 9 percent) are nearly three times more likely to have severe periodontitis than those without diabetes.

Heart Helper	Vitamin C Power (Percent of the Daily Value)
Yellow bell pepper (1 cup, chopped)	365%
Broccoli (1 stalk)	142%
Papaya (1 cup, cubed)	115%
Strawberries (1 cup, whole)	113%
Brussels sprouts (1 cup, whole)	100%
Kiwifruit (1 medium)	94%
Oranges (1 medium)	93%

with high blood pressure levels to refrain from salting their foods and eating obviously salted snacks, such as potato chips and salted peanuts. The result: After 6 weeks, their systolic blood pressure decreased by 8 percent, which is a drop the researchers say cuts stroke risk by 33 percent and heart disease and heart failure by 25 percent. If going cold turkey is too hard, fill half the saltshaker with pepper and gradually cut back to no added salt.

GO BANANAS FOR BETTER BP

To lower your blood pressure, don't just eat less sodium. You should also increase your potassium intake, because it speeds up the body's sodium excretion, say researchers at the Hypertension Institute of Nashville. Lead author Mark Houston, MD, says most Americans consume more sodium than potassium, but it should be the other way around. Here are some pop-

ular potassium-rich foods to help fix this: baked potatoes, tomato paste, lima beans, yogurt, cantaloupe, and bananas.

AVOID STROKE WITH C

Pile your plate high with vitamin C–rich foods to slash your stroke risk. UK scientists tracked more than 20,000 people for almost 10 years. Those who ate the most vitamin C had a 42 percent lower risk of stroke than people who ate the least. Because your body doesn't store C, it's safe to get up to 25 times the daily value (75 milligrams) each day.

CLOBBER DISEASE WITH CAPERS

These tiny buds may play a big role in preventing heart disease and cancer. When researchers from the Università di Palermo in Italy added caper extracts to cooked meat and simulated how the food would be broken down in the stomach, the capers helped prevent the formation of compounds that damage DNA. Look for jarred capers in the condiments aisle, near the pickles. Make like a chef and sprinkle on foods such as chicken piccata and smoked salmon, or drain them and add them to your favorite pasta, meat, or fish dish.

◾ WEIGH YOUR CANCER RISK

Keeping track of your BMI can help your body fight off colon cancer, say National Cancer Institute researchers who studied the health history of more than 200,000 women. They found that 50- to 71-year-olds who were just slightly overweight increased their odds of developing the disease by 29 percent, compared with their leaner peers. Being moderately overweight raised the risk by 31 percent; being obese, by 49 percent.

Fat cells produce and release hormones that may promote cancer cell growth, says the study's lead researcher Kenneth F. Adams, PhD. Women over 50 years of age who carry extra weight should consider having a screening colonoscopy.

AVOID COMPLICATIONS— KNOW YOUR NUMBERS

There is a lot you and your healthcare team can do to reduce the risks for the complications of diabetes. The most common complications may involve your heart, blood vessels, feet, eyes, kidneys and nerves. Keeping blood glucose levels in target range is only a first step. Controlling blood pressure and cholesterol is also important. Learn about the key tests or exams for staying healthy. Know when they should be done. Ask about the numbers or results and what they mean.

■ A1C

What is it? A blood test that shows the average blood glucose over the past 2 to 3 months

Why? It's the best way to measure overall glucose control

How often? Two to four times a year

Target goal: Less than 7 percent. Your goal may be different. Ask!

Action steps: Check your blood glucose levels; use the results and discuss with your healthcare provider.

Ask if your medicines need changing.

Review your meal plan and activity plan.

■ BLOOD PRESSURE

What is it? A test that measures the pressure against the walls of your blood vessels

Why? High blood pressure is more common in diabetes.

Having high blood pressure increases the risk of stroke, heart attack, kidney disease, and eye disease.

How often? At every check-up or at least once a year

Target goal: Less than 130/80mmHg— both numbers should be in target

Action steps: Be more active.

If you weigh too much, even losing a few pounds can help.

Use less salt and eat fewer salty foods.

Ask about medicines that can help lower your blood pressure.

■ CHOLESTEROL (LDL)

What is it? A blood test that measures the amount of fat that has built up on artery walls (LDL = "lousy" or "bad" cholesterol)

Why? Diabetes increases your risk of having heart disease.

LDL cholesterol can clog the walls of arteries.

If you catch problems early, they can be treated.

How often? Once a year—more often if levels are high

Target goal: LDL less than 100 (or lower if you have heart disease)

Action steps: If you smoke, try to stop.

Be more active.

Eat less saturated and trans fats.

Lose weight.

Ask about medicines to lower your blood cholesterol.

MICROALBUMINURIA

What is it? A urine test that measures how well your kidneys are working. "Micro" means tiny; "albumin" is a kind of protein. This test measures the protein in your urine.

Why? High blood glucose levels can damage kidneys.

If you catch problems early, they can be treated.

How often? At least once a year

Target goal: Less than 30

Action steps: Keep A1C in target range of less than 7 percent.

Keep blood pressure below 130/80mmHg.

Ask about medicines called ACE inhibitors that help control blood pressure and also help control microalbumin.

OTHER TIPS FOR STAYING HEALTHY

- Check your **blood glucose** regularly. Learn what results are too high for you and what results are too low. Know what to do when they fall out of range.
- Inspect your **feet** every day at home. Look for any redness, cracks, sores, or open areas. Make sure your healthcare provider checks your feet often, especially if you have any problems with circulation or vascular disease or if you have had a history of foot problems.
- Have a dilated **eye exam** every year.
- **Take medicines** as prescribed. Talk to your healthcare provider if you experience any side effects or decide to stop taking them for any reason.
- Ask about taking a daily **aspirin**.
- See your **dentist** for regular teeth and gum checkups.
- Have a **flu** shot each year. Ask if you need a Pneumovax shot.

CHAPTER
24

Know Your
RISK

Millions of Americans are *living* with diabetes. But the most important way to live well with diabetes is to manage your condition and remain vigilant for signs of complications. **Here's how.**

G etting a diagnosis of diabetes or struggling with existing complications can be scary and often overwhelming. You may have heard of stories of someone with diabetes who lost a foot or who went blind. You might be fearful whether it is inevitable that these complications will happen to you. The answer is no. Millions of people live long, healthy lives with diabetes, but it takes work on your part to learn about diabetes and take the right steps to stay healthy. The following are some important pointers about the complications of diabetes and what you can do to prevent them.

What's the Big Deal about Diabetes?

Blood glucose levels that run high for long periods of time can cause a number of complications, including heart disease, stroke, blindness, kidney disease, nerve damage, foot problems, and sexual dysfunction. The good news is that, accord-

ing to the Centers for Disease Control and Prevention (CDC), the rates of foot amputations and cases of blindness among people with diabetes have actually dropped in recent years. Also, many research studies focused on heart disease show lower rates of heart attack and stroke among people with diabetes than expected. Diabetes experts think that one explanation for this is that healthcare providers and patients are doing a better job of controlling risk factors such as blood pressure, LDL cholesterol, and A1C.

Diabetes Complications: Acute and Chronic

There are two types of complications that can occur in diabetes: acute and chronic. The acute complications of diabetes are those that can happen right away. Examples of acute complications are very low or very high blood glucose levels. Either of these situations can cause problems, but they are very treatable. The chronic complications of diabetes, on the other hand, are those that can happen over time, and they are a result of high blood glucose levels that are left untreated. These chronic complications include problems with the heart, brain, nerves, kidneys, eyes, and circulation. High blood pressure and high LDL (bad) cholesterol can make these complications even worse, so it is important to control blood glucose levels and cholesterol and blood pressure as well. Understanding the difference between acute and chronic complications is also important.

Acute Complications

LOW BLOOD GLUCOSE

A low blood glucose is a reading on your glucose meter of less than 70. You're at risk for low blood glucose if you take certain types of diabetes pills and/or insulin. Ask your healthcare provider if you are on a medicine that can cause low blood glucose. Low blood glucose is sometimes called "hypoglycemia" or "insulin reaction" and is very treatable. You may feel hungry, shaky, nervous, dizzy, weak, or irritable. If your blood glucose gets too low without treating it, you can become confused, fall, have an accident, or in some rare cases, even pass out or have a seizure. That's why it's important to know how to recognize and treat low blood glucose.

HIGH BLOOD GLUCOSE

High blood glucose levels can happen if you are not taking enough diabetes medi-

TREATING LOW BLOOD GLUCOSE

1. Check your blood glucose if you are feeling shaky, nervous, sweaty, confused, or weak.

2. If your glucose is less than 70, take any ONE of the following:

- 3 or 4 glucose tablets
- Half a cup of juice (4 ounces)
- Half of a 12 ounce can of regular soda (NOT diet)
- 1 tablespoon sugar, jelly, or honey

3. Check your blood glucose again in 15 minutes; if it's over 80, have a small snack so that you don't go low again. If it's still under 80, repeat step 2.

4. Try to figure out why you went low. Sometimes it can be from doing more physical activity or from eating less than usual. If you can't figure it out, let your healthcare provider know.

cation or if you eat more than your meal plan indicates, but also when you are sick or have an infection. If you have type 1 diabetes and your blood glucose gets too high, a serious condition called diabetic ketoacidosis can develop. In people with type 2 diabetes, a rare but serious condition called hyperglycemic hyperosmolar syndrome can occur. These conditions can be life threatening, which is why it's important to pay close attention to your diabetes when you are sick.

People with diabetes will often ask how high is too high, and that's a hard question to answer! Some people can go several months with blood glucose levels in the 200s and 300s and feel fine, while others will not feel well when their blood glucose is that high. In general, if your blood glucose is high (over 250) and you have an infection or are sick, for example, with the flu, you can get dehydrated more quickly than the average person. Your illness or infection can become more severe. It also takes longer to heal or recover from an illness when you have diabetes. That's why it's so important for people with diabetes to get a flu shot every year and a pneumonia shot once before the age of 65. It's also important to have a sick day plan in place so that you know what to do if you do become ill. Your provider or diabetes educator can help you develop your own individualized sick day plan.

Chronic Complications

Unlike acute complications, chronic complications happen over time and are a result of untreated or undertreated high blood glucose. High blood glucose (over 130 before meals and over 180 two hours after meals) along with high blood pressure and high LDL cholesterol can cause changes in the small and large blood vessels in the body. These changes can lead to high blood pressure and increased plaque in your arteries, putting you at higher risk for heart attack, stroke, kidney disease, nerve problems, blindness, and foot problems.

You can lower your chances of getting diabetes complications by:

1. Keeping your A1C less than 7 percent

2. Keeping your blood pressure less than 130/80mmHg

3. Keeping your LDL less than 100 mg/dl

4. Getting a urine test for microalbumin once a year

5. Checking your feet every day

6. Getting a dilated eye exam once a year

1. KEEP YOUR A1C BELOW 7 PERCENT

The A1C is one of the most important tests for people with diabetes. This test tells you the average of your glucose results over the past 2 to 3 months. For most people with diabetes, the A1C goal is less than 7 percent.

Two large studies done in the 1990s proved that controlling blood glucose reduces diabetes complications. One of these studies, the Diabetes Control and Complications Trial (DCCT), involving people with type 1 diabetes, showed that patients who kept their A1C at less than 7 percent reduced their risk of eye disease (retinopathy) by 76 percent and nerve problems by 60 percent. The second study, called the United Kingdom Prospective Diabetes Study (UKPDS), which looked at people with type 2 diabetes, demonstrated that keeping the A1C less than 7 percent reduced complications of the eyes, kidneys, and nerves by 37 percent. The UKPDS also showed that blood pressure and cholesterol control in diabetes were important factors in reducing the risk of heart disease and stroke.

2. KEEP YOUR BLOOD PRESSURE BELOW 130/80

People with diabetes are two to three times more likely to have a heart attack and twice as likely to have a stroke compared with people without diabetes. Circulation problems in the legs are also very common among people with diabetes. Aside from keeping blood glucose at tar-get, keeping your LDL under 100 and blood pressure less than 130/80 is the best way for you to prevent these complications.

People with diabetes are two and a half times more likely to have high blood pressure than people without diabetes. High blood pressure is a problem because if left untreated, it can damage the large vessels leading to your heart and brain and put

WHAT TO DO IF YOU'RE SICK

If you have diabetes, follow this sick-day plan.

- Check your blood glucose at least four times a day when you are ill or have an infection.
- Drink plenty of sugar-free, caffeine-free liquids to prevent dehydration.
- If you have type 1 diabetes, check for ketones in your urine if your blood glucose is over 250 and you are ill. If you are unsure of how to do this, ask your healthcare provider.
- If you have type 2 diabetes, ask your healthcare provider if you need to check for ketones in your urine.

Call your healthcare provider if:

- You are vomiting and unable to keep fluids down
- You have a temperature of greater than 101°F for more than 2 days
- Your blood glucose is over 250 for more than two readings in a row
- You are unsure of what to do
- Your infection is worsening

you at higher risk for heart attack and stroke. For people with diabetes, the goal is a blood pressure lower than 130/80. You will notice that this goal is lower than the target set for most people, which is less than 140/90. This is because people with diabetes have a higher risk for heart attack, stroke, and heart disease than people without diabetes.

Take the following steps to lower your blood pressure to less than 130/80.

- Have your blood pressure checked at every office visit and keep track of your numbers.

- If your blood pressure is over 130/80, talk to your healthcare provider about taking medication to lower it. Some people need to take several different types of blood pressure pills to get their blood pressure to target.

- Walk for 30 to 60 minutes every day.

- Eat a diet that is high in fresh fruits and vegetables and low in sodium (less than 2,400 mg per day). For more information, see the description of the DASH diet below.

- If you already have high blood pressure, buy a home blood pressure cuff and check it at home regularly.

- If you are overweight, even modest weight loss can help.

- If you smoke, talk to your healthcare provider about ways to quit.

3. KEEP YOUR LDL CHOLESTEROL BELOW 100

LDL (low-density lipoprotein) is a type of protein that carries cholesterol in your body. Too much LDL cholesterol is not good because it can cause plaque to build

THE DASH DIET

Dietary Approaches to Stop Hypertension (DASH diet) is a diet rich in fruits, vegetables, low-fat dairy products, whole grains, poultry, fish, and nuts, and low in red meat, sweets, and added sugar. The following is based on a 2,000-calorie-per-day diet:

- 7 to 8 servings of grains/starches/breads, with at least 3 servings from whole grain sources (1 slice bread or about 1/2 cup grain or cereal)
- 4 to 5 servings of fruit (about 1 small piece or 1/2 to 1 cup)

- 4 to 5 servings of vegetables (about 1 cup raw or 1/2 cup cooked)
- 2 to 3 servings of low-fat dairy products, such as milk and yogurt (about 1 cup)
- 2 servings lean meat, fish, or poultry (about 3 to 4 ounces per serving)
- 4 to 5 servings of nuts and seeds per week
- Limit fats and sweets

Following the DASH diet can lower the systolic blood pressure by 8 to 14 points.

up on your blood vessel walls, putting you at higher risk for heart attack and stroke. When you have diabetes, high LDL cholesterol can also lead to problems with your kidneys and eyes and decrease circulation to your feet. That's why it's very important to keep LDL less than 100 mg/dl (and less than 70 mg/dl if you have both diabetes and heart disease).

Eating a diet low in saturated and trans fat can help, but many people with diabetes need to take medication to lower their LDL to less than 100. Don't be discouraged if your provider prescribes cholesterol-lowering medication. Remember that your goal is to get your LDL to target.

Here's what can you do to lower your LDL cholesterol.

- See a dietitian to help you with a heart-healthy meal plan.

- Be physically active at least several times a week

- If prescribed, take your cholesterol-lowering medication as directed

- If you smoke, talk to your provider about how to quit

- Try to reach and maintain a healthy weight

4. GET A MICROALBUMIN TEST ONCE A YEAR

According to the National Kidney Foundation, about one-third of people with diabetes may get kidney disease. The best way to prevent kidney disease is to keep your blood pressure less than 130/80, your A1C less than 7 percent and your LDL cholesterol less than 100.

Early screening for kidney disease is also important. The best way to screen for early kidney disease is to get a urine test called the "microalbumin." This urine test is ordered by your healthcare provider and should be checked once a year if you have type 2 diabetes. If you have type 1 diabetes, it should be checked once a year as well, but usually only after you have had type 1 for 5 years. If your kidneys are damaged, small amounts of protein start to leak into the urine. The microalbumin test measures how much protein is in your urine. The goal for the microalbumin test is a reading of less than 30. Make sure your healthcare provider specifically orders this test; it is not the same as a routine urinalysis. High

microalbumin levels can be caused by other problems, such as a urinary tract infection or doing a lot of physical activity, so if the number is high, it may need to be rechecked 2 to 3 months later.

You can do the following things to slow or stop kidney problems, especially if the problem is caught early.

- Keep your A1C and blood glucose in target range as much as possible.

- Keep your blood pressure at or below target goal.

- Talk to your provider about taking an ACE inhibitor or an ARB. These are medicines that can keep your microalbumin from rising. They can also help control blood pressure.

5. CHECK YOUR FEET

The CDC estimates that one third of all people with diabetes over the age of 40 have some impaired feeling in their feet. High blood glucose can damage nerve endings. This damage is called neuropathy and usually starts in the feet. The big problem with neuropathy is that if you step on something sharp or have an infection, you may not feel pain, and pain is one of the best ways the body protects itself against infection and injury. Diabetes can also cause open cuts to heal more slowly, putting you at higher risk for infection. Checking your feet every day is one of the most important steps you can take to prevent foot problems.

Take the following steps to keep your feet healthy.

- Look at your feet every day for dry skin, cracks, or cuts.

- Wash your feet in warm (not hot) soapy water every day. *Do not* soak your feet.

- Use talcum powder if your feet tend to sweat. Dust off any extra powder.

- Put lotion on your feet (but not between your toes) to keep the skin from getting dry.

- File your toenails with an emery board and round the edges. Avoid cutting or clipping the nails because you can cut your skin instead of the nail.

- See a foot doctor (called a podiatrist) if you have corns or thick calluses, poor circulation, nerve damage, or thick toenails, or if you are unable to reach or see your feet.

- Do not use over-the-counter treatments for your corns, calluses, or toenails. These treatments can burn healthy tissue.

- Avoid going barefoot. This will protect your feet from injury.

- Wear cotton socks with shoes. (Cotton helps absorb sweat.)

- Have your healthcare provider check your feet at every visit.

- Quit smoking. Smoking decreases the amount of blood flowing to the feet.

Keep Your Sexual Function Healthy

Erectile dysfunction in men and sexual dysfunction in women is quite common with diabetes, yet it is often not discussed. Having a healthy sex life is important and can affect a person's sense of well being, so it is important for you to let your provider know if you are having problems. Problems with sexual function can be caused by hormonal imbalances, certain medications, and psychological issues, along with uncontrolled diabetes. People who have chronic high blood glucose levels, high cholesterol, and high blood pressure are at greater risk for having sexual dysfunction. Keeping your numbers at target is the best way to prevent this complication.

- Take care of cuts and sores right away by washing with soap and water and using a gentle antibiotic ointment on the area. If the cut is not healing, have your healthcare provider look at it. Check the cut at least twice a day.

Call your healthcare provider if:

- Cuts or scratches do not start to heal within 24 to 48 hours.

- You notice any drainage, increased redness, swelling, or pain.

- You are not sure what to do

6. GET A DILATED EYE EXAM ONCE A YEAR

The most common eye complication of diabetes is called retinopathy, a condition in which the blood vessels leading to the retina become leaky or overgrown. It is estimated that 40 percent of people with diabetes who are over the age of 40 have some form of retinopathy. If retinopathy is undetected and untreated (and there usually are no symptoms with retinopathy), it can lead to vision loss.

One of the best ways to screen for retinopathy is to have a yearly dilated eye exam. This is an exam in which drops are placed in the eye to dilate the pupil. You might have blurred vision for a couple of hours after the exam, but it is the best way for your eye doctor to get a good look at the retina. It is important to remember these two points: First, if you do have retinopathy, there are ways to treat it, and second, there are no symptoms with retinopathy, so don't assume that because your vision is good, you can skip the dilated eye exam.

You can keep your eyes healthy by:

- Getting a yearly dilated eye exam

- Keeping blood pressure, LDL cholesterol, and A1C in target

- Stopping smoking, if you do smoke

Staying Healthy with Diabetes

Remember, there are a lot of ways to prevent and treat the complications of diabetes and what you do makes a difference. Get the recommended tests, know your numbers, and if you are at increased risk, find out what you can do to get back on track. It is never too late to reap the benefits of living a healthier lifestyle.

Diabetes Danger:

BRAIN ATTACK

Two thirds of people with diabetes die of heart disease and stroke. So why do doctors overlook the danger? **Here's what you must know to protect yourself.**

T he statistics regarding stroke and diabetes are sobering. According to the American Diabetes Association, two out of three people with diabetes die of heart disease and stroke. The risk for stroke is two to four times higher among people with diabetes.

But that's not common knowledge. In the popular imagination, strokes happen at senior centers, not at motorcycle rallies. They're certainly not supposed to befall a woman like Sandra Thornburg. In 2001, Thornburg was a vibrant, 43-year-old exercise fanatic attending nursing school in Phoenix. Newly divorced, she embraced singlehood by meeting new people and trying new things, including riding Harley-Davidson bikes.

Thornburg was sleeping after a day's ride in northern Arizona when a sharp pain knifed through her head. She tried to get up, but her left side didn't work and her mind was in a fog. "I had no idea what was going on," she says. When she got to the hospital, her prognosis was grim. "They told my family I wasn't going to survive," she says.

A decade ago, it took a massive effort by researchers and others to alert women—and doctors—to the long-overlooked risk of female heart attacks. Now, experts say, it's time to turn the spotlight on another lurking danger: The devastation that can occur from a stroke, or "brain attack." More than 100,000 American women under age 65 suffer strokes every year, according to the American Stroke Association. That eclipses the 83,000 women in that age range who have heart attacks.

Even more surprising: The risk surges between ages 45 and 54. In those years, women are more than twice as likely as men to have strokes. And at every age, strokes are harder on women. They're more likely than men to wind up physically and mentally impaired.

"We all learned in medical school that

TWO TESTS THAT COULD SAVE YOU . . . AND WHEN TO ASK FOR THEM

THE ANKLE-BRACHIAL INDEX

A doctor compares the blood pressure in your ankle with the pressure in your arm.

If your pressure is lower at your ankle, it's a powerful sign of clogged arteries, which can foretell a stroke.

Consider it if: You've been told you're at increased risk of clogged arteries—perhaps because you're over age 50 and have diabetes or another condition that can threaten circulation.

A BLOOD TEST FOR A CLOTTING DISORDER

A blood draw can show if you have a disorder that encourages blood clots.

Consider it if: You or a family member has had deep vein thrombosis or another clotting problem.

strokes and heart attacks are male problems," says Lewis Morgenstern, MD, director of the stroke program at the University of Michigan Medical School. "The reality is far different."

Those grim statistics reflect plenty of missed opportunities: Doctors often overlook chances to prevent strokes in women, especially those that hit at relatively young ages. If a woman does have a stroke, studies show that her physicians will almost certainly take longer to diagnose it than they would for a man. And even after a woman's problem is recognized, she's less likely to get all the treatments and tests that can improve her chances of a successful recovery.

But it doesn't have to be that way. Here is what's behind the gender bias—and the facts that can save your life.

Who's Vulnerable

Thornburg felt perfectly healthy before her stroke, but a simple medical exam would have shown the ingredients for a catastrophe. "If the right risk factors are in place, a woman can have a stroke in her forties instead of her seventies," says David Katz, MD, MPH, director of the Prevention Research Center at Yale University. "But if she takes care of herself, the chances are very remote."

Thornburg's vulnerability started with high blood pressure and high cholesterol. Each encourages a buildup of arterial plaque, which is the raw material for a

stroke-inducing clot. (Most strokes occur when a clot chokes off blood to the brain; another type, caused by a burst blood vessel in the brain, is rare.) Studies show that women nearly halve their risk of stroke simply by bringing high blood pressure under control.

Lowering high cholesterol is just as helpful. But doctors are less likely to check women's cholesterol than men's, and if it's high, they treat it less aggressively. As for hypertension, it's undertreated in men and women. (For other risk factors that your doctor might miss, see "Are You at Risk? Six Surprising Signs" on opposite page.)

Thornburg's bad numbers were particularly unfortunate because she was on birth control pills. Most healthy women in their thirties and forties can take the Pill without worry as long as they don't smoke, says Cheryl Bushnell, MD, an associate professor of neurology at Wake Forest University. But even nonsmokers like Thornburg should steer clear of oral contraceptives if they already have a couple of stroke risk factors, such as diabetes, high cholesterol, hypertension, or obesity.

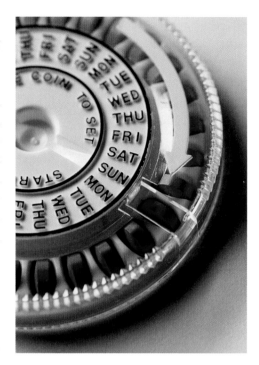

Where Docs Fall Short

Speed is critical in treating a stroke: There's just a 3-hour window to use a clot-busting drug called tissue plasminogen activator, or tPA, which greatly improves a victim's chances of avoiding death or lifelong disability. But gender differences in stroke symptoms can throw doctors off track. Delays in diagnosis help explain why a study of more than 2,000 patients in Michigan found that women were only about half as likely as men to get tPA.

Lori Manning knows what it's like to be on the wrong side of the gender divide. A 35-year-old multitasking machine before a stroke suddenly left her confused and capable of saying only "I'm okay," Manning was a prime example of women who stray from classic stroke symptoms. Several supposedly telltale signs—loss of

balance and sudden weakness, numbness, or paralysis on one side of the body—are less common in women than in men, a 2002 study showed. At the same time, women are more likely to suffer pain, confusion, or loss of consciousness, which are less familiar signs of stroke.

The symptom gap isn't the only thing that slows diagnosis. On average, women get to the emergency room an hour later than men when a stroke hits, partly because stroke isn't on their mental checklist of ER-worthy dangers. And when they reach the hospital, it takes women about an hour longer to be examined by a neurologist.

In Manning's case, doctors lost time checking for meningitis. They diagnosed the stroke after several hours, which is

ARE YOU AT RISK? SIX SURPRISING SIGNS

1. **High cholesterol** encourages a buildup of arterial plaque, raw material for a stroke-inducing clot. Yet like high blood pressure (which is a better-known stroke risk), it's undertreated.

2. **Birth control pills** may double the odds of having a stroke. Even in their thirties and forties, smokers and women with other risk factors should think twice.

3. **Hormone therapy** for menopause symptoms contains far less estrogen than even low-dose oral contraceptives—but still slightly increases stroke risk.

4. **Sleep apnea** interrupts breathing during sleep, raising both blood pressure and stroke danger. Yet doctors often overlook it in women.

5. **Migraine with aura** (the visual changes that can occur before migraines) doubles the risk of stroke in women under 55, though it's not clear why. Also unknown: what causes aura. What is clear: Women with migraine-plus-aura outnumber men 3 to 1.

6. **Blood clotting disorders** affect up to 8 percent of Americans, but they often go unrecognized. If you've had more than one miscarriage, you may tend to form blood clots. Other red flags include deep vein thrombosis (DVT)—a blood clot in the leg sometimes called economy class syndrome, because sitting for long periods in cramped seats can raise the risk.

too late for tPA. Manning has spent the past 5 years relearning how to talk and read, and only recently started to volunteer for the American Heart Association.

Even after diagnosis and treatment, women continue to get short shrift. In 2005, Dr. Morgenstern reported that female stroke patients often miss out on two critical tests that can help prevent further problems: They get imaging of the carotid arteries in the neck, which feed the brain, only 57 percent as often as men do, and an echocardiograph, which gives a detailed view of the heart, 64 percent as often. (Why is that important? Because abnormalities in heart rhythm can increase the risk of stroke.) One in seven stroke patients has a second stroke within

a year, Dr. Morgenstern says, and these tests are crucial in preventing that blow.

Thornburg was lucky: Her doctors eventually realized she had a clotting disorder and put her on a blood thinner to prevent a recurrence. Every step still takes concentration, but a few years ago, she was able to walk 15 miles in an American Stroke Association marathon.

How to Protect Yourself

While doctors catch up, take the following simple steps to stay healthy now and for decades to come.

Don't smoke. The habit roughly doubles the likelihood of having a stroke.

Get regular exercise. If you keep your

circulatory system in good shape, then your blood pressure stays low—slashing your stroke risk.

Watch your numbers. Your doctor should check your blood pressure every other year and cholesterol levels every 5 years (more often if your numbers are high). When you get your cholesterol tested, ask your doctor to also check your levels of highly sensitive C-reactive protein, or hs-CRP. Raised levels signal inflammation. An hs-CRP over 3 mg/l means an increased stroke risk, no matter how low your cholesterol, says Paul Ridker, MD, director of the Center for Cardiovascular Disease Prevention at Brigham and Women's Hospital in Boston.

Pick produce. Two large studies have found that each daily serving of fruits or vegetables trims your stroke risk by 6 percent.

Frequent the fish counter. A 2005 Harvard study concluded that people who ate fish even occasionally were about 12 percent less likely than seafood avoiders to suffer strokes. Eat fish at least once a week or ask your doctor if it makes sense

NOTES FROM JOSLIN | The National Stroke Association advises all to think FAST if you think you or someone else might be having a stroke:

Face: Ask the person to smile. Look to see if one side of the face drops.

Arms: Ask the person to raise both arms to see if one arm drifts downward.

Speech: Ask the person to repeat a simple sentence. Check to see if words are slurred and if the sentence is repeated correctly.

Time: If a person shows any of these signs, time is of the essence. Get to the hospital as quickly as possible. Call 9-1-1. Act FAST!

What the LDL?

Sixty-three percent of American women say they're worried about high cholesterol, but only 32 percent of them actually know their numbers, according to the Society for Women's Health Research. Ask your doctor to order a reading of your four most important cholesterol numbers—total cholesterol level, LDL, HDL, and triglyceride/blood fat level—and to explain to you what they mean.

to take a fish-oil supplement daily, researchers suggest.

Talk before taking hormones. If you're considering using the Pill or hormone therapy for menopause, make sure that your doctor knows your habits and history—especially if you smoke or if you have had a blood clot (or if a family member has ever had one).

Ask about aspirin. A 10-year study of nearly 40,000 women found that taking a low-dose aspirin (100 milligrams) every other day reduced the risk of stroke by 17 percent. Women over age 65 should talk with their doctors and consider a daily low-dose aspirin, says Dr. Ridker, who led the study.

PART

7

DIABETES

Here are 100 delicious and nutritious recipes,

COOKBOOK

CHAPTER

26

THE RECIPES

Here are 100 of the very best of this year's _Prevention_ recipes, specifically selected for people with diabetes. They're healthy, and they all taste great, too.

We selected recipes for meals with fewer than 40 grams of carbohydrates, and we chose snacks and sides with fewer than 25 grams. If you eat more than one dish per meal, take that into account. And be sure to coordinate your medicine with your meals.

Note that recipe analyses—and therefore the carb counts—don't include ingredients that are marked as "optional" or serving suggestions, such as "try this dish over rice." Take those additional foods into account when counting your carbs.

BREAKFASTS

"Open-Faced" Broccoli and Jack Omelet   245

Peach Breakfast Parfait   246

Red Pepper–Scallion Corn Muffins   247

Breakfast Bread Pudding   248

Sour Cream Waffles   249

Chocolate Oatmeal   250

Omelet Italian-Style   251

Mediterranean Breakfast Bake   252

Cinnamon Chip Muffins   254

Texas Breakfast Burritos   255

"OPEN-FACED" BROCCOLI AND JACK OMELET

MAKES 4 SERVINGS

- 3 large eggs
- 6 large egg whites
- 3 Tbsp 1% milk
- 2 cups Wok-Seared Broccoli (see recipe on page 298)
- 2 oz reduced-fat Monterey Jack cheese, grated (½ cup lightly packed)

1. Preheat the broiler and place the rack in the top setting (4" to 5" from heat). Whisk the eggs, egg whites, and milk in a medium bowl. Stir in the broccoli and half of the cheese.

2. Place a medium nonstick, broiler-safe skillet over medium-high heat. Pour the egg mixture into the hot pan. Reduce the heat to medium and let the omelet set for 2 minutes. Carefully lift one side of the omelet with a spatula and tilt the pan toward that side. Repeat on the other side. Continue tilting the pan until the center is almost set.

3. Sprinkle the remaining cheese over the omelet. Broil 2 to 3 minutes, until the omelet is set and the cheese is bubbly and golden on top.

PER SERVING:
155 CAL

| 16 g pro |
| 5 g carb |
| 8.5 g fat |
| 3 g sat fat |
| 2 g fiber |
| 348 mg sodium |

PEACH BREAKFAST PARFAIT

MAKES 2 SERVINGS

  1 cup canned peach slices (water or juice-packed), drained

$^2/_3$ cup fat-free vanilla yogurt

$^1/_4$ cup low-fat granola

    Ground cinnamon

PER SERVING:

176 CAL

6 g pro
39 g carb
0.8 g fat
22 g sat fat
2 g fiber
91 mg sodium

1. Divide the peaches between 2 cereal bowls and spoon the yogurt on top.
2. Top with the granola and sprinkle with cinnamon to taste.

RED PEPPER–SCALLION CORN MUFFINS

MAKES 6 TEXAS SIZE OR 12 REGULAR SIZE MUFFINS

$\frac{1}{2}$ cup canola oil, divided

1 medium red bell pepper, coarsely chopped

4 scallions, thinly sliced

$1\frac{1}{2}$ cups yellow cornmeal

$\frac{1}{2}$ cup white whole wheat or whole grain pastry flour

2 tsp baking powder

$\frac{1}{2}$ tsp salt

$\frac{1}{4}$ tsp baking soda

$\frac{1}{8}$ tsp freshly ground black pepper

$\frac{1}{2}$ cup fat-free plain yogurt

$\frac{1}{4}$ cup unsweetened applesauce

1 large egg

2 large egg whites

$\frac{3}{4}$ cup canned vacuum-packed corn kernels (about $\frac{1}{2}$ an 11-oz can), drained

1. Preheat the oven to 350°F. Coat a Texas-size, 6-cup muffin tin with cooking spray or line with paper baking cups.
2. Warm 2 tablespoons of the oil in a medium skillet over medium heat. Add the bell pepper and cook, stirring, for 5 minutes or until tender. Add the scallions. Cook, stirring, for 1 minute or until softened. Remove from the heat and let cool for 5 minutes.
3. Stir together the cornmeal, flour, baking powder, salt, baking soda, and black pepper in a large bowl.
4. In a medium bowl, whisk together the yogurt, applesauce, egg, egg whites, and remaining 6 tablespoons oil. Fold in the bell pepper mixture and corn. Fold into the dry ingredients until just moistened.
5. Divide the batter evenly among the prepared muffin cups. Bake 25 to 30 minutes or until a wooden pick inserted in the center comes out clean. Cool in the pan on a wire rack for 5 minutes. Remove the muffins from the pan to cool completely on the wire rack.

PER MUFFIN:

363 CAL

8 g pro
40 g carb
21 g fat
2 g sat fat
4 g fiber
472 mg sodium

When you buy canned corn, look for "vacuum-packed" on the label. That variety is higher in fiber, which helps quell hunger.

BREAKFAST BREAD PUDDING

MAKES 8 SERVINGS

- 2 cups evaporated skim milk
- 1 cup fat-free egg substitute
- $^2/_3$ cup sugar
- 1 tsp vanilla
- $^1/_2$ tsp ground cinnamon
- $^1/_2$ cup chopped mixed dried fruit
- $^1/_3$ cup currants
- 4 cups cubed multigrain bread, lightly toasted

PER SERVING:
204 CAL

11 g pro
38 g carb
2 g fat
0.5 g sat fat
2 g fiber
220 mg sodium

1. Preheat the oven to 350°F. Coat a 1$^1/_2$-quart baking dish with cooking spray.
2. In a large bowl, whisk together the evaporated milk, egg substitute, sugar, vanilla, cinnamon, dried fruit, and currants. Add the bread cubes and stir to coat. Transfer the mixture to the baking dish, making sure that the dried fruit is evenly distributed.
3. Bake 1 hour or until puffed and a knife inserted in the center of the pudding comes out clean. Serve warm.

You'll never guess that this custardy pudding has less than a gram of saturated fat per serving. Vary the pudding according to the dried fruit that you use. Apples, apricots, cherries, cranberries, figs, peaches, pears, and prunes are delicious options.

The pudding can be covered with plastic and stored in the refrigerator for up to 3 days. You can use any slightly stale bread, bagels, or hamburger buns for bread pudding. Store your leftover bread in the freezer until needed.

SOUR CREAM WAFFLES

MAKES 10

- ³⁄₄ cup fat-free milk
- ¹⁄₂ cup fat-free vanilla yogurt
- ¹⁄₄ cup fat-free sour cream
- 2 egg yolks
- 1 Tbsp canola oil
- 1 tsp vanilla
- 1³⁄₄ cups cake flour or 1¹⁄₂ cups all-purpose flour mixed with 3 Tbsp cornstarch
- 2 tsp baking powder
- ¹⁄₂ tsp baking soda
- ¹⁄₄ tsp salt
- ¹⁄₂ cup sugar
- 4 egg whites

1. Preheat a waffle iron according to the manufacturer's directions.
2. In a small bowl, combine the milk, yogurt, sour cream, egg yolks, oil, and vanilla. Mix well.
3. In a large bowl, combine the flour, baking powder, baking soda, salt, and ¹⁄₄ cup of the sugar. Mix well to combine. Add the egg-yolk mixture and stir until the batter is smooth.
4. Place the egg whites in a medium bowl. Using an electric mixer, beat on medium speed until foamy. Gradually beat in the remaining ¹⁄₄ cup sugar. Increase the speed to high and continue to beat until soft peaks form. Fold the egg-white mixture into the batter.
5. Spoon a scant ³⁄₄ cup batter into the center of the waffle iron. Cook until the waffle is golden brown and crispy. (Do not press on the iron during cooking or the waffle will collapse.) Repeat to make a total of 10 waffles.

PER WAFFLE:
181 CAL
6 g pro
33 g carb
2.5 g fat
0.5 g sat fat
0.5 g fiber
264 mg sodium

To save time in the morning, partially prepare the batter the night before. In a small bowl, combine the liquid ingredients except for the eggs. Cover the bowl and refrigerate. In a large bowl, combine the dry ingredients and cover with plastic wrap. In the morning, mix the egg yolks into the liquid ingredients, beat the egg whites and sugar, and follow the rest of the directions.

CHOCOLATE OATMEAL

MAKES 2 SERVINGS

- 1 cup old-fashioned oats
- 2 cups water
- 2 Tbsp freshly ground flaxseed
- 2 Tbsp unsweetened cocoa powder
- 4 tsp Splenda or sugar
- ¼ cup chopped walnuts

PER SERVING:

312 CAL

12 g pro
35 g carb
16 g fat
1.5 g sat fat
8 g fiber
6 mg sodium

1. Place the oats and water in large microwaveable bowl or container. Cover loosely with a lid or vented plastic wrap and microwave on high, stirring once or twice, for 6 minutes or until the oats are softened. Mix in the flaxseed, cocoa, and Splenda or sugar until well blended.

2. Spoon into 2 bowls, and sprinkle evenly with the walnuts.

OMELET ITALIAN-STYLE

MAKES 1 SERVING

- 1 Tbsp chopped onion
- 1 Tbsp chopped green bell pepper
- 1 Tbsp chopped tomatoes + more tomatoes for garnish
- 1 egg, beaten
- 2 egg whites, beaten
- ½ tsp Italian seasoning
- 1 tsp grated Parmesan cheese

1. In a medium nonstick skillet coated with cooking spray over medium heat, add the onion and peppers. Cook, stirring, for about 2 minutes or until sizzling.
2. Add the tomatoes. Cook for about 1 minute longer, or until just starting to soften. Add the egg and egg whites. Sprinkle with the seasoning. Reduce the heat to low and cook for about 5 minutes, lifting the cooked edges of the egg mixture with a fork so the uncooked egg can run underneath, or until the bottom is set. Cook 1 to 2 minutes or until the eggs are cooked through. Sprinkle with the cheese and fold the omelet in half.

PER SERVING:

123 CAL

15 g pro
3 g carb
5.5 g fat
2 g sat fat
0.5 g fiber
208 mg sodium

MEDITERRANEAN BREAKFAST BAKE

MAKES 4 SERVINGS

- 1 container (15 oz) fat-free ricotta cheese
- 1 tsp olive oil
- 1½ cups sliced scallions
- 1 clove garlic, minced
- 2 oz feta cheese, crumbled
- ¼ tsp ground allspice or nutmeg
- 3 small yellow squash, thinly sliced
- Salt
- Freshly ground black pepper
- 1 egg
- 4 egg whites
- ½ tsp dried Italian herb seasoning
- 5 sheets phyllo dough, thawed if frozen
- 1 cup shredded reduced-fat mozzarella cheese
- 2 sweet red peppers, roasted
- 1 Tbsp grated Parmesan cheese

PER SERVING:

364 CAL

36 g pro	
30 g carb	
12 g fat	
6 g sat fat	
3 g fiber	
830 mg sodium	

1. Set a sieve over a small bowl. Pour in the ricotta and drain for 10 minutes.
2. Warm the oil in a large nonstick skillet over medium heat. Add the scallions and garlic. Cook 2 to 3 minutes or until tender. Add the feta and cook 1 minute or until almost melted. Transfer to a large bowl. Stir in the ricotta and allspice or nutmeg.
3. Coat the same skillet with cooking spray. Add the squash and cook over medium heat, stirring occasionally, for 3 to 4 minutes or until softened. Season with the salt and black pepper. Transfer to a medium bowl.
4. Coat the skillet with cooking spray. Place over medium heat. In a small bowl, lightly beat the egg, egg whites, and Italian herb seasoning. Pour into the skillet, cover, and cook 2 minutes or until the eggs are almost set. Flip the omelet over and cook 2 minutes or until the eggs are set. Transfer to a plate.
5. Preheat the oven to 400°F. Coat a 9″× 9″ baking dish with cooking spray.

6. Drape 2 sheets of the phyllo across the baking dish; press into place along the bottom and over the sides. Mist with cooking spray. Working in the opposite direction, drape 2 more sheets of the phyllo across the baking dish. Mist with cooking spray. (The phyllo should overhang all sides of the baking dish.)

7. Sprinkle with $1/2$ cup of the mozzarella. Top with the ricotta mixture. Layer the omelet, roasted peppers, squash, and the remaining $1/2$ cup mozzarella. Sprinkle with the Parmesan.

8. Cut the last sheet of phyllo in half and place on top of the dish. Fold the overhanging phyllo over the top to completely cover the mixture. Mist lightly with cooking spray.

9. Bake 40 to 45 minutes or until golden brown and hot throughout. Serve warm or at room temperature.

You can easily assemble this dish a day in advance and bake it just before serving. If you assemble it in advance, refrigerate it until baking time. Add 5 to 7 minutes to the final baking time. You can also freeze the unbaked assembled dish for up to 1 month. If baking the frozen dish, add 30 minutes to the final baking time.

CINNAMON CHIP MUFFINS

MAKES 12

- 1 Tbsp cinnamon sugar
- 1½ cups unbleached all-purpose flour
- ½ cup sugar
- 3 tsp baking powder
- ½ tsp salt
- ½ cup fat-free milk
- 1 egg, lightly beaten
- ¼ cup light butter or margarine, melted
- 3 oz cinnamon baking chips

PER MUFFIN:
173 CAL

3 g pro	
26 g carb	
6 g fat	
4 g sat fat	
1 g fiber	
225 mg sodium	

1. Preheat the oven to 400°F. Line a 12-cup muffin tin with paper liners. Dust the bottoms with the cinnamon sugar.
2. In a large bowl, combine the flour, sugar, baking powder, and salt. Add the milk, egg, and butter and stir until just combined. Stir in the cinnamon chips. Evenly divide the batter among the muffin cups.
3. Bake 20 minutes or until a wooden pick inserted in the center of a muffin comes out clean.

TEXAS BREAKFAST BURRITOS

MAKES 4 SERVINGS

- 1 tsp olive oil
- 1/2 cup chopped onion
- 3 1/2 oz reduced-fat turkey sausage
- 2 cups fat-free hash-brown potatoes
- 1 can (4 oz) chopped green chile peppers
- 1/4 tsp freshly ground black pepper
- 2 eggs
- 4 egg whites
- 2 Tbsp fat-free milk
- 1/4 tsp ground red pepper
- 4 flour tortillas (8" diameter)
- 1/2 cup shredded reduced-fat Monterey Jack cheese
- 4 Tbsp salsa
- 2 Tbsp sliced black olives

1. Warm the oil in a large nonstick skillet over medium heat. Add the onion. Crumble the sausage into the pan. Cook, stirring occasionally, for 4 to 5 minutes or until the onions are soft and the sausage is browned. Add the potatoes and cook, stirring occasionally, for 5 to 8 minutes or until the potatoes begin to brown. Stir in the chile peppers and black pepper. Transfer to a large bowl.
2. In a small bowl, whisk together the eggs, egg whites, milk, and red pepper. Pour into the same skillet and place over medium heat. Cook, stirring occasionally, for 3 to 4 minutes or until lightly scrambled. (Do not overcook.) Stir in the potato mixture.
3. Wrap the tortillas in plastic wrap. Microwave on high for 1 minute.
4. Sprinkle each tortilla with 2 tablespoons of the cheese. Divide the egg mixture among the tortillas. Roll to enclose the filling. Top with the salsa and olives.

PER SERVING:
316 CAL

20 g pro
29 g carb
13 g fat
5 g sat fat
2 g fiber
852 mg sodium

You can buy fat-free hash-brown potatoes in the dairy or freezer section of most grocery stores. If using frozen ones, thaw them first. Try using English muffins instead of tortillas to make an open-faced breakfast dish.

APPETIZERS AND SNACKS

Spinach-Pesto Dip	257
Three-Bean Avocado Dip	258
Yogurt and Cucumber Dip	259
Creamy Veggie Dip	260
215-Calorie Taco Snack	261
Cranberry-Apple Chutney	262
Honey Barbecue Drummettes	263
Incredible Crab Canapes	264
Feta-Walnut Stuffed Cucumbers	265

SPINACH-PESTO DIP

MAKES 6 SERVINGS

- 1 package (10 oz) frozen chopped spinach, thawed and squeezed dry
- 3 scallions, thinly sliced (about 1/2 cup)
- 1/2 yellow bell pepper, finely chopped (about 1/2 cup)
- 1/4 cup + 2 Tbsp pesto sauce
- 1/3 cup reduced-fat sour cream
- 1/3 cup fat-free plain yogurt
- 1 1/2 Tbsp mayonnaise
- 1 large clove garlic, minced
- 1/2 tsp salt

1. Combine all ingredients in a bowl.
2. Cover and chill at least 1 hour before serving.

PER SERVING
(1/3 CUP):
140 CAL

6 g pro	
7 g carb	
10.5 g fat	
3 g sat fat	
2 g fiber	
391 mg sodium	

THREE-BEAN AVOCADO DIP

MAKES 12 SERVINGS

- 2 cans (15 oz each) red beans, rinsed and drained
- 2 cans (15 oz each) low-sodium black beans, rinsed and drained
- 2 cans (8.75 oz each) red kidney beans, rinsed and drained
- 2 tomatoes, chopped, or 1 can (14.5 oz) low-sodium diced tomatoes
- 2 cloves garlic, crushed
- 4 Tbsp chopped cilantro
- 2 tsp chili powder
- 2 cups picante sauce
- 1 Haas avocado, peeled, pitted, and chopped
  Low-fat Cheddar cheese, shredded (optional)

PER SERVING
(¾ CUP):

148 CAL

8 g pro

27 g carb

2 g fat

0.25 g sat fat

11 g fiber

472 mg sodium

1. Combine the red beans, black beans, kidney beans, tomatoes, garlic, cilantro, chili powder, and picante sauce in a slow cooker.
2. Cover. Cook on low about 4 hours. Stir in the avocado and serve. Top with cheese, if desired.

YOGURT AND CUCUMBER DIP

MAKES 4 SERVINGS

- 1 cup fat-free plain Greek-style yogurt
- ½ cup tahini (sesame seed paste)
- 3 Tbsp freshly squeezed lemon juice
- 2 large cloves garlic, minced
- 1 medium seedless cucumber (with skin), finely chopped (about 1 cup)
- 2 Tbsp finely chopped fresh mint
- 1 Tbsp finely chopped fresh dill
- ½ tsp salt
- ⅛ tsp freshly ground black pepper

1. Stir together the yogurt, tahini, lemon juice, and garlic in large bowl until well combined. Mix in the cucumber, mint, and dill.
2. Add the salt and pepper. Cover and chill for at least 1 hour before serving.

PER SERVING
(½ CUP):
217 CAL

| 11 g pro |
| 11 g carb |
| 16 g fat |
| 2 g sat fat |
| 2 g fiber |
| 323 mg sodium |

CREAMY VEGGIE DIP

MAKES 4 SERVINGS

- $1/3$ cup reduced-fat sour cream
- $1/4$ cup safflower oil
- 1 cup 1% small curd cottage cheese
- $1/4$ medium red onion, finely chopped (about $1/4$ cup)
- 1 jalapeño chile pepper, seeded and finely chopped
- 1 large clove garlic, minced
- 1 Tbsp freshly squeezed lemon juice
- $1/2$ tsp Worcestershire sauce
- $1/4$ tsp salt

PER SERVING
($1/2$ CUP):

200 CAL

8 g pro
5 g carb
17 g fat
3 g sat fat
0.5 g fiber
395 mg sodium

1. Whisk together the sour cream and oil in large bowl until creamy. Stir in the cottage cheese, onion, chile pepper, garlic, lemon juice, and Worcestershire.
2. Add the salt. Cover and chill for at least 1 hour before serving.

215-CALORIE TACO SNACK

MAKES 2 SERVINGS

- 2 soft corn tortillas (6" diameter)
- 2 Tbsp natural peanut butter
- 1 cup mixed berries or chopped fruit, such as kiwifruit, pineapple, banana, and mango
- 1 Tbsp shredded coconut

1. Warm the tortillas in the microwave for 10 seconds.
2. Spread each tortilla with 1 tablespoon of the peanut butter. Fill each with half of the fruit, and sprinkle evenly with the coconut.

PER SERVING:

215 CAL

5 g pro
27 g carb
10 g fat
1.6 g sat fat
4 g fiber
102 mg sodium

CRANBERRY-APPLE CHUTNEY

MAKES 6 SERVINGS

  2 cups fresh cranberries
  1 medium apple, peeled and cut into $1/4$" cubes (about 1 cup)
$1/3$ cup brown sugar
$1/4$ cup orange juice
  3 Tbsp cider vinegar
$1/2$ tsp salt
$1/4$ tsp grated fresh ginger or $1/8$ tsp ground ginger
$1/4$ tsp freshly grated lime zest
$1/8$ tsp ground cinnamon

PER SERVING:
($1/3$ CUP):

77 CAL

0 g pro

20 g carb

0 g fat

0 g sat fat

2 g fiber

167 mg sodium

1. Boil all the ingredients in a 2-quart saucepan over medium heat. Reduce the heat and simmer vigorously for 15 minutes, until the mixture is thickened.
2. Let cool and refrigerate.

HONEY BARBECUE DRUMMETTES

MAKES 4 SERVINGS

- 2 lb chicken drummettes
- 1/3 cup honey
- 1/3 cup tomato sauce
- 1 tsp grated ginger
- 1 tsp soy sauce
- 1 tsp Worcestershire sauce

1. Pull the skin off the drummettes and discard it; place the drummettes in a large, resealable plastic bag.
2. In a mixing bowl, combine the honey, tomato sauce, ginger, soy sauce, and Worcestershire. Pour over the drummettes. Refrigerate for 2 hours.
3. Preheat the oven to 350°F. Line a rimmed baking sheet with aluminum foil and coat it with cooking spray. Remove the drummettes from the marinade and arrange them on the baking sheet. Bake 15 minutes.

PER SERVING:
362 CAL

47 g pro
24 g carb
8 g fat
2 g sat fat
0.5 g fiber
431 mg sodium

INCREDIBLE CRAB CANAPES

MAKES 8 SERVINGS

2 cans (5½ oz each) flaked crabmeat, drained

2 Tbsp light mayonnaise

8 oz fat-free cream cheese, at room temperature

¼ tsp garlic powder

¼ tsp salt

Fresh parsley, chopped

PER SERVING:

78 CAL

7 g pro	
8 g carb	
2 g fat	
0.5 g sat fat	
0.5 g fiber	
586 mg sodium	

1. In a medium bowl, combine the crabmeat, mayonnaise, cream cheese, garlic powder, and salt. Stir gently until thoroughly mixed.
2. Line a small plate with a piece of plastic wrap and place the crab mixture in the center. Gently shape the mixture into a log, roll in the plastic wrap, and twist the ends to secure. Refrigerate for 2 hours.
3. Unwrap the cheese log, roll it in the parsley, and serve.

FETA-WALNUT STUFFED CUCUMBERS

MAKES 4 SERVINGS

- ½ cup walnut halves
- ¼ cup chopped fresh parsley
- ½ cup crumbled feta cheese (about 2 oz)
- ¼ cup fat-free milk
- 1 small clove garlic, minced (½ tsp)
- ½ tsp mild paprika
- ⅛ tsp ground red pepper
- 4 medium cucumbers, peeled, halved lengthwise, and seeded

1. Combine the walnuts and parsley in a blender or food processor and pulse until powdery in texture. Add the cheese, milk, garlic, paprika, and ground red pepper and puree until smooth.
2. Fill the cucumbers with the feta-walnut mixture, patting into place with a fork or spoon. Slice into wedges and lightly sprinkle with a little extra paprika.

PER SERVING:
164 CAL

6 g pro

8 g carb

12.5 g fat

3.5 g sat fat

3 g fiber

222 mg sodium

SALADS

Leafy Grilled Chicken Salad with Creamy
    Balsamic Dressing   267

Oriental Spinach Salad   268

Fresh Corn and Tomato Bruschetta Salad   269

Roasted Vegetable Salad   270

Quick Pasta Salad   271

Watermelon Salad   271

Roasted Butternut and Spinach Salad   272

Balsamic Tomato and Roasted Pepper Salad   273

LEAFY GRILLED CHICKEN SALAD WITH CREAMY BALSAMIC DRESSING

MAKES 4 SERVINGS

- ½ cup canned no-salt-added great Northern beans, rinsed and drained
- ¼ cup extra-virgin olive oil
- 3 Tbsp balsamic vinegar
- 2 large cloves garlic
- 8 large fresh basil leaves
- ⅛ tsp salt
- 5 oz mixed baby greens
- 1½ cups pre-grilled chicken breast strips
- ¼ large red onion, thinly sliced (¼ cup)
- 1 cup grape tomatoes or halved cherry tomatoes

1. Prepare the dressing: Puree the beans, oil, vinegar, garlic, basil, and salt in a blender until smooth. (Makes 1 cup.)

2. Arrange the greens among 4 plates. Top evenly with the chicken, onion, and tomatoes. Drizzle with ¼ cup of the dressing.

PER SERVING:
256 CAL

15 g pro	
14 g carb	
15.5 g fat	
2.5 g sat fat	
3 g fiber	
533 mg sodium	

ORIENTAL SPINACH SALAD

MAKES 4 SERVINGS

- 2 tsp cornstarch
- 1/3 cup defatted reduced-sodium chicken broth
- 3 Tbsp seasoned rice vinegar
- 1 Tbsp reduced-sodium soy sauce
- 1 Tbsp honey
- 1 tsp toasted sesame oil
- 1 tsp minced fresh ginger
- 1 clove garlic, minced
- 1 orange
- 5 cups lightly packed spinach leaves
- 1 cup thinly sliced mushrooms
- 1 cup mung bean sprouts
- 1 tsp toasted sesame seeds

PER SERVING:
77 CAL

3 g pro	
14 g carb	
2 g fat	
0.5 g sat fat	
2 g fiber	
204 mg sodium	

1. Prepare the dressing: Place the cornstarch in a small saucepan. Whisk in the broth until smooth. Add the vinegar, soy sauce, honey, oil, ginger, and garlic. Mix well.

2. Grate 1 teaspoon rind from the orange into the saucepan; cut the orange in half and squeeze the juice into the pan. Discard the orange. Bring the dressing to a boil over medium heat. Cook, whisking often, for 3 to 5 minutes or until thickened and translucent. Remove from heat and let cool slightly.

3. In a large bowl, combine the spinach, mushrooms, sprouts, and sesame seeds. Add the dressing and toss to combine.

FRESH CORN AND TOMATO BRUSCHETTA SALAD

MAKES 4 SERVINGS

- 1 cup fresh (uncooked) corn kernels, cut from 2 ears corn
- 1 cup grape tomatoes, halved
- 1 cup yellow pear or cherry tomatoes, halved
- 1 cup seeded and chopped tomato (about 1 large)
- ½ cup chopped Vidalia or other sweet onion (about ¼ large)
- ¼ cup chopped fresh mint
- 2 Tbsp chopped fresh basil
- 1½ Tbsp extra-virgin olive oil
- 1 Tbsp balsamic vinegar
- 1 Tbsp drained nonpareil capers
- ½ tsp salt
- ⅛ tsp freshly ground black pepper
- 4 slices (1 oz each) multigrain bread
- 1 clove garlic

1. Combine the corn, grape tomatoes, yellow tomatoes, chopped tomato, onion, mint, basil, oil, vinegar, capers, salt, and pepper in large bowl. Toss well.
2. Grill or toast the bread. Rub 1 side of each slice briefly with the garlic. To serve as a salad, place 1 slice of bread rubbed side up on each of 4 plates. Top each with 1 cup of the corn mixture. To serve as an appetizer, cut bread slices into small pieces, and top evenly with the corn mixture.

PER SERVING:
187 CAL

| 6 g pro |
| 27 g carb |
| 7 g fat |
| 1 g sat fat |
| 7 g fiber |
| 488 mg sodium |

ROASTED VEGETABLE SALAD

MAKES 4 SERVINGS

1½ lb small red potatoes, quartered

12 oz green beans, cut into 1" pieces

2 red bell peppers, thinly sliced

1 red onion, thinly sliced crosswise and separated into rings

½ cup defatted chicken broth

2 cloves garlic

2 Tbsp red-wine vinegar

1½ Tbsp olive oil

1 tsp crushed dried rosemary

¼ tsp freshly ground black pepper

8 kalamata olives, pitted and sliced

2 Tbsp lemon juice

PER SERVING:

225 CAL

5 g pro
37 g carb
7 g fat
1 g sat fat
7 g fiber
196 mg sodium

1. Preheat the oven to 425°F.

2. Coat a 9″ × 13″ baking dish with cooking spray. Add the potatoes, beans, red peppers, onion, broth, and garlic. Mix well. Roast, stirring every 10 minutes, for 20 to 30 minutes or until the vegetables are tender. Set aside.

3. Transfer the garlic to a small bowl and mash. Whisk in the vinegar, oil, rosemary, and black pepper.

4. Place the vegetables in a large bowl. Add the dressing and olives. Toss to mix well. Sprinkle with the lemon juice just before serving. Serve warm or chilled.

QUICK PASTA SALAD

MAKES 4 SERVINGS

- 1 1/2 cups whole wheat rotini
- 1 finely chopped plum tomato
- 1/2 cucumber, sliced, halved lengthwise, and seeded
- 2 Tbsp crumbled feta cheese
- 2 Tbsp light Italian dressing

1. Cook the pasta according to the package directions. Drain, rinse in cold water, and drain again.
2. In a large bowl, combine the pasta with the tomato and cucumber. Gently fold in the feta and toss with the dressing to coat. Serve at room temperature or refrigerate for 30 minutes before serving.

PER SERVING:
137 CAL

6 g pro
27 g carb
1.6 g fat
0.8 g sat fat
3 g fiber
185 mg sodium

WATERMELON SALAD

MAKES 4 SERVINGS

- 1 bag (4 oz) arugula, stems removed and roughly torn
- 2 cups cubed watermelon
- 1 package (3 oz) feta cheese, crumbled
- 2 Tbsp olive oil
  Freshly ground black pepper

1. In a large bowl, combine the arugula, watermelon, and feta.
2. Gently mix in the oil and pepper to taste.

PER SERVING:
146 CAL

4 g pro
8 g carb
12 g fat
4 g sat fat
1 g fiber
246 mg sodium

ROASTED BUTTERNUT AND SPINACH SALAD

MAKES 4 SERVINGS

- $^3/_4$ lb precut butternut squash cubes ($^3/_4$") or $^1/_2$ medium butternut squash, peeled, seeded, and cubed (2 cups)
- 1 large red bell pepper, cut into $^3/_4$" pieces
- 2 Tbsp extra-virgin olive oil
- 1 tsp chopped fresh thyme or $^1/_2$ tsp dried thyme
- $^1/_2$ tsp salt
- $^1/_4$ tsp freshly ground black pepper
- 2 Tbsp freshly squeezed lemon juice (about 1 lemon)
- 2 tsp honey
- $^1/_4$ small red onion, chopped (about $^1/_4$ cup)
- 4 cups loosely packed baby spinach (4 oz)
- 1 small Gala or Golden Delicious apple, cored and thinly sliced
- 1 cup thinly sliced radicchio
- $^1/_2$ cup unsalted sunflower seed kernels

PER SERVING:
238 CAL

5 g pro
25 g carb
15 g fat
2 g sat fat
7 g fiber
338 mg sodium

1. Preheat the oven to 425°F. Coat a rimmed baking sheet with olive oil spray.
2. Toss the squash and bell pepper with 2 teaspoons of the oil, thyme, $^1/_4$ teaspoon of the salt, and $^1/_8$ teaspoon of the black pepper in a medium bowl. Arrange in a single layer on the prepared baking sheet. Roast 25 to 30 minutes, stirring occasionally to prevent sticking, until tender and lightly browned. Let cool for 10 minutes.
3. Whisk the lemon juice, honey, and remaining 4 teaspoons oil, $^1/_4$ teaspoon salt, and $^1/_8$ teaspoon black pepper in a large salad bowl while the squash roasts. Stir in the onion. Add the spinach, apple, radicchio, sunflower seeds, and squash mixture and toss to combine.

BALSAMIC TOMATO AND ROASTED PEPPER SALAD

MAKES 4 SERVINGS

- 1½ tsp balsamic vinegar
- 1 tsp extra-virgin olive oil
- 1 tsp flaxseed oil
- 1 small clove garlic, minced
- ¼ tsp salt
- ⅛ tsp freshly ground black pepper
- 2 large red bell peppers, halved and seeded
- 2 large tomatoes, cut into ½"-thick slices
- ⅓ cup fresh basil leaves, julienned

1. Preheat the broiler. Coat a broiler-pan rack with cooking spray.
2. In a cup, whisk together the vinegar, olive oil, flaxseed oil, garlic, salt, and pepper; set aside.
3. Place the bell peppers, skin side up, on the prepared rack. Broil, without turning, for 8 to 12 minutes, or until the skins are blackened and blistered in spots.
4. Place the peppers in a bowl and cover with a kitchen towel. Let stand 10 minutes or until cool enough to handle. Peel the skin from the peppers and discard. Cut the peppers into ½"-wide strips.
5. Arrange the tomato slices on a platter. Scatter the pepper strips on top and sprinkle with the basil. Drizzle the dressing over the salad. Let stand at least 15 minutes to allow the flavors to blend.

PER SERVING:

66 CAL

2 g pro	
9 g carb	
3 g fat	
0.5 g sat fat	
3 g fiber	
172 mg sodium	

SOUPS

Creamy Honeydew Soup — 275

Spiced Cauliflower Soup — 276

Cream of Broccoli Soup — 277

Quick Thai Seafood Soup — 278

Tuscan Chicken Soup — 279

Tex-Mex Tomato Soup — 280

White Chicken Chili — 282

Black and White Bean Soup — 283

CREAMY HONEYDEW SOUP

MAKES 4 SERVINGS

- 4 cups cubed honeydew melon
- ¼ cup reduced-fat plain Greek-style yogurt (We used Fage Total 2%.)
- 1 Tbsp light floral or orange blossom honey
- 1 Tbsp freshly squeezed lime juice (½ lime)
- ½ tsp freshly grated lime zest (about ½ lime)

1. Puree the melon, yogurt, honey, and lime juice in blender until smooth.
2. Pour into 4 small bowls and sprinkle with lime zest before serving.

This cool, fruity soup is an ideal way to start or finish a light dinner. The key is a juicy, ripe melon; immature honeydew is hard and tasteless. Look for a creamy white rind, a velvety (not smooth) skin, and an overall heavy feel. If a melon is underripe, place on the counter out of direct sunlight for a few days. See photo insert.

PER SERVING:
87 CAL

2 g pro	
21 g carb	
0.5 g fat	
0.5 g sat fat	
1 g fiber	
35 mg sodium	

SPICED CAULIFLOWER SOUP

MAKES 4 SERVINGS

- 1 tsp canola oil
- 2 cinnamon sticks
- 2 tsp mild curry powder
- 1 medium onion, halved and sliced
- 2 cloves garlic, minced
- 2 Tbsp water
- 3 cups vegetable broth
- ½ head cauliflower, cut into small florets
- 1 cup thinly sliced mustard greens

PER SERVING:
92 CAL

5 g pro
16 g carb
2 g fat
0 g sat fat
6 g fiber
391 mg sodium

1. Warm the oil in a large saucepan over medium heat. Add the cinnamon sticks and cook until they are fragrant and begin to unfurl, about 2 minutes. Stir in the curry powder and reduce heat to medium low. Add the onion, garlic, and water. Cook, stirring occasionally, until the onion is soft and translucent, about 8 minutes.

2. Add the broth and cauliflower. Bring to a boil. Reduce heat and simmer, covered, for 25 minutes or until cooked through.

3. Stir in the mustard greens and cook until wilted, about 30 seconds. Discard the cinnamon sticks.

CREAM OF BROCCOLI SOUP

MAKES 4 SERVINGS

- 1 bag (14 oz) frozen loose-pack broccoli (4$\frac{1}{2}$ cups)
- 1 Tbsp butter or trans fat–free margarine
- $\frac{1}{4}$ cup finely chopped onion
- 1 Tbsp all-purpose flour
- 2 cups fat-free reduced-sodium chicken broth
- 1 cup fat-free evaporated milk
- $\frac{1}{2}$ tsp salt
- $\frac{1}{4}$ tsp freshly ground black pepper
- $\frac{1}{2}$ cup shredded reduced-fat sharp Cheddar cheese

1. Cook the broccoli according to the package directions. Drain and set aside.
2. In a large heavy saucepan over medium heat, warm the butter or margarine. Add the onion. Cook, stirring occasionally, for 2 minutes or until tender.
3. Place the flour in a bowl. Gradually add the broth, whisking constantly, until the flour is dissolved. Add the broth mixture and milk to the saucepan. Cook, stirring constantly, for 5 to 7 minutes or until bubbly and slightly thickened. Add the reserved broccoli, salt, and pepper. Simmer 5 minutes.
4. In a blender or food processor, puree the soup, in batches if necessary, and return to the saucepan. Stir in the cheese. Cook, stirring, over low heat for about 1 minute or until cheese melts.

PER SERVING:

157 CAL

12 g pro

15 g carb

6 g fat

3.5 g sat fat

3 g fiber

853 mg sodium

QUICK THAI SEAFOOD SOUP

MAKES 4 SERVINGS

- 1 Tbsp vegetable or canola oil
- 1 Tbsp minced garlic (3 large cloves)
- 1½ cups sliced button mushrooms (about 10)
- 1 medium red bell pepper, julienned
- 4 cups low-sodium chicken broth
- 1 cup clam juice
- ½ lb sea scallops, halved
- 3 scallions, thinly sliced on diagonal
- 2 small (2") pieces lemongrass (from bottom of stalk), smashed
- 1 large carrot, grated
- ½ lb haddock or cod fillet, cut into 2" chunks
  Freshly grated zest of 1 lime
  Freshly squeezed juice of 1 lime
- ½ cup cilantro leaves, chopped
- 1 tsp grated fresh ginger
- 1 tsp reduced-sodium soy sauce
- ½–1 tsp red-pepper flakes

PER SERVING
(2 CUPS):

200 CAL

26 g pro	
10 g carb	
5.5 g fat	
1 g sat fat	
2 g fiber	
476 mg sodium	

1. Heat the oil in a stockpot over medium heat. Add the garlic and sauté 1 to 2 minutes, being careful not to burn it. Add the mushrooms and sauté 2 minutes. Add the bell pepper and sauté 2 to 3 minutes longer or until softened.

2. Pour in the broth and clam juice. Add the scallops, scallions, lemongrass, and carrot and simmer gently for 5 minutes. Add the haddock, lime zest, and lime juice. Simmer 5 minutes longer.

3. Stir in the cilantro, ginger, soy sauce, and red-pepper flakes to taste. Remove and discard lemongrass before serving.

TUSCAN CHICKEN SOUP

MAKES 6 SERVINGS

 2 carrots, chopped (about 1 cup)
 1 rib celery, chopped (about 1/2 cup)
1/4 cup water
 2 Tbsp olive oil
 1 medium onion, chopped (about 1 cup)
 4 large cloves garlic, minced (about 1 1/2 Tbsp)
 1 large bay leaf (or 2 small)
 8 cups low-sodium chicken broth
 3 cups shredded roasted skinless chicken breast (1 lb)
 3 plum tomatoes, diced
1/2 cup grated zucchini (about 1 medium)
 1 can (15 oz) no-salt-added cannellini beans, rinsed and drained
 1 can (14 oz) artichoke hearts in water, drained, rinsed, and roughly chopped
 1 Tbsp chopped fresh oregano or 1/2 Tbsp dried
 1 Tbsp finely chopped fresh sage or 1/2 Tbsp dried
 1 Tbsp fresh thyme or 1/2 Tbsp dried
12 thin slices Parmesan cheese, cut with vegetable peeler (optional)

1. Place the carrots and celery in a small microwaveable bowl. Add the water and cover the top of the bowl loosely with plastic wrap. Microwave on high for 5 minutes or until the vegetables are almost tender.
2. Heat the oil in a stockpot over medium heat. Add the onion and sauté 5 to 7 minutes. Add the garlic and sauté another 1 to 2 minutes. Add the steamed vegetables and bay leaf. Sauté 4 to 5 minutes longer.
3. Pour in the broth. Add the chicken, tomatoes, zucchini, beans, and artichoke hearts. Simmer for 30 minutes. Remove and discard the bay leaf. Add the oregano, sage, and thyme and simmer for an additional 5 minutes. Top each bowl with 2 slices of cheese, if desired.

PER SERVING:
(2 CUPS)
218 CAL

22 g pro	
19 g carb	
6.5 g fat	
1.5 g sat fat	
5 g fiber	
503 mg sodium	

TEX-MEX TOMATO SOUP

MAKES 6 SERVINGS

  2 carrots, chopped (about 1 cup)
  2 ribs celery, chopped (about 1 cup)
  1 red bell pepper, chopped (about $^3/_4$ cup)
2$^1/_4$ cups water
  1 Tbsp olive oil
  1 medium onion, chopped (about 1 cup)
$^1/_4$ tsp salt
  1 large can (28 oz) no-salt-added diced tomatoes
  1 can (15 oz) no-salt-added black beans, rinsed and drained
$^1/_2$ cup cilantro leaves, chopped
  2 Tbsp chipotle chile pepper sauce (We used Tabasco brand.)
     Freshly squeezed juice of 1 small lime
  3 corn tortillas (6" diameter), sliced into $^1/_4$" strips
$^1/_4$ cup + 2 Tbsp fat-free sour cream (optional)

PER SERVING:
(1 CUP)

138 CAL

5 g pro

23 g carb

3 g fat

0.5 g sat fat

6 g fiber

186 mg sodium

1. Place the carrots, celery, and bell pepper in a small microwaveable bowl. Add $^1/_4$ cup of water, cover the top of the bowl loosely with plastic wrap, and microwave on high for 5 minutes or until the vegetables are just tender.

2. Heat the oil in a stockpot over medium heat. Add the onion and sauté until translucent, about 5 minutes. Add the steamed vegetables and season with the salt. Sauté an additional 5 minutes or until the vegetables are just slightly caramelized.

3. Add the tomatoes (with juice) and the remaining 2 cups water. (Depending on the brand of tomatoes, you may need to add more water.) Add the beans, cilantro, and chipotle sauce. Stir to blend, bring to a simmer, reduce heat to low, and cook 25 to 30 minutes. Add the lime juice and top each serving with tortilla strips and a tablespoon of sour cream (if desired) right before serving.

WHITE CHICKEN CHILI

MAKES 10 SERVINGS

1 Tbsp olive oil

3 lb boneless, skinless chicken breasts, cut into bite-sized chunks

2 onions, chopped

2 cloves garlic, minced

2 cans (14 oz each) fat-free, reduced-sodium chicken broth

4 cans (15.5 oz each) cannellini beans, rinsed and drained

1 can (4.5 oz) chopped green chile peppers

1 tsp salt

1 tsp ground cumin

$3/4$ tsp dried oregano

$1/2$ tsp chili powder

$1/2$ tsp freshly ground black pepper

$1/8$ tsp ground cloves

$1/8$ tsp cayenne pepper

PER SERVING:
257 CAL

37 g pro
22 g carb
2.5 g fat
0.5 g sat fat
6 g fiber
787 mg sodium

1. Heat the oil in a large pot over medium-high heat. Add the chicken, onion, and garlic and sauté until the chicken is lightly browned, 5 to 7 minutes. Transfer the chicken mixture to 4-quart or larger slow cooker. Add the broth, beans, chile peppers (with juice), salt, and remaining spices. Stir to combine.

2. Cover. Cook on low for 4 to 6 hours. Uncover and cook 1 more hour, stirring occasionally, until flavors are blended.

BLACK AND WHITE BEAN SOUP

MAKES 9 SERVINGS

- 1 Tbsp olive oil
- 1 cup chopped onion
- 1 cup chopped red and green bell peppers
- ½ cup sliced carrots
- 1½ tsp chopped garlic
- 4 cups reduced-sodium vegetable broth
- 1 cup canned black beans, rinsed and drained
- 1 cup canned cannellini beans, rinsed and drained
- 1 cup frozen corn kernels
- 1 tsp ground cumin
- 1 tsp ground coriander
- 1 Tbsp chopped fresh Italian parsley

1. Warm the oil in a large saucepan over medium heat. Add the onion and cook 5 minutes or until soft. Add the red and green peppers, carrot, garlic, and ½ cup of the broth. Cook 10 minutes, stirring often.
2. Add the black beans, cannellini beans, corn, cumin, coriander, and the remaining 3½ cups broth. Simmer 15 to 20 minutes or until vegetables are tender. Stir in the parsley.

Canned beans make this a quick soup to assemble. You can store this soup in the refrigerator for up to 5 days or in the freezer for up to 3 months. For a little Southwestern fire, try adding minced jalapeño peppers or reconstituted dried chipotle peppers.

PER SERVING:

96 CAL

4 g pro
18 g carb
2 g fat
0.5 g sat fat
4 g fiber
343 mg sodium

VEGETARIAN AND SIDE DISHES

Tex-Mex Stuffed Acorn Squash — 285

Dramatically Seared Green Beans — 286

Green Bean and Macadamia Nut Casserole — 287

Open-Faced Grilled Vegetable Sandwiches — 288

Grilled Almond Butter and Berry Sandwiches — 289

Mediterranean Salad-Wraps — 290

Four-Veggie Pizza — 291

Edamame with Asparagus, Scallions, and Egg — 292

Sweet Potatoes with Brown Sugar–Pecan Topping — 293

Portobello Parmesan — 294

Savory Fruit and Nut Stuffing — 295

Peanut Noodles with Tofu — 296

Sesame Tofu with Bok Choy and Corn — 297

Wok-Seared Broccoli — 298

Southeast-Asian-Style Eggplant — 299

TEX-MEX STUFFED ACORN SQUASH

MAKES 4 SERVINGS

- 2 medium acorn squash (about 1¼ lb each), halved and seeded
- 2 tsp olive oil
- ½ tsp freshly ground black pepper
- 1 cup canned black beans, rinsed and drained
- ½ cup pine nuts, toasted
- 1 large tomato (6 oz), coarsely chopped
- 2 scallions, thinly sliced
- 1 tsp ground cumin
- 2 oz reduced-fat Monterey Jack cheese, shredded (about ½ cup)

1. Preheat the oven to 425°F. Coat a rimmed baking sheet with olive oil spray.
2. Brush the cut sides and cavity of the squash with the oil. Sprinkle with ¼ teaspoon of the pepper. Place the squash cut-side down on the prepared baking sheet. Bake 30 to 40 minutes, until tender. (Don't pierce with a fork.) Turn the squash cut-side up.
3. Mix the beans, pine nuts, tomato, scallions, cumin, and remaining ¼ teaspoon pepper in a medium bowl. Spoon a heaping ½ cup of the bean mixture into each squash half, pressing down gently to get all of the filling in. Sprinkle evenly with the cheese.
4. Bake 10 to 15 minutes, until the cheese is melted and golden brown.

PER SERVING:
324 CAL

| 12 g pro |
| 38 g carb |
| 17.5 g fat |
| 3 g sat fat |
| 8 g fiber |
| 363 mg sodium |

DRAMATICALLY SEARED GREEN BEANS

MAKES 4 SERVINGS

- 2 Tbsp canola or peanut oil
- 1 lb whole green beans, trimmed
- 2 large cloves garlic, minced (1 Tbsp)
- $\frac{1}{8}$–$\frac{1}{4}$ tsp red-pepper flakes

PER SERVING:

98 CAL

2 g pro	
8 g carb	
7 g fat	
0.5 g sat fat	
4 g fiber	
7 mg sodium	

1. Place a large, deep skillet or wok over medium heat. After about 2 minutes, add the oil and swirl to coat the pan.
2. Raise the heat to high and wait about 30 seconds. Add the green beans and season with salt to taste. Cook 3 minutes, shaking the pan and/or using tongs to turn and move the beans so they cook quickly and evenly. Carefully taste the beans (may be crunchy) and cook until desired doneness.
3. Season with the garlic and red-pepper flakes to taste. Cook 1 minute longer. Serve hot, warm, or at room temperature.

GREEN BEAN AND MACADAMIA NUT CASSEROLE

MAKES 6 SERVINGS

1½ lb fresh green beans, trimmed

1 Tbsp olive oil

1 package (10 oz) sliced white button mushrooms

½ tsp dried thyme

½ tsp freshly ground black pepper

⅛ tsp salt

4 medium scallions, sliced (about ½ cup)

1 clove garlic, minced

1 cup reduced-sodium, fat-free chicken broth

½ cup 1% milk

2 Tbsp cornstarch

¾ cup chopped unsalted macadamia nuts

1. Preheat the oven to 375°F.
2. Steam the green beans in a steamer basket over a large saucepan of boiling water for about 10 to 12 minutes, until tender. Drain and transfer to an 8″× 8″ or 9″× 9″ baking dish.
3. Warm the oil in a large nonstick skillet over medium-high heat while the green beans cook. Add the mushrooms, thyme, pepper, and salt. Cook, stirring often, until the mushrooms are tender and lightly browned, for 6 to 8 minutes. Add the scallions and garlic and cook 1 minute longer. Add the mushrooms to the green beans.
4. Add the broth to the same skillet and bring to a boil over medium heat.
5. In a small bowl, whisk together the milk and cornstarch until the cornstarch is dissolved and add to the broth. Simmer until thickened, about 1 to 2 minutes. Pour over the green beans and mushrooms and stir to combine. Sprinkle with the nuts. Bake 15 to 20 minutes until heated and bubbly and the nuts are browned.

PER SERVING:
208 CAL
6 g pro
16 g carb
15.5 g fat
2.5 g sat fat
6 g fiber
161 mg sodium

OPEN-FACED GRILLED VEGETABLE SANDWICHES

MAKES 4

- 1 small eggplant (8 oz), cut into 8 slices
- 1 zucchini (8 oz), quartered lengthwise
- 1 red onion, cut into 4 slices
- 1 red bell pepper, quartered
- 5 tsp extra-virgin olive oil
- ¼ tsp salt
- ¼ tsp freshly ground black pepper
- ¾ cup canned white beans (such as cannellini), rinsed and drained
- 1 Tbsp freshly squeezed lemon juice (½ lemon)
- 2 multigrain submarine rolls (about 3 oz each), halved lengthwise
- 8 fresh basil leaves

PER SANDWICH:
240 CAL

8 g pro
39 g carb
8 g fat
1 g sat fat
9 g fiber
573 mg sodium

1. Preheat the grill to medium-high.
2. Brush the eggplant, zucchini, onion, and bell pepper with 4 teaspoons of the oil. Sprinkle with salt and black pepper and grill 6 to 7 minutes per side. Separate the onion into rings and slice the peppers.
3. Place the beans, lemon juice, and remaining 1 teaspoon oil in a small bowl while the vegetables cook. Lightly mash the beans with a fork until combined.
4. Grill the rolls until lightly toasted, 45 seconds per side. Spread the halves with the bean mixture and top each with 2 eggplant slices, 1 zucchini slice, one-fourth of the onion rings and pepper strips, and 2 basil leaves.

GRILLED ALMOND BUTTER AND BERRY SANDWICHES

MAKES 4

1	package (6 oz) fresh raspberries (1–1½ cups)
¼	cup raspberry fruit spread
8	slices light-style whole grain bread or whole grain cinnamon swirl bread
½	cup creamy almond butter

1. Mash the fresh raspberries into a raspberry spread in a small bowl with a fork. Spread 4 slices of the bread with 2 tablespoons each of the almond butter. Spread about 3 tablespoons each of the berry mixture over the almond butter and top with the remaining bread slices. Lightly coat the outsides of the bread with cooking spray.

2. Place the sandwiches on a large nonstick griddle or skillet over medium-low heat (in batches, if necessary). Cook 5 to 7 minutes, turning halfway through, to brown both sides. Cut each sandwich in half.

PER SANDWICH:
355 CAL
9 g pro
40 g carb
19.4 g fat
2 g sat fat
7 g fiber
334 mg sodium

MEDITERRANEAN SALAD-WRAPS

MAKES 4

$^1/_2$ cup green olive tapenade

2 Tbsp freshly squeezed lemon juice (about 1 lemon)

4 cups salad greens (4 oz)

$^1/_2$ cup canned no-salt-added chickpeas, rinsed and drained

$^1/_2$ cup drained and sliced jarred roasted red peppers (blotted dry)

$^1/_4$ medium seedless cucumber, halved and thinly sliced ($^1/_2$ cup)

$^1/_2$ small red or sweet onion, thinly sliced ($^1/_4$ cup)

2 oz crumbled goat cheese

4 whole wheat wraps or tortillas (8" diameter)

PER WRAP:
297 CAL

11 g pro
37 g carb
6 g fiber
12 g fat
3.5 g sat fat
684 mg sodium

1. Mix the tapenade and lemon juice in a large bowl with a fork. Add the greens, chickpeas, peppers, cucumber, and onion, and toss to mix well. Add the cheese and toss gently.

2. Warm the wraps or tortillas per the package directions.

3. Arrange one-quarter of the salad mixture onto the bottom of a wrap and roll up. Cut in half on an angle, placing a wooden pick in each half. Repeat with remaining wraps.

FOUR-VEGGIE PIZZA

MAKES 4 SERVINGS

- 1 thin whole wheat pizza crust (12" diameter) (We used Boboli.)
- 1/4 cup sun-dried tomato pesto
- 1 small zucchini, sliced (1 cup)
- 1 medium orange or yellow bell pepper, cut into thin strips (about 1 cup)
- 1 cup sliced cremini or button mushrooms
- 1/2 medium red onion, thinly sliced (1/2 cup)
- 2 tsp olive oil
- 2 oz fresh mozzarella cheese, thinly sliced
- 2 Tbsp grated Parmesan cheese
- 3/4 cup quartered grape or cherry tomatoes
- 1/2 cup thinly sliced fresh basil leaves

1. Preheat the oven to 425°F.
2. Put the crust on a baking sheet or pizza pan. Spread the crust with the pesto.
3. In a medium bowl, toss the zucchini, pepper, mushrooms, and onion with the oil. Place in a medium skillet over medium-high heat and sauté until the vegetables are soft and excess liquid has evaporated, about 6 to 8 minutes.
4. Top the crust evenly with the mozzarella and Parmesan. Arrange the sautéed vegetables over the cheese and top with the tomatoes. Bake 18 to 20 minutes, until the crust is baked through and slightly crisp. Sprinkle with the basil. Let stand a few minutes before cutting into quarters.

PER SERVING
(1 SLICE):
301 CAL
16 g pro

42 g carb

11 g fat

3 g sat fat

7 g fiber

600 mg sodium

EDAMAME WITH ASPARAGUS, SCALLIONS, AND EGG

MAKES 4 SERVINGS

2	large egg whites
1	large egg
¼	tsp freshly ground black pepper
2½	tsp toasted sesame oil
1	lb fresh asparagus, trimmed and cut on diagonal into 1" pieces
1	bunch scallions (about 6), trimmed and cut into 1" pieces
1½	cups frozen shelled edamame, thawed
3	cloves garlic, minced
1	Tbsp finely chopped fresh ginger
2½	Tbsp reduced-sodium soy sauce
¼	cup chopped fresh cilantro

PER SERVING:
159 CAL
13 g pro

11 g carb

7 g fat

1 g sat fat

6 g fiber

388 mg sodium

1. Whisk together the egg whites, egg, and pepper in a small bowl. Set aside.
2. Heat the oil in a wok or large nonstick skillet over high heat. Add the asparagus, scallions, edamame, garlic, and ginger. Stir-fry for 6 minutes.
3. Add the egg mixture and soy sauce. Stir-fry until the egg is just cooked through, about 30 seconds. Toss with cilantro.

SWEET POTATOES WITH BROWN SUGAR–PECAN TOPPING

MAKES 6 SERVINGS

2¼ lb sweet potatoes, scrubbed

Salt (optional)

Freshly ground black pepper (optional)

⅔ cup chopped pecans

2 Tbsp brown sugar

¼ tsp ground cinnamon

1. Preheat the oven to 375°F.
2. Place the potatoes on a rimmed baking sheet. Bake 1 to 1½ hours, depending on size, until soft when squeezed with a gloved hand. Let cool slightly and then cut in half.
3. Scoop the insides into a medium bowl (discard skin). Mash with a potato masher until smooth. Add salt and freshly ground black pepper to taste, if desired. Coat 9" glass pie plate with cooking spray. Transfer the mashed potatoes to the prepared pie plate. Smooth the surface.
4. Mix the pecans, sugar, and cinnamon in small bowl. Sprinkle evenly over the sweet potatoes.
5. Cover with foil and bake 20 to 25 minutes, until the potatoes are heated through. Uncover and bake 10 minutes longer, until the pecans are lightly browned and the top is crusty.

You can bake these sweet potatoes and assemble the dish earlier in the day. Just cover them and refrigerate. Let them stand for a few minutes on the counter before placing in oven about 45 minutes before dinnertime.

PER SERVING:
202 CAL

| 3 g pro |
| 28 g carb |
| 9.7 g fat |
| 1 g sat fat |
| 5 g fiber |
| 39 mg sodium |

PORTOBELLO PARMESAN

MAKES 4 SERVINGS

- 1 Tbsp extra-virgin olive oil
- 4 firm portobello mushrooms (4" diameter), stems and gills removed (leave edges of caps intact)
- ¾ cup fat-free ricotta cheese
- ½ cup shredded reduced-fat mozzarella cheese
  Freshly ground black pepper
- 1 large clove garlic, minced (1 tsp)
- 1 medium firm-ripe tomato, thinly sliced
- 1 Tbsp fresh thyme leaves
- 3 Tbsp grated Parmesan cheese

PER SERVING:

156 CAL

| 12 g pro |
| 11 g carb |
| 7 g fat |
| 2.5 g sat fat |
| 2 g fiber |
| 214 mg sodium |

1. Place a large ovenproof skillet over medium heat. After about a minute, add the oil and swirl to coat the pan. Place the mushrooms in the skillet cap-side down and cook undisturbed for about 10 minutes. Turn and cook on other side for 10 minutes. Turn over again.
2. Combine the ricotta, mozzarella, and garlic in a small bowl. Season with the pepper to taste.
3. Spoon about 3 tablespoons of the ricotta mixture into each mushroom cap (leave in pan), spreading gently into place.
4. Preheat the broiler.
5. Arrange a few tomato slices on each mushroom and sprinkle evenly with the thyme and Parmesan. Broil about 5 minutes or until the tops turn golden brown. (Watch carefully to prevent burning.)

SAVORY FRUIT AND NUT STUFFING

MAKES 6 SERVINGS

- 6 slices whole wheat bread, cut into 1/2" cubes
- 1 Tbsp olive oil
- 1 large onion, chopped
- 2 large ribs celery (with some leaves), coarsely chopped
- 1½ tsp dried sage
- ½ tsp freshly ground black pepper
- ¼ tsp salt
- 1 can (14.5 oz) reduced-sodium, fat-free chicken broth
- ¾ cup chopped hazelnuts
- ⅓ cup snipped unsweetened dried apricot halves
- ⅓ cup unsweetened dried cherries

1. Preheat the oven to 425°F. Coat an 8 × 8" or 9 × 9" baking dish (or 9" deep-dish pie plate) with cooking spray.
2. Place the bread cubes in an 11"× 7"baking pan. Bake, stirring often, until the cubes are golden and lightly crisp, 10 to 12 minutes. Set aside to cool in the pan. Reduce heat to 375°F.
3. Warm the oil in a medium nonstick skillet over medium heat. Add the onion, celery, sage, pepper, and salt and cook, stirring often, until the vegetables are tender, 8 to 10 minutes. Add broth, 1 tablespoon at a time, if the pan gets dry.
4. Put the onion mixture in a large bowl. Add the bread cubes, hazelnuts, apricots, cherries, and remaining broth. Mix well and transfer to the prepared baking dish. Cover with foil.
5. Bake 15 minutes, until heated through. Uncover and bake 20 to 25 minutes more, until crisp and browned.

PER SERVING:
241 CAL

| 8 g pro |
| 28 g carb |
| 12 g fat |
| 1 g sat fat |
| 7 g fiber |
| 411 mg sodium |

PEANUT NOODLES WITH TOFU

MAKES 4 SERVINGS

 4 oz soba noodles

 $^{1}/_{2}$ cup creamy reduced-sodium natural peanut butter

 3 Tbsp reduced-sodium soy sauce

 3 Tbsp rice wine vinegar

 $^{1}/_{2}$ Tbsp toasted sesame oil

 2 tsp chile paste with garlic (optional), see note above

 1 tsp sesame seeds, toasted

 4 oz light firm tofu, drained, patted dry, and cut into $^{1}/_{2}$" cubes

 2 cups shredded or grated carrots (about 2 large)

 3 scallions, thinly sliced ($^{1}/_{4}$ cup)

PER SERVING:

377 CAL

16 g pro	
36 g carb	
19.5 g fat	
3.5 g sat fat	
5 g fiber	
551 mg sodium	

1. Prepare the noodles according to the package directions.
2. Place the peanut butter in a small microwaveable bowl and microwave on high for 15 seconds to soften.
3. Whisk together the peanut butter, soy sauce, vinegar, oil, chile paste (if desired), and sesame seeds in a large bowl while the noodles cook. Set aside.
4. Heat a medium skillet coated with cooking spray over medium heat. Add the tofu and sauté until lightly browned, about 5 minutes.
5. Drain the noodles and add to the peanut sauce along with all but $^{1}/_{2}$ cup of the carrots. Mix until well combined. Top with the tofu and remaining carrots and sprinkle with the scallions. Serve immediately or chill and serve cold.

SESAME TOFU WITH BOK CHOY AND CORN

MAKES 4 SERVINGS

- 2 Tbsp sesame seeds
- 1 package (16 oz) firm tofu, drained (see note below) and cut into bite-size cubes
- 4 tsp toasted sesame oil
- 1½ lb baby bok choy, cut into 1" pieces
- 2 Tbsp finely chopped fresh ginger
- 3 cloves garlic, minced
- 1 can (15 oz) baby corn, rinsed and drained

1. Place the sesame seeds in a medium bowl. Add the tofu and gently roll around to coat the cubes.
2. Heat 2 teaspoons of the oil in a medium nonstick skillet over medium heat. Add the tofu and cook, turning occasionally, until golden brown on all sides, about 10 minutes.
3. Heat the remaining 2 teaspoons oil in a wok or large nonstick skillet over high heat. Add the bok choy, ginger, and garlic and stir-fry for 4 minutes. Add the baby corn and stir-fry for 2 minutes longer. Toss in the tofu and heat through.

PER SERVING:
241 CAL
17 g pro
11 g carb
14.5 g fat
2 g sat fat
3 g fiber
368 mg sodium

To drain tofu, place it between two plates lined with paper towels. Let the towels absorb the excess liquid for about 30 minutes.

WOK-SEARED BROCCOLI

MAKES 8 SERVINGS

- 1½ Tbsp canola oil
- 12 cups bite-size broccoli florets (about 4 medium bunches)
- ¼ tsp freshly ground black pepper
- 1 cup low-sodium chicken or vegetable broth
- 2 Tbsp reduced-sodium soy sauce
- 1 Tbsp orange juice

PER SERVING:
61 CAL

4 g pro	
7 g carb	
3 g fat	
0.5 g sat fat	
3 g fiber	
171 mg sodium	

1. Heat a wok or large skillet with cover over high heat. Add the oil and swirl to coat the pan.
2. Place the broccoli in the pan and toss to coat with the oil. Reduce heat to medium-high and sauté 4 minutes, allowing the broccoli to brown in spots. Season with pepper. Add the broth, cover, and cook 2 minutes longer, until crisp-tender.
3. Add the soy sauce and orange juice and toss the broccoli for 2 to 4 minutes, until all the liquid has evaporated and the broccoli is tender. Chill the leftovers in an airtight container for up to 4 days.

SOUTHEAST-ASIAN-STYLE EGGPLANT

MAKES 4 SERVINGS

- 2 Tbsp canola or peanut oil
- 2 large eggplants (about 3 lb—2.4 lb peeled weight), peeled and sliced lengthwise ($1/2$" thick) and then crosswise into $1/2$"-thick sticks
- 1 medium red onion, sliced (1 cup)
- $1/4$ tsp salt
- 3 large cloves garlic, minced (2 Tbsp)
- 3 serrano chile peppers, thinly sliced (Use plastic gloves when handling; avoid touching eyes.)
- $1/3$ cup dry sherry or $1/4$ cup rice wine vinegar
- $1/4$ cup water
- 2 Tbsp packed brown sugar
- 2 Tbsp reduced-sodium soy sauce
- 2 Tbsp freshly squeezed lime juice (1 lime)
- 1 cup (packed) fresh mint leaves, coarsely chopped

PER SERVING:
197 CAL

4 g pro	
29 g carb	
7.7 g fat	
6 g sat fat	
11 g fiber	
423 mg sodium	

1. Place a large skillet or wok over medium heat. Swirl in the oil to coat the pan. Add the eggplant, onion, and salt and cook, stirring, for about 5 minutes.
2. Add the garlic, peppers, and sherry or vinegar and cook, stirring constantly, for 5 minutes longer.
3. Combine the water, sugar, soy sauce, and lime juice in a small bowl and stir until the sugar dissolves. Stir into the eggplant mixture. Cover, reduce heat to low, and cook, stirring frequently, for 10 minutes or until the eggplant has reduced in volume by about half.
4. Remove from heat and stir in the mint.

CHICKEN DISHES

Capellini with Pine Nuts, Sun-Dried Tomatoes,
and Chicken   301

Grilled Chicken Breasts with Plum and Walnut Relish 302

Chicken, Broccoli, and Cashew Stir-Fry   303

Chicken-Olive Sauté   304

Chicken and Salad Pizza   305

Turkey Sausage and Peppers   306

Zesty Skillet Turkey and Noodles   307

Turkey Burgers with Chili Beans   308

Turkey Meatballs   309

CAPELLINI WITH PINE NUTS, SUN-DRIED TOMATOES, AND CHICKEN

MAKES 4 SERVINGS

- 4 oz whole wheat capellini or angel hair pasta
- 3 oz dry-packed sun-dried tomatoes
- 1½ Tbsp olive oil
- 8 oz chicken breast tenderloins, cut into bite-size pieces
- ⅛ tsp salt
- 3 cloves garlic, minced
- ¼–½ tsp red-pepper flakes
- ¼ cup sliced fresh basil
- ½ cup pine nuts, toasted

1. Prepare the pasta according to the package directions, without adding salt.
2. Meanwhile, soak the tomatoes in hot water for 10 minutes or until soft. Drain, reserving ½ cup of the water, and chop.
3. Heat the oil in a large skillet over medium-high heat while the pasta cooks. Season the chicken with the salt. Add the chicken, garlic, and red-pepper flakes to the skillet. Cook, stirring, until the garlic turns golden, 1½ minutes. Stir in the tomatoes and reserved water and cook 2 to 3 minutes, until chicken is completely cooked.
4. Drain the pasta, add to skillet, and toss. Add the basil and toss. Divide the pasta equally among 4 bowls and sprinkle each with 2 tablespoons of the pine nuts. Top with more basil, if desired.

PER SERVING:

387 CAL

22 g pro
36 g carb
19 g fat
2 g sat fat
6 g fiber
562 mg sodium

GRILLED CHICKEN BREASTS WITH PLUM AND WALNUT RELISH

MAKES 4 SERVINGS

- 2 medium black plums, pitted and chopped (1½ cups)
- ½ cup orange juice
- ¼ small red onion, chopped (2 Tbsp)
- 1 Tbsp honey
- 1½ tsp freshly grated orange zest
- ½ cup chopped walnuts
- 2 tsp olive oil
- ¼ tsp salt
- ¼ tsp red-pepper flakes
- 4 boneless, skinless chicken breast halves (6 oz each)

PER SERVING:

362 CAL

37 g pro	
18 g carb	
16 g fat	
2.5 g sat fat	
2 g fiber	
228 mg sodium	

1. Prepare the relish: Combine the plums, ¼ cup of the orange juice, and the onion, honey, and ½ teaspoon of the orange zest in a medium bowl. Stir in the walnuts (yields 2 cups).

2. Mix the oil, salt, red-pepper flakes, and remaining ¼ cup orange juice and 1 teaspoon orange zest in a pie plate or shallow dish with fork. Add the chicken and turn to coat. Let the relish and chicken stand 10 to 20 minutes.

3. Heat the grill to medium-high or coat a grill pan with cooking spray and heat 3 minutes over medium heat. Grill the chicken, turning once, about 10 minutes or until the chicken is browned and the internal temperature is 170°F and juices run clear. Serve with the relish.

CHICKEN, BROCCOLI, AND CASHEW STIR-FRY

MAKES 4 SERVINGS

- 3 cups small broccoli florets with short stems (about ½ lb crowns)
- 2 large carrots, cut into thin diagonal slices (2 cups)
- 5 oz soba noodles
- 1 Tbsp olive oil
- 1 Tbsp minced fresh ginger
- 3 large cloves garlic, minced
- 2 boneless, skinless chicken breast halves (6 oz each), sliced crosswise
- 1 Tbsp reduced-sodium soy sauce
- 1 tsp toasted sesame oil
- 3 medium scallions, thinly sliced (about ½ cup)
- ½ cup reduced-sodium, fat-free chicken broth
- ½ cup raw, unsalted cashews (2 oz), lightly toasted

1. Bring a large pot of water to a boil. Add the broccoli, carrots, and noodles. Cover and cook until the vegetables are crisp-tender, 3 to 5 minutes. Drain, transfer to a medium bowl, and cover loosely with wax paper.
2. Heat the olive oil, ginger, and garlic in a wok or large nonstick skillet over medium-high heat. Cook, stirring, until the garlic starts to turn golden, 1 to 2 minutes. Add the chicken, soy sauce, and sesame oil. Stir-fry for 4 to 5 minutes or until the chicken is cooked through. Add the scallions and stir-fry for 1 minute.
3. Stir in the noodles, vegetables, and broth and heat through. Sprinkle each portion with 2 tablespoons of the cashews.

PER SERVING:
376 CAL

27 g pro
40 g carb
13.6 g fat
2.3 g sat fat
5 g fiber
290 mg sodium

CHICKEN-OLIVE SAUTÉ

MAKES 4 SERVINGS

- 1 Tbsp olive oil
- 1 large onion, coarsely chopped
- 3 large cloves garlic, minced
- 1 tsp chopped fresh rosemary or $3/4$ tsp dried rosemary, crumbled
- 1 lb boneless, skinless chicken breast, cut into 1" pieces
- $1/4$ tsp freshly ground black pepper
- 40 large pitted kalamata olives, sliced (about $1^1/_3$ cups)
- 8 oz large cherry tomatoes, halved, or 2 medium tomatoes, cut into $1/2$" pieces (about $1^1/_2$ cups)

PER SERVING:

286 CAL

25 g pro	
10 g carb	
16 g fat	
2.5 g sat fat	
2 g fiber	
671 mg sodium	

1. Warm the oil in a large nonstick skillet over medium-high heat. Add the onion, garlic, and rosemary and cook, stirring often, until the onion and garlic are tender and just starting to brown, 3 to 4 minutes.

2. Add the chicken, sprinkle with the pepper, and stir. Cook, turning often, until the chicken is no longer pink, 5 to 7 minutes. Add the olives. Cook and stir for 1 minute until heated and fragrant. Stir in the tomatoes. Reduce heat to medium-low, cover, and cook 4 to 5 minutes longer, until the tomatoes are heated and juicy.

Note the sodium content in the recipe. Strive to limit your sodium intake to less than 2,300 mg per day.

CHICKEN AND SALAD PIZZA

MAKES 4 SERVINGS

- 1/4 cup extra-virgin olive oil
- 1 Tbsp + 2 tsp red wine vinegar
- 1/2 tsp dried oregano
- 1/4 tsp freshly ground black pepper
- 1/8 tsp salt
- 2 cups skinless shredded rotisserie chicken breast (8 oz) or leftover roasted chicken breast
- 2 medium tomatoes (8 oz), cut into 1/2" pieces
- 1/2 cup coarsely chopped jarred roasted red peppers, blotted dry
- 1/2 small red onion, chopped (1/4 cup)
- 1/2 package (10 oz) Italian salad mix (5 cups loosely packed)
- 2 oz reduced-fat goat cheese, crumbled
- 4 whole grain flatbread wraps (10" rectangle) (We used Flatout.)
- 2 cloves garlic, crushed

1. Preheat the oven to 350°F.
2. Mix 2 tablespoons of the oil with the vinegar, oregano, black pepper, and salt in large bowl. Stir in the chicken, tomatoes, red peppers, and onion. Toss to mix. Place the greens and cheese on top (don't toss).
3. Place the wraps on 2 baking sheets. Pour the remaining 2 tablespoons oil into small bowl and stir in the garlic. Spoon the oil over each wrap and spread evenly. Bake 10 to 12 minutes until lightly crisped.
4. Place a wrap on each of 4 plates. Toss the salad and spoon about 1 1/2 cups on each wrap.

PER SERVING:
377 CAL

30 g pro
24 g carb
20.5 g fat
3.5 g sat fat
10 g fiber
637 mg sodium

TURKEY SAUSAGE AND PEPPERS

MAKES 4 SERVINGS

- 2 Tbsp olive oil
- 1 large red bell pepper, cut into thin strips
- 1 large green bell pepper, cut into thin strips
- 2 medium yellow onions, cut into thin strips
- 3 cloves garlic, finely chopped
- 1 lb mild or hot Italian turkey sausage, cut into 4 equal pieces
- 1 can (28 oz) crushed tomatoes in thick puree
- 1 tsp dried Italian seasoning
- 1 tsp red-pepper flakes (optional)
-   Pinch of salt

PER SERVING:

356 CAL

24 g pro	
26 g carb	
20 g fat	
1 g sat fat	
6 g fiber	
997 mg sodium	

1. In a large, deep nonstick skillet over medium heat, warm the oil. Add the bell peppers, onion, and garlic. Cook, stirring frequently, for about 10 minutes, or until the peppers are softened. Transfer the vegetables to a bowl. Set aside.

2. Add the sausage to the same skillet. Cook, turning as needed, for 5 to 6 minutes or until browned on all sides. Add the tomatoes, the reserved pepper-and-onion mixture, seasoning, pepper flakes (if desired), and salt. Bring to a boil, then reduce to a simmer. Simmer for about 1 hour, or until the sausage is fork-tender.

ZESTY SKILLET TURKEY AND NOODLES

MAKES 6 SERVINGS

8 oz (4 cups) yolk-free medium-wide noodles

2 tsp olive oil

1 bunch scallions, all parts, sliced (about 8 scallions)

1 lb lean ground turkey breast

2 cans (14½ oz each) no-salt-added diced tomatoes

½ tsp Italian seasoning

¼ tsp salt

¼ tsp red-pepper flakes

¼ cup grated Parmesan/Romano cheese blend

2 Tbsp chopped parsley

1. Cook the pasta according to the package directions. Drain the pasta and return it to the cooking pot to keep warm.

2. In a large nonstick skillet over high heat, warm the oil. Add the scallions. Cook, stirring, for 1 minute. Add the turkey. Cook, breaking up the turkey with the back of a spoon, for 4 to 5 minutes or until no pink remains. Add the tomatoes, seasoning, salt, and red-pepper flakes. Reduce heat to medium-low. Cover and simmer for 10 to 15 minutes.

3. Toss the noodles with the turkey mixture. Top with the cheese and parsley.

PER SERVING:
291 CAL
27 g pro
34 g carb
5 g fat
1.5 g sat fat
3 g fiber
302 mg sodium

TURKEY BURGERS WITH CHILI BEANS

MAKES 4 SERVINGS

1 large onion, chopped

1 tsp olive oil

2-2$\frac{1}{2}$ tsp chili powder

$\frac{1}{2}$ tsp whole cumin seeds

$\frac{1}{8}$-$\frac{1}{4}$ tsp ground red pepper

1 can (15-16 oz) navy beans, rinsed and drained

1 can (15-16 oz) red kidney beans, rinsed and drained

1 can (8 oz) no-salt-added tomato sauce, plus $\frac{1}{2}$ can water

$\frac{1}{2}$ cup jarred roasted red peppers, chopped and drained

1$\frac{1}{4}$ lb ground turkey breast

$\frac{1}{4}$ cup jarred roasted red peppers, chopped, drained, and blotted dry

2 scallions, chopped

2 Tbsp plain dried bread crumbs

2 Tbsp chopped fresh parsley

1 Tbsp Dijon mustard

$\frac{1}{2}$ tsp coarsely ground black pepper

PER SERVING:
(WITHOUT
BUN)

369 CAL

47 g pro	
39 g carb	
4 g fat	
0.5 g sat fat	
12 g fiber	
667 mg sodium	

1. Prepare the beans: In a large nonstick skillet, combine the onion and oil. Cook over medium heat, stirring, 5 to 6 minutes. Add the chili powder, cumin seeds, and ground red pepper. Cook, stirring, for 30 seconds.

2. Stir in the navy and kidney beans, tomato sauce and water, and $\frac{1}{2}$ cup roasted peppers and bring to a boil. Reduce the heat to low, cover, and simmer for 10 minutes. Remove from heat, cover, and keep warm.

3. Make burgers: Preheat the grill to medium and oil the grate with cooking spray.

4. In a large bowl, combine the turkey, $\frac{1}{4}$ cup roasted peppers, scallions, bread crumbs, parsley, mustard, and black pepper. Mix gently but thoroughly until blended. Shape into four 1"-thick patties.

5. Grill the patties 10 to 12 minutes, turning once, or until a thermometer inserted into the thickest part registers 165°F and the meat is no longer pink. Serve each burger with 1 cup of beans.

Ground turkey makes a mean lean burger—if you're choosy about the meat. Make sure the label reads "ground turkey breast" (or specifies "99 percent fat free").

TURKEY MEATBALLS

MAKES 6 SERVINGS

1½ lb lean ground turkey breast

¾ cup quick-cooking oats

½ cup chopped onion

½ cup tomato sauce

1 egg

1½–2 cups tomato sauce

1. Preheat the oven to 400°F.
2. Mix the turkey, oats, onion, tomato sauce, and egg in a medium bowl. Roll into 1″ balls and place in a shallow pan. Bake about 20 minutes.
3. Place the tomato sauce in a large saucepan. Add the meatballs and simmer in the tomato sauce to heat throughout.

PER SERVING:

199 CAL

32 g pro

13 g carb

3.2 g fat

0.3 g sat fat

3 g fiber

505 mg sodium

BEEF AND PORK DISHES

Gingered Beef with Broccolini and Walnuts	311
Roast Beef Sandwiches	312
Beef and Mushroom Noodles	313
Homestyle Roast Beef	314
Orange Beef and Broccoli	315
Stuffed Pork Roast	316
Sweet and Sour Chinese Pork	317
Pork Kebabs Italiano	318
Grilled Pork Tacos with Avocado-Radish Salad	319

GINGERED BEEF WITH BROCCOLINI AND WALNUTS

MAKES 4 SERVINGS

PER SERVING:
289 CAL
27 g pro

16 g carb

14.5 g fat

3 g sat fat

3 g fiber

300 mg sodium

- 2 Tbsp oyster sauce
- 2 Tbsp finely chopped fresh ginger
- 1 Tbsp reduced-sodium soy sauce
- 1 tsp chile paste with garlic
- ¼ cup + 1 Tbsp water
- 2½ tsp toasted sesame oil
- 1½ lb broccolini, trimmed and cut into bite-size pieces
- ¾ lb lean flank steak, cut into thin strips
- 1 bunch scallions (about 6), trimmed and cut into 1"pieces
- ⅓ cup walnut pieces, toasted and coarsely chopped

1. Whisk together the oyster sauce, ginger, soy sauce, chile paste, and 2 table-spoons of the water in a small bowl.
2. Heat the oil in a wok or large nonstick skillet over high heat. Add the broccolini and stir-fry for 3 minutes. Add the remaining 3 tablespoons water and stir-fry for 2 minutes. Add the steak, scallions, and oyster sauce mixture and stir-fry for 1 minute or until the beef is rosy and just cooked through. Stir in the walnuts and serve immediately.

ROAST BEEF SANDWICHES

MAKES 4

- 1/3 cup fat-free cream cheese, at room temperature
- 2 Tbsp fat-free mayonnaise
- 2 Tbsp mango chutney
- 2 tsp prepared horseradish
- Freshly ground black pepper
- 4 crusty rolls, halved
- 1 lb thinly sliced lean roast beef
- 4 leaves lettuce
- 4 slices tomato
- 4 very thin slices red onion
- 4 spears kosher dill pickles (optional)

PER
SANDWICH:
316 CAL

| 30 g pro |
| 34 g carb |
| 6 g fat |
| 2 g sat fat |
| 2 g fiber |
| 1,398 mg sodium |

1. Make the horseradish spread: In a small bowl, stir together the cream cheese, mayonnaise, chutney, and horseradish until well combined. Season with the pepper.

2. Make the roast beef sandwiches: Spread the horseradish mixture on the top and bottom half of each roll. Divide the roast beef among the bottom halves of the rolls. Top with the lettuce, tomato, and onion. Top with the remaining roll halves. Serve with pickles (if desired).

Note the sodium content in the recipe. Strive to limit your sodium intake to less than 2,300 mg per day.

BEEF AND MUSHROOM NOODLES

MAKES 4 SERVINGS

- 4 oz whole wheat noodles
- 2 Tbsp cornstarch
- 2 cups fat-free reduced-sodium beef broth
- 1 Tbsp soy sauce
- 1 lb beef top round steak
- 2 Tbsp canola oil
- 12 oz baby bella mushrooms, sliced
- 1 large sweet onion, halved and sliced
- 1 cup thinly sliced carrots
- 2 Tbsp chopped fresh parsley (optional)
- 2 tsp salt-free seasoning blend
- ½ tsp freshly ground black pepper
- 4 tsp reduced-fat sour cream (optional)

1. Cook the noodles according to the package directions. Drain the noodles and return them to the cooking pot to keep warm.
2. Meanwhile, place the cornstarch in a small bowl. Gradually add the broth while whisking constantly until the cornstarch is dissolved. Add the soy sauce and set aside.
3. Cut the beef into thin slices across the grain. Set aside.
4. In a large nonstick skillet over high heat, warm 1 tablespoon of the oil. Add the mushrooms, onion, and carrots. Stir to mix. Cook, stirring frequently, for about 4 minutes or until the vegetables start to soften. Transfer to a plate and set aside.
5. Return the skillet to high heat. Add the remaining 1 tablespoon oil. Scatter the beef in the skillet. Cook, tossing frequently, for about 4 minutes or until browned. Add the parsley (if desired), seasoning blend, pepper, the reserved vegetables, and the broth mixture. Cook, stirring, for 4 minutes or until bubbling and thickened.
6. Reduce heat to medium-low. Simmer for about 10 minutes for the flavors to blend. Serve over the noodles. Garnish each serving with 1 teaspoon of the sour cream, if desired.

PER SERVING:
433 CAL

34 g pro	
35 g carb	
17 g fat	
4 g sat fat	
4 g fiber	
478 mg sodium	

HOMESTYLE ROAST BEEF

MAKES 8 SERVINGS

- 1 boneless beef tri-tip roast (bottom sirloin) (1½–2 lb)
- 2 cups frozen pearl onions, thawed
- 2 cups baby carrots
- 1 Tbsp canola oil
- 2 tsp garlic herb seasoning blend
- ½ tsp salt
- 1 cup fat-free reduced-sodium beef broth

PER SERVING:
182 CAL

19 g pro	
10 g carb	
7 g fat	
1.5 g sat fat	
0.5 g fiber	
272 mg sodium	

1. Preheat the oven to 375°F. Coat the inside of a heavy roasting pan with cooking spray.
2. Place the roast, onions, and carrots in the pan. Drizzle the oil over the meat and vegetables. Toss with clean hands to coat. Sprinkle with the seasoning blend and salt. Rub the seasonings all over the roast.
3. Roast for about 50 minutes or until an instant read thermometer inserted into the center registers 155°F. Remove the roast and vegetables to a platter. Let stand for 10 minutes.
4. Meanwhile, place the roasting pan over medium heat. Add the broth and cook, scraping the pan bottom with a spatula to release the browned particles. Boil a few minutes to reduce the sauce. Slice the roast. Serve the beef and vegetables drizzled with the pan juices.

ORANGE BEEF AND BROCCOLI

MAKES 4 SERVINGS

- 1/4 cup chicken broth
- 3 Tbsp dry sherry or chicken broth
- 1/2 cup orange juice
- 2 Tbsp soy sauce
- 1 Tbsp grated fresh ginger
- 2 tsp cornstarch
- 1 tsp toasted sesame oil
- 1/2 tsp red-pepper flakes
- 3/4 lb beef sirloin, trimmed of all visible fat and cut into 1/4"-thick strips
- 2 tsp vegetable oil
- 1 large bunch broccoli, cut into florets
- 1 bunch scallions, cut into 1/4"-thick diagonal slices
- 3 cloves garlic, minced
- 2 cups cooked basmati rice

1. In a medium bowl, combine the broth, sherry or broth, orange juice, soy sauce, ginger, cornstarch, sesame oil, and red-pepper flakes. Add the beef, tossing to coat. Let stand for 10 minutes.

2. Heat 1 teaspoon of the oil in a large skillet over medium-high heat. Add the beef to the skillet; reserve the marinade. Cook the beef, stirring, for 3 minutes or until browned. Transfer to a plate.

3. Add the remaining 1 teaspoon vegetable oil to the skillet. Add the broccoli, scallions, and garlic; cook, stirring, for 2 minutes. Add 2 tablespoons water. Cover and cook 2 minutes or until the broccoli is tender-crisp. Add the reserved marinade and cook, stirring, for 3 minutes or until the mixture boils and thickens slightly. Return the beef to the pan and cook, stirring, for 2 minutes or until heated through.

4. Serve over the rice.

PER SERVING:

341 CAL

27 g pro
36 g carb
10 g fat
2.5 g sat fat
5 g fiber
590 mg sodium

STUFFED PORK ROAST

MAKES 8 SERVINGS

¾ cup Cranberry-Apple Chutney (see recipe on page 262)

2 ½ lb boneless, center-cut pork loin, butterflied and trimmed of fat

2 oz blue cheese crumbles

1 tsp olive oil

½ tsp salt

¼ tsp freshly ground black pepper

PER SERVING:
250 CAL

| 33 g pro |
| 6 g carb |
| 10 g fat |
| 4 g sat fat |
| 1 g fiber |
| 359 mg sodium |

1. Preheat the oven to 350°F.
2. Spread the chutney on the loin (lay flat, cut-side up), leaving a 1/2″ border. Top with the cheese. Roll the loin back into shape and tie with twine at 1″ intervals.
3. Rub the loin with the oil and sprinkle with the salt and pepper. Place on a rack in a roasting pan and roast for 1 hour and 15 minutes or until the internal temperature registers 155°F. Let sit for 10 minutes before slicing.

SWEET AND SOUR CHINESE PORK

MAKES 4 SERVINGS

- 2 Tbsp reduced-sodium soy sauce
- 1 Tbsp white or rice vinegar
- 1 Tbsp cornstarch
- 1 cup reduced-sodium chicken broth
- 1 Tbsp canola oil
- 12 oz pork loin, cut into 1" cubes
- 1 cup chopped red onion
- 1 red or yellow bell pepper, thinly sliced
- 1 Tbsp minced garlic
- 1 cup canned-in-juice pineapple chunks, drained

1. In a small bowl, whisk the soy sauce, vinegar, cornstarch, and about $\frac{1}{4}$ cup of the broth until smooth. Gradually add the remaining $\frac{3}{4}$ cup broth, whisking constantly, until smooth. Set aside.

2. Heat a nonstick wok or large skillet over medium-high heat for 2 minutes. Add $\frac{1}{2}$ tablespoon of the oil. Add the pork. Cook, tossing constantly, for 3 to 4 minutes longer or until the pork is no longer pink. Remove and set aside.

3. Add the remaining $\frac{1}{2}$ tablespoon oil to the pan. Add the onion, pepper, and garlic. Cook, tossing constantly, for 3 to 4 minutes or until crisp-tender. Add the pineapple and the reserved pork to the pan. Add the reserved cornstarch mixture. Cook, stirring constantly, for 3 to 4 minutes longer or until the mixture thickens and is heated through.

PER SERVING:
233 CAL

19 g pro	
17 g carb	
10 g fat	
3 g sat fat	
2 g fiber	
749 mg sodium	

PORK KEBABS ITALIANO

MAKES 4 SERVINGS

- ¼ cup dry bread crumbs
- 2 Tbsp grated Pecorino Romano cheese
- 2 tsp Italian seasoning
- 2 tsp minced garlic (2 medium cloves)
- ½ tsp salt
- ¼ tsp freshly ground black pepper
- 12 oz boneless pork loin, cut into 1" cubes
- ½ carton (5 oz) grape or cherry tomatoes (about 1 cup)
- 1½ cups frozen pearl onions, thawed
- 1 Tbsp olive oil

PER SERVING:

292 CAL

24 g pro	
28 g carb	
9.5 g fat	
3 g sat fat	
5 g fiber	
467 mg sodium	

1. Preheat the grill.
2. In a small bowl, combine the bread crumbs, cheese, seasoning, garlic, salt, and pepper. Toss to mix. Set aside.
3. In a medium bowl, combine the pork, tomatoes, and onions. Toss with the oil to coat.
4. Thread the meat, tomatoes, and onions alternately on 8 metal or soaked bamboo skewers. Put an even number of ingredients on each skewer. Place on a tray. Sprinkle with the seasoning mixture, making sure that all surfaces are coated evenly.
5. Grill the skewers, turning often, for about 10 minutes or until the pork is no longer pink and the juices run clear.

If you prefer, instead of grilling the kebabs, you can cook them in a 375°F oven or on a stove-top grill pan. If you're using bamboo skewers, soak them in water first.

GRILLED PORK TACOS WITH AVOCADO-RADISH SALAD

MAKES 4 SERVINGS

- 1½ tsp paprika
- ¼ tsp salt
- ¼ tsp garlic powder
- ¼ tsp dry mustard
- ¼–½ tsp ground red pepper
- 1 trimmed pork tenderloin (about 1¼ lb)
- 1 Tbsp olive oil
- 8 whole grain tortillas (6"–7" diameter)
- ¼ tsp dried oregano
- 1 ripe medium avocado, halved, pitted, peeled, and cut into ¼" chunks
- ½ cup sliced radishes (about 4 large)
- 2 scallions, thinly sliced
- 1 Tbsp freshly squeezed lime juice (about ½ lime)

1. Preheat the grill to medium.
2. Prepare pork: In a small bowl, mix the paprika, salt, garlic powder, mustard, and red pepper. Rub all over the pork. Drizzle the pork with the oil.
3. Grill the pork, turning two or three times, for 20 to 25 minutes or until a meat thermometer inserted into the thickest part registers 150°F. Transfer the pork to a cutting board and let stand, covered, for 10 minutes.
4. Meanwhile, wrap the tortillas in foil and place on a cooler corner of the grill to warm for about 10 minutes.
5. Make salad: In small skillet over medium heat, toast the oregano, stirring often, for 2 to 3 minutes. Set aside.
6. In a medium bowl, mix the avocado, radishes, scallions, lime juice, and toasted oregano.
7. Cut the pork on an angle into thin slices. Place a tortilla on a work surface. Arrange a few pork slices on the bottom half, top with some of the salad, and roll up, folding in the sides. Repeat with the rest of tortillas, pork, and salad.

PER SERVING:

382 CAL

41 g pro

28 g carb

19 g fat

3 g sat fat

20 g fiber

562 mg sodium

FISH AND SEAFOOD DISHES

Salmon and Herb Penne — 321

Parmesan-Crusted Tilapia — 322

Zesty Baked Fish — 323

Roasted Fish with Crisp Potatoes — 324

Sweet and Tangy Wild Salmon with Onion
and Tomatoes — 325

Chile Sautéed Shrimp — 326

Baked Spaghetti Squash with Shrimp — 327

Stir-Fried Rice Noodles with Shrimp — 328

Garlic Shrimp with Spinach and Shiitake Mushrooms — 329

Southwestern Shrimp Pizza — 330

SALMON AND HERB PENNE

MAKES 4 SERVINGS

- 4 oz whole wheat penne
- ¼ cup olive oil
- 1 cup grape tomatoes (12–15), halved
- 5 cloves garlic, minced
- ½ cup white wine or low-sodium chicken broth
- ¾ lb boneless, skinless wild salmon fillet, cut into bite-size pieces
- 2 Tbsp chopped fresh basil
- 1 Tbsp chopped fresh oregano
- 1 Tbsp capers, rinsed and drained

1. Prepare the pasta according to the package directions, without adding salt.
2. Heat the oil in a large skillet over medium-high heat while the pasta cooks. Add the tomatoes and garlic and cook 1 to 2 minutes. Raise the heat to high and add the wine or broth and the salmon, basil, oregano, and capers and cook until the salmon is just opaque, about 4 minutes.
3. Drain the pasta and add to the skillet. Toss with the tomatoes and salmon to combine. Divide equally among 4 bowls. Sprinkle with additional basil and oregano, if desired.

Don't add oil (and extra calories) to the pasta cooking water. Using enough water and stirring often will prevent sticking.

PER SERVING:
385 CAL
21 g pro
25 g carb
20 g fat
2.5 g sat fat
3 g fiber
111 mg sodium

PARMESAN-CRUSTED TILAPIA

MAKES 4 SERVINGS

- 4 tilapia or salmon fillet (6 oz each)
- 2 Tbsps olive oil
- ½ cup quick-cooking oats
- 3 Tbsps grated Parmesan cheese
- ½ tsp ground nutmeg

PER SERVING:

282 CAL

37 g pro
7 g carb
11.6 g fat
2.8 g sat fat
1 g fiber
146 mg sodium

1. Preheat the oven to 350°F.
2. Coat the tilapia or salmon fillets with the oil.
3. In a shallow dish, combine the oats, cheese, and nutmeg. Roll the fish in the mixture.
4. Place the fish on a rimmed baking sheet, sprayed with cooking spray. Bake 10 minutes per inch of thickness, until fish is completely opague.

ZESTY BAKED FISH

MAKES 4 SERVINGS

- 1 lb orange roughy fillets
- 1/3 cup reduced-fat mayonnaise
- 2 Tbsp grated Parmesan cheese
- 1 scallion, thinly sliced
- 1/2 tsp Worcestershire sauce

1. Preheat the oven to 450°F.
2. Coat a 9″ × 13″ baking pan with cooking spray and arrange the fillets in the pan.
3. In a small bowl, stir together the mayonnaise, cheese, scallion, and Worcestershire sauce. Spread the mixture over the fish fillets.
4. Bake uncovered for 15 minutes or until the fish flakes easily with a fork.

PER SERVING:

165 CAL

| 20 g pro |
| 2 g carb |
| 8 g fat |
| 1.5 g sat fat |
| 0 g fiber |
| 287 mg sodium |

ROASTED FISH WITH CRISP POTATOES

MAKES 4 SERVINGS

- 4 medium Yukon gold potatoes, scrubbed and cut into 1/4" slices
- 2 Tbsp extra-virgin olive oil
- 4 skinless halibut or other fish fillets (4–6 oz each)
- 1 bunch (about 12 oz) slender asparagus, trimmed
- 6 plum tomatoes, chopped (about 1 cup)
- 2 Tbsp chopped fresh basil or cilantro
- 1 Tbsp fresh lime juice
- ½ tsp minced garlic

PER SERVING:

356 CAL

30 g pro

36 g carb

10 g fat

1.5 g sat fat

4 g fiber

118 mg sodium

1. Preheat oven to 400°F. Coat a 13"× 9"baking dish with cooking spray.
2. Place the potatoes in the prepared baking dish, drizzle with the oil, and spread in an even layer.
3. Roast the potatoes until they are browned on the bottom, for 30 to 45 minutes. Remove from the oven. Turn the potatoes so the browned side is up.
4. Increase the oven temperature to 450°F. Place the fish on the potatoes. Place the asparagus between the fish fillets.
5. Return the pan to the oven and roast until the fish is opaque in the center, 8 to 10 minutes for thin fillets and 12 to 15 minutes for thicker fillets.
6. Let the fish stand while making salsa: Combine the tomatoes, basil, lime juice, and garlic.
7. Use a wide spatula to serve potatoes with a portion of the fish. Distribute asparagus evenly. Top each serving with a spoonful of salsa.

SWEET AND TANGY WILD SALMON WITH ONION AND TOMATOES

MAKES 4 SERVINGS

2½ tsp toasted sesame oil
1 medium red onion, halved and thinly sliced
½ tsp chile paste with garlic
4 plum tomatoes, cored and chopped
3 Tbsp packed brown sugar
2 Tbsp reduced-sodium soy sauce
2 tsp rice wine vinegar
3 cups mung bean sprouts (8 oz)
1 lb boneless, skinless wild salmon, cut into bite-size cubes
1 Tbsp finely chopped fresh ginger
¼ cup chopped fresh cilantro

1. Heat the oil in a wok or large nonstick skillet over high heat. Add the onion and chile paste. Stir-fry for 2 minutes to brown the onion. Stir in the tomatoes, sugar, soy sauce, and vinegar. Cook 3 minutes, stirring occasionally.
2. Add the sprouts, salmon, and ginger. Cook, stirring often (but gently to avoid breaking the salmon), for 3 minutes or until the salmon is only slightly pink in the center. Sprinkle with the cilantro.

PER SERVING:
279 CAL

26 g pro	
21 g carb	
10.5 g fat	
1.5 g sat fat	
3 g fiber	
336 mg sodium	

CHILE SAUTÉED SHRIMP

MAKES 8 SERVINGS

- 2 Tbsp canola oil
- 3 lb large shrimp, peeled and deveined
- 2 jalapeño chile peppers, thinly sliced
  Freshly ground black pepper
- 4 tsp sugar
- ½ tsp sea salt

PER SERVING:

184 CAL

28 g pro	
4 g carb	
6 g fat	
1 g sat fat	
0 g fiber	
349 mg sodium	

1. Heat the oil in a large skillet over high heat.
2. Add the shrimp, chile peppers, and black pepper to taste. Sauté 3 to 5 minutes, stirring constantly. Add the sugar and cook 1 to 2 minutes longer until the shrimp are pink. Toss with the salt.

BAKED SPAGHETTI SQUASH WITH SHRIMP

MAKES 4 SERVINGS

- 1 spaghetti squash (about 3 lb), halved and seeded
- 1 Tbsp extra-virgin olive oil
- ½ large onion, chopped (¾ cup)
- 3 cloves garlic, minced
- 1 can (14.5 oz) no-salt-added diced tomatoes
- ½ tsp dried oregano
- ¼ tsp red-pepper flakes (optional)
- 2 oz mild feta cheese, crumbled, divided (We used Athenos.)
- 8 kalamata olives, halved lengthwise and pitted
- 16 Chile Sautéed Shrimp, halved lengthwise (about 1 cup) (see recipe on page 326)

1. Preheat the oven to 350°F.
2. Place the squash cut-side down on a baking sheet. Bake 45 to 50 minutes, until the flesh just yields to pressure. Remove the baking sheet from the oven and let the squash cool enough to touch.
3. Heat the oil in a medium saucepan over medium heat. Add the onion and garlic and sauté 5 minutes until softened. Pour in the tomatoes (with juice), oregano, and red-pepper flakes (if desired) and bring to a simmer. Stir in half of the cheese. Reduce heat to medium-low and cook 4 minutes longer.
4. Scrape a fork against the flesh of the cooled squash in long, diagonal motions to yield long strands (4 cups total). Add the squash, olives, and shrimp to the tomato mixture. Cook 2 minutes until the sauce clings to the squash. Crumble the remaining cheese over top.

PER SERVING:
224 CAL

14 g pro
18 g carb
11 g fat
3 g sat fat
4 g fiber
442 mg sodium

STIR-FRIED RICE NOODLES WITH SHRIMP

MAKES 4 SERVINGS

4 oz rice-flour noodles, broken into 3" pieces

1/2 cup low-sodium chicken or vegetable broth

2 Tbsp water

1 Tbsp oyster sauce

2 tsp reduced-sodium soy sauce

2 tsp rice wine vinegar

1 tsp chile paste

1 tsp cornstarch

1 1/2 Tbsp canola oil

1/2 lb small shrimp, peeled and deveined

2 cloves garlic, minced

1 large egg, lightly beaten

3 cups Wok-Seared Broccoli (see recipe on page 298)

1 cup frozen peas

1 oz low-sodium lean cooked ham, cut into 1/4" cubes (1/3 cup)

PER SERVING:

326 CAL

21 g pro	
37 g carb	
11 g fat	
1.5 g sat fat	
4 g fiber	
517 mg sodium	

1. Soak the noodles in a bowl of hot water for 10 minutes. Drain and set aside. (You should have 1 3/4 cups of noodles.)

2. Whisk the broth, water, oyster sauce, soy sauce, vinegar, chile paste, and cornstarch in a small bowl and set aside.

3. Heat 1/2 tablespoon of the oil over high heat in large wok or wide skillet. Add the shrimp and garlic and stir-fry for 1 to 2 minutes until the shrimp is just pink. Turn onto a plate.

4. Pour the remaining 1 tablespoon oil into a pan and swirl to coat. Add the noodles and cook 3 to 4 minutes, until softened. Push to one side of the pan and pour in the egg. Let set for 30 seconds and then chop coarsely with a spatula. Stir in the broccoli, peas, and ham and toss to combine. Add the shrimp back to the pan, pour in the broth mixture, and toss again to coat. Cook 3 minutes longer or until heated through.

GARLIC SHRIMP WITH SPINACH AND SHIITAKE MUSHROOMS

MAKES 4 SERVINGS

- 2 Tbsp reduced-sodium soy sauce
- 2 Tbsp sherry or 1 Tbsp rice wine vinegar
- 1 tsp packed brown sugar
- 2½ tsp toasted sesame oil
- ½ lb fresh shiitake mushroom caps, sliced ¼" thick
- 1 lb medium shrimp, peeled and deveined
- 4 cloves garlic, minced
- 1 Tbsp finely chopped fresh ginger
- 9 oz baby spinach leaves (about 12 cups)

1. Whisk together the soy sauce, sherry or vinegar, and sugar in small bowl.
2. Heat the oil in a wok or large nonstick skillet over medium-high heat. Add the mushrooms and stir-fry for 2 minutes. Add the shrimp, garlic, and ginger and stir-fry for 1 minute. Add the spinach and soy mixture and continue stir-frying until the spinach has just wilted (shrimp will be cooked), about 1 minute.

PER SERVING:

203 CAL

| 27 g pro |
| 13 g carb |
| 5 g fat |
| 1 g sat fat |
| 4 g fiber |
| 540 mg sodium |

SOUTHWESTERN SHRIMP PIZZA

MAKES 4 SERVINGS

- 1 thin whole wheat pizza crust (12" diameter) (We used Boboli.)
- 8 oz medium shrimp, peeled, deveined, and tails removed
- ¾ tsp ground cumin
- ¼–½ tsp ground ancho chile pepper
- ¼ cup tomato sauce
- Pinch of ground red pepper (optional)
- 2 plum tomatoes (about 12 oz), sliced crosswise and drained on paper towels
- ½ medium sweet white onion, thinly sliced (1 cup)
- 2 Tbsp canned diced mild green chiles, rinsed and drained
- 2 oz reduced-fat shredded pepper-Jack cheese
- ½ cup chopped Florida avocado

PER SERVING:
(2 SLICES)
343 CAL

25 g pro	
40 g carb	
11.8 g fat	
3.3 g sat fat	
8 g fiber	
672 mg sodium	

1. Preheat oven to 425°F.
2. Put the pizza crust on a baking sheet or pizza pan.
3. Mix the shrimp with the cumin and ancho chile pepper in a small bowl.
4. Spread the tomato sauce evenly on the crust and sprinkle with the ground red pepper (if desired). Top with the tomatoes, onion, and green chiles. Distribute the shrimp over the pizza and sprinkle evenly with the cheese. Bake 20 to 23 minutes until the shrimp are firm and opaque.
5. Top the pizza with the avocado and let stand for 10 minutes before cutting into slices.

DESSERTS

Watermelon Granita | 333

Grilled Banana Split | 334

Crunchy Frozen Banana | 334

Broiled Red Grapefruit with Pomegranate Syrup | 335

Mixed Berry Ice Pops | 336

Chocolate-Strawberry Ice Pops | 337

Berry and Peach Sundaes | 338

Strawberry Cream Clouds | 339

Vanilla Poppy Seed Biscotti | 341

Blueberry-Chocolate Parfaits | 342

Raspberry and Chocolate Ice Cream Pielettes | 343

Blueberry-Cheesecake Parfaits | 344

Clementine and Grapefruit Compote | 345

Banana-Chocolate Tartlets | 346

Tangelo Tiramisu | 347

Orange and Pear Crisp | 348

Berry and Yogurt Crepes | 349

Holiday Sugar Cookies with Royal Icing | 350

Ginger Cashew Pillows | 351

Peanut Butter Cookies with Chocolate Chunks | 352

Chocolate-Coconut Rum Balls | 353

Double Chocolate Cherry Chews | 354

WATERMELON GRANITA

MAKES 4 SERVINGS

  6 cups seedless watermelon chunks or balls (about 4 lb with rind)
  1 Tbsp freshly squeezed lemon juice (½ lemon)
  1 Tbsp freshly squeezed lime juice (½ lime)
  ½ cup ginger ale

1. Puree the watermelon, lemon juice, and lime juice in a blender. Slowly pour in the ginger ale.

2. Freeze in an 8″ × 8″ baking pan. During freezing, rake with a fork or stir with a whisk (be sure to scrape sides of pan) every 30 minutes for 2½ hours or until nearly frozen but not completely solid. Rake with a fork and serve.

PER SERVING:
82 CAL

1 g pro
21 g carb
0.5 g fat
0 g sat fat
1 g fiber
5 mg sodium

GRILLED BANANA SPLIT

MAKES 4 SERVINGS

PER SERVING:
145 CAL

1 g pro	
28 g carb	
3.5 g fat	
2.1 g sat fat	
3 g fiber	
5 mg sodium	

- 2 bananas, unpeeled
- ¼ cup dark chocolate chips
- ¼ cup crushed pineapple
- ¼ cup strawberry sorbet
- 20 mini marshmallows

1. Slice the bananas lengthwise in half, and place each half on a large square of foil. Top each half with 1 tablespoon each of the dark chocolate chips and pineapple.

2. Wrap the banana in foil and grill 3 to 4 minutes. Remove the foil, place the banana on a plate, and slice through.

3. Top each with 1 tablespoon of the sorbet and 5 marshmallows.

CRUNCHY FROZEN BANANA

MAKES 4 SERVINGS

PER SERVING:
123 CAL

3 g pro	
29 g carb	
0.7 g fat	
0.2 g sat fat	
3 g fiber	
12 mg sodium	

- 4 small bananas, peeled
- ¼-½ cup fat-free vanilla yogurt, softened
- 2 Tbsp rolled oats

1. On a plate, spread 1 tablespoon of yogurt directly onto a banana with a pastry brush.

2. Sprinkle it with the oats and cover with waxed paper.

3. Chill in the freezer for at least 4 hours. Unwrap the bananas, discard the paper, and eat immediately.

BROILED RED GRAPEFRUIT WITH POMEGRANATE SYRUP

MAKES 4 SERVINGS

$^3/_4$ cup pomegranate juice

$^1/_4$ cup sugar, divided

2 red grapefruits, peeled (white pith removed) and each cut into 4–6 round slices

1. Combine the juice and $^1/_4$ cup of the sugar in a small saucepan. Bring to a boil, reduce heat, and simmer, stirring occasionally, for 15 to 20 minutes or until reduced to $^1/_3$ cup. Cool to room temperature.
2. Preheat the broiler with rack about 4" from the heat.
3. Arrange the grapefruit slices in a single layer in a large baking dish. Sprinkle with the remaining 2 tablespoons sugar. Broil 6 minutes or until the grapefruit is flecked with brown. Arrange on a serving platter or individual plates and drizzle with the pomegranate syrup.

PER SERVING:

112 CAL

1 g pro

28 g carb

0.1 g fat

0 g sat fat

1 g fiber

6 mg sodium

MIXED BERRY ICE POPS

MAKES 6

²/₃ cup fresh blueberries

30 small fresh mint leaves

1¹/₃ cups raspberries

1¹/₂ cups seltzer

2 Tbsp light floral honey, such as acacia

2 Tbsp freshly squeezed lemon juice (1 lemon)

PER POP:

47 CAL

1 g pro
12 g carb
0 g fat
0 g sat fat
2 g fiber
1 mg sodium

1. Fill 6 ice pop molds evenly with blueberries, then mint, then raspberries.

2. Stir together the seltzer, honey, and lemon juice gently in a measuring cup until the honey dissolves. Pour very slowly over the berries and mint. (Note: There should be about ¹/₂" of space at the top of each mold to allow for expansion during freezing. Adjust the liquid accordingly.) Insert the handles or sticks into the molds.

3. Freeze for at least 4 hours.

CHOCOLATE-STRAWBERRY ICE POPS

MAKES 6

    1 cup thinly sliced fresh strawberries
    ½ cup premium semisweet chocolate chips
    1½ cups chocolate soy milk

1. Fill 6 ice pop molds evenly with strawberries, then chocolate chips, then soy milk. (Note: There should be about ½″ of space at the top of each mold to allow for expansion during freezing. Adjust the soy milk accordingly.) Insert the handles or sticks into the molds.
2. Freeze for at least 4 hours.

PER POP:

151 CAL

3 g pro

21 g carb

6 g fat

3.5 g sat fat

1 g fiber

19 mg sodium

BERRY AND PEACH SUNDAES

MAKES 4 SERVINGS

- ¹⁄₂ cup fresh raspberries
- ¹⁄₂ cup fresh blueberries
- ¹⁄₂ cup fresh peach slices (about 1 medium)
- 1 Tbsp sugar
- 2 cup low-fat vanilla ice cream
- 2 Tbsp seedless strawberry jam, warmed
- 2 Tbsp walnuts, coarsely chopped
- 4 maraschino cherries

PER SERVING:

223 CAL

5 g pro	
39 g carb	
6 g fat	
2.5 g sat fat	
3 g fiber	
57 mg sodium	

1. Combine the raspberries, blueberries, peaches, and sugar in a medium bowl. Refrigerate for 1 to 2 hours, stirring occasionally.
2. Scoop ¹⁄₂ cup of the ice cream into each of 4 small sundae cups. Top each with one-quarter of the fruit mixture, 1 tablespoon of the jam, ¹⁄₂ tablespoon of the walnuts, and 1 cherry.

STRAWBERRY CREAM CLOUDS

MAKES 8 SERVINGS

- 3 large egg whites, at room temperature
- ¼ tsp salt
- ½ cup + 1 Tbsp granulated sugar
- 2 cups sliced fresh strawberries
- ¾ cup heavy cream
- ¼ cup confectioners' sugar
- ¼ tsp almond extract
- 2 Tbsp sliced almonds, toasted

1. Preheat the oven to 200°F. Line 2 large baking sheets with parchment.
2. Add the egg whites and salt to the bowl of an electric mixer. Beat on high speed until the whites hold soft peaks. Gradually beat in ½ cup of the granulated sugar until the whites are glossy and hold stiff peaks. With a small spatula, spoon the whites onto baking sheets, making eight 4"-diameter mounds. Make a small hollow in each mound with the back of a spoon. Bake 1½ hours. Turn off the oven and let cool in the oven for 1 hour longer.
3. Combine the strawberries and the remaining granulated sugar in a medium bowl. Chill until ready to use.
4. Place the cream, confectioners' sugar, and almond extract in the bowl of an electric mixer just before removing the meringues from the oven. Beat on high speed until the cream holds stiff peaks, 2 to 3 minutes.
5. Remove the meringues from the oven and place on 8 small serving plates. Spoon ¼ cup of the strawberries over each and then top with ¼ cup of the cream. Sprinkle with the almonds.

PER SERVING:

175 CAL

2 g pro
22 g carb
9 g fat
5 g sat fat
1 g fiber
102 mg sodium

VANILLA POPPY SEED BISCOTTI

MAKES 3 DOZEN

- 3 cups all-purpose flour
- 1/2 cup poppy seeds
- 1 1/4 tsp baking powder
- 1/2 tsp salt
- 1 cup sugar
- 1/2 cup canola oil
- 2 large eggs
- 2 large egg whites
- 2 Tbsp vanilla extract

1. Preheat oven to 350°F. Put the oven rack in the middle position.
2. Whisk together the flour, poppy seeds, baking powder, and salt in a large bowl. Set aside.
3. Combine the sugar and oil in a medium bowl. Using an electric mixer, blend in the eggs, egg whites, and vanilla extract. Add the poppy seed mixture and blend until just mixed.
4. Divide the dough into 3 equal portions and, working on a lightly floured surface, shape each portion into a free-form log about 2″ wide and 10″ long. Arrange the logs several inches apart on a large ungreased baking sheet. Bake 25 minutes or until the logs are golden. Remove from the oven (do not turn off).
5. Use a metal spatula to gently loosen the logs from the baking sheet. Transfer to a cutting board and let cool for 5 minutes. Cutting crosswise on a slant with a sharp knife, slice each log into 1/2″-wide crescents. Arrange half of the crescents, standing upright, on a clean, ungreased baking sheet and bake 10 minutes longer. Cool on a rack. Repeat the process with the remaining crescents.

PER COOKIE:
107 CAL

2 g pro	
14 g carb	
4.5 g fat	
0.5 g sat fat	
1 g fiber	
48 mg sodium	

BLUEBERRY-CHOCOLATE PARFAITS

MAKES 4 SERVINGS

- 1 cup frozen wild blueberries
- 2 cups cooked oatmeal
- 2 oz dark chocolate chips (about 60 chips)

PER SERVING:

167 CAL

4 g pro
27 g carb
5.7 g fat
2.5 g sat fat
3 g fiber
10 mg sodium

1. Place the blueberries in an ovenproof baking dish. Cover with the cooked oatmeal and top with the chocolate chips.
2. Microwave on high for 30 seconds. Divide into serving bowls.

RASPBERRY AND CHOCOLATE
ICE CREAM PIELETTES

MAKES 4 SERVINGS

- ½ cup graham cracker crumbs
- 2 tsp sugar
- 1 Tbsp trans fat–free spread
- 1 cup 50%-less-fat light vanilla ice cream, softened (We used Breyers.)
- ½ cup fresh or frozen raspberries
- 1 Tbsp dark chocolate shavings (¼ oz)

1. Preheat the oven to 350°F.
2. Combine the graham cracker crumbs and sugar in a medium bowl. Mix in the spread until the crumbs are coated. Press a quarter of the mixture onto the bottoms of 4 tartlet pans (4″ diameter) with removable bottoms. Bake 5 minutes and cool completely.
3. Fill each crust with ¼ cup of the ice cream and smooth with a spoon. Top 2 of the pielettes with about 8 raspberries each. Sprinkle the remaining 2 pielettes with the chocolate. Freeze until set, 15 to 20 minutes. Remove the sides of the tartlet pans before serving.

PER SERVING:

146 CAL

3 g pro
22 g carb
6 g fat
2 g sat fat
2 g fiber
111 mg sodium

To shave the chocolate, use a vegetable peeler and let the curls fall onto a sheet of parchment.

BLUEBERRY-CHEESECAKE PARFAITS

MAKES 4 SERVINGS

4	oz Neufchâtel cheese, softened
1/2	cup reduced-fat sour cream
1/4	cup confectioners' sugar
1/2	tsp vanilla extract
4	gingersnaps, crushed (2–3 Tbsp)
1 1/2	cups fresh or frozen and thawed blueberries

PER SERVING:
200 CAL

5 g pro
24 g carb
10 g fat
6 g sat fat
1 g fiber
190 mg sodium

1. Combine the cheese and sour cream in the bowl of an electric mixer and beat on high speed until smooth. Add the sugar and vanilla extract and beat until well combined. Reserve 4 teaspoons of the mixture and set aside. (You should have 1 cup for the parfaits.)

2. Fill each of 4 small parfait glasses or champagne flutes with layers, starting with 2 tablespoons of the cheese mixture, then some cookie crumbs, and then a layer of blueberries. Repeat the pattern once more using the remaining cheese mixture, crumbs, and blueberries. Finish by dabbing 1 teaspoon of the reserved cheese mixture on top of each parfait. Use any extra berries and crumbs to garnish, if desired. Chill for at least 30 minutes before serving.

CLEMENTINE AND GRAPEFRUIT COMPOTE

MAKES 4 SERVINGS

4 clementines
1 grapefruit
Grated zest of 1 lime
3 Tbsp honey

1. Remove the peel and white pith from the clementines and grapefruit and cut sections from the membranes into a large bowl. Squeeze the juice from the membranes over the fruit. Add the lime zest and honey and mix gently.
2. Serve in small cups or bowls and top with additional lime zest, if desired.

PER SERVING:
113 CAL

1 g pro

29 g carb

0.1 g fat

0 g sat fat

2 g fiber

1 mg sodium

BANANA-CHOCOLATE TARTLETS

MAKES 12 SERVINGS

1 refrigerated piecrust (We used Pillsbury.)
¼ cup dark chocolate shavings (1½ oz)
2 medium bananas, thinly sliced
1 Tbsp apple jelly

PER SERVING:

114 CAL

1 g pro
16 g carb
5.5 g fat
2.5 g sat fat
1 g fiber
67 mg sodium

1. Preheat the oven to 425°F. Line a large baking sheet with parchment.
2. Roll out the dough on a lightly floured surface to a 15″ diameter. With a 4″-diameter biscuit cutter, or the top of a widemouthed jar, cut out 12 circles, rerolling the scraps if necessary. Discard any leftover dough.
3. Top each circle with ½ teaspoon of the chocolate. Add a layer of banana, leaving a ½″ border around the edges. Fold the sides of the dough and pleat the edges, pressing firmly with your fingers to seal the pleats, forming a rustic tart.
4. Place the jelly in a small microwaveable bowl and microwave on high for 15 to 20 seconds. Lightly brush the bananas with the jelly. Sprinkle the tops with the remaining chocolate.
5. Bake until the tops are lightly browned and the bananas have softened, for 14 to 15 minutes. Remove from the oven and cool on the baking sheet for 15 minutes before serving.

TANGELO TIRAMISU

MAKES 6 SERVINGS

- 6 Minneola tangelos (2¼ lb)
- ⅓ cup sugar
- ⅓ cup fat-free cream cheese, softened
- ¼ cup mascarpone cheese
- 1 package (3 oz) ladyfingers (about 12)

1. Remove the peel and white pith from the tangelos and cut sections from the membranes. Place the sections in a medium bowl. Squeeze the juice from the membranes into a small bowl.
2. Beat the sugar, cream cheese, and mascarpone until smooth in a medium bowl.
3. Split the ladyfingers lengthwise in half.
4. Pour half of the tangelo juice into a pie plate or shallow dish. Dip the flat sides of half of the ladyfingers into the juice. Arrange the ladyfingers flat-side up in an 8″ × 8″ baking dish. Spread half of the cheese mixture over the top and cover with half of the tangelo sections. Repeat with the remaining juice, ladyfingers (place flat-side down on the fruit), cheese mixture, and fruit. Cover with plastic wrap and chill for 2 to 24 hours to allow the flavors to blend.

PER SERVING:

237 CAL

6 g pro

35 g carb

10.5 g fat

3 g fiber

5 g sat fat

101 mg sodium

ORANGE AND PEAR CRISP

MAKES 8 SERVINGS

- $\frac{1}{2}$ cup all-purpose flour
- $\frac{1}{4}$ cup + 2 Tbsp granulated sugar
- $\frac{1}{4}$ cup packed brown sugar
- $\frac{1}{4}$ cup cold trans fat–free margarine, cut into small pieces
- 8 medium seedless (navel) oranges
- 2 large pears (1 lb), peeled, cored, and cut into $1\frac{1}{2}$"–2" chunks
- 1 Tbsp cornstarch
- $\frac{1}{4}$ tsp freshly grated nutmeg

PER SERVING:

227 CAL

2 g pro
46 g carb
4.5 g fat
0.5 g sat fat
5 g fiber
46 mg sodium

1. Preheat the oven to 400°F.
2. Combine the flour, $\frac{1}{4}$ cup of the granulated sugar, and brown sugar in a food processor. Add the margarine and process until crumbly.
3. Remove the peel and white pith from the oranges and cut into sections from the membranes; place in a large bowl. Squeeze the juice from the membranes over the fruit. Add the pears, cornstarch, nutmeg, and the remaining 2 tablespoons granulated sugar. Mix gently. Spoon the mixture into eight 6-ounce ramekins or an 8″ × 8″ baking pan. Sprinkle with the flour mixture. Bake the individual ramekins for 15 minutes or the square pan for 30 minutes or until golden brown.

BERRY AND YOGURT CREPES

MAKES 6 SERVINGS

- 1 cup all-purpose flour
- 1 Tbsp sugar
- ½ tsp salt
- 2 large eggs
- 1½ cups 1% milk
- 2 Tbsp butter, melted
- ¼ tsp + ½ tsp vanilla extract
- 1 cup low-fat Greek-style yogurt (We used Fage 2%.)
- 2 Tbsp no-sugar-added fruit spread
- 1 cup fresh blueberries

1. Mix the flour, sugar, and salt in a large bowl.
2. Place the eggs, milk, butter, and ¼ teaspoon of the vanilla extract in a blender. Add the flour mixture and blend until it reaches the consistency of cream. Allow the batter to stand at room temperature for 15 minutes.
3. Whisk the yogurt, honey, and remaining ½ teaspoon vanilla extract in a small bowl.
4. Coat a 7" to 8" nonstick skillet with cooking spray and heat over medium-high heat. Pulse the blender a few times to stir the batter. Pour a scant ¼ cup of the batter into the center of the hot pan and swirl. When the batter is just set and bubbling all over, 40 to 60 seconds, flip with a spatula and cook 20 to 30 seconds longer. Transfer to a plate and repeat to create 12 crepes.
5. Spread each crepe with 1½ tablespoons of the yogurt (leaving a ½" border) and spoon ½ tablespoon of fruit spread down the centers. Top with a heaping tablespoon of blueberries. Roll up the crepes from the bottom. Place 2 crepes on each of 6 plates.

PER SERVING
(2 CREPES):
218 CAL
9 g pro

29 g carb

7 g fat

3.9 g sat fat

1 g fiber

249 mg sodium

HOLIDAY SUGAR COOKIES WITH ROYAL ICING

MAKES 4 DOZEN 3" COOKIES

2 cups white whole wheat flour (We used King Arthur.)
1/2 tsp baking powder
1/2 tsp baking soda
1/2 tsp salt
1/2 cup (1 stick) unsalted butter, softened
3/4 cup sugar
1 large egg
2 Tbsp 2% milk
1/2 tsp lemon extract
1/3 cup pasteurized egg whites
1/2 tsp vanilla extract
1/4 tsp cream of tartar
1 package (1 lb) confectioners' sugar (about 4 cups)

PER COOKIE:
88 CAL

1 g pro	
17 g carb	
2 g fat	
1 g sat fat	
0.5 g fiber	
42 mg sodium	

1. Make the cookies: Whisk together the whole wheat flour, baking powder, baking soda, and salt in a medium bowl.

2. Place the butter and sugar in a large bowl and, using an electric mixer, beat until the mixture is light and fluffy, about 1 minute. Beat in the egg, followed by the milk and lemon extract. Add the flour mixture and blend until just mixed. Form the dough into a disk, wrap tightly in wax paper, and chill for at least 1 hour.

3. Preheat the oven to 375°F. Put the oven rack in the middle position. Remove the dough from the refrigerator and roll out to a 1/4" thickness on a lightly floured surface. Cut the dough into the desired shapes with lightly floured cookie cutters. Place the cookies on an ungreased baking sheet, spacing them 2" apart, and bake 10 minutes or until pale brown around edges. Cool completely on a rack.

4. Prepare the icing while the cookies cool. Using an electric mixer at low speed, blend the egg whites, vanilla extract, and cream of tartar in a medium bowl until frothy. Gradually add the sugar and beat at medium-high speed until the icing thickens and stiffens, about 4 to 6 minutes. Tint with food coloring if desired. Spread or pipe the icing onto the cooled cookies.

GINGER CASHEW PILLOWS

MAKES 3 DOZEN

- ½ cup old-fashioned rolled oats
- ½ cup whole wheat pastry flour
- ⅓ cup toasted unsweetened wheat germ
- 2 tsp ground ginger
- ½ tsp salt
- ¾ cup sugar
- ½ cup cashew butter
- ¼ cup trans fat–free vegetable oil spread, softened (We used Earth Balance.)
- 2 tsp vanilla extract
- ⅓ cup ground flaxseed or ¼ cup whole flaxseed, ground in coffee or spice grinder
- ½ cup water
- 18 lightly salted roasted cashew halves
- 18 small pieces crystallized ginger

1. Preheat the oven to 350°F. Put the oven rack in the middle position.
2. Place the oats, flour, wheat germ, ginger, and salt in a food processor. Pulse until finely ground. Set aside.
3. Combine the sugar, cashew butter, spread, and vanilla extract in a medium bowl. Using an electric mixer, beat until well blended.
4. Put the flaxseed in a small bowl and stir in the water. Beat into the cashew butter mixture. Beat in the oat mixture. (The dough will be sticky.)
5. Roll a heaping teaspoonful of dough gently to form a ball. Place on an ungreased baking sheet. Repeat with the remaining dough, spacing the balls 2″ apart. Lightly press a cashew half, flat-side down, on half of the balls. Press a piece of crystallized ginger on the remaining balls. Bake 16 minutes or until puffed and golden around the edges. Cool completely on a wire rack.

PER COOKIE:

75 CAL

| 2 g pro |
| 9 g carb |
| 4 g fat |
| 1 g sat fat |
| 1 g fiber |
| 65 mg sodium |

PEANUT BUTTER COOKIES WITH CHOCOLATE CHUNKS

MAKES 3 DOZEN

- $\frac{1}{4}$ cup + 2 Tbsp packed dark brown sugar
- $\frac{1}{3}$ cup trans fat–free spread or vegetable shortening
- $\frac{1}{4}$ cup chunky natural peanut butter
- 1 large egg yolk
- $\frac{1}{2}$ tsp vanilla extract
- $\frac{1}{2}$ cup all-purpose flour
- $\frac{1}{2}$ tsp baking powder
- $\frac{1}{8}$ tsp salt
- 2 oz semisweet baking chocolate, broken into 36 small chunks

PER SERVING
(3 COOKIES):
141 CAL

2 g pro

15 g carb

8 g fat

2.5 g sat fat

1 g fiber

105 mg sodium

1. Preheat the oven to 350°F. Line 2 large baking sheets with parchment.
2. Combine the sugar, spread or shortening, peanut butter, egg yolk, and vanilla extract in a large bowl and mix until well combined.
3. In a medium bowl, combine the flour, baking powder, and salt. Add to the peanut butter mixture and stir until well combined. Divide the dough into 36 cookies, using 1 generous teaspoon per cookie, and place on the prepared baking sheets. Lightly press each cookie down with fingers until slightly larger than a quarter and about $\frac{1}{4}$″ thick. Bake until lightly golden, 9 to 11 minutes.
4. Remove the cookies from the oven and immediately press a chocolate chunk onto the center of each. Cool completely on the baking sheets or place in the refrigerator for 15 minutes to firm the chocolate.

To keep the size of these cookies uniform, use a measuring teaspoon.

CHOCOLATE-COCONUT RUM BALLS

MAKES 3 DOZEN

- 4 oz honey-sweetened graham crackers
- 8 whole, pitted dried apricots
- 8 whole, pitted dried Medjool dates
- ½ cup brown rice syrup
- ¼ cup Dutch cocoa powder
- Freshly grated zest of 1 orange
- 2 Tbsp dark rum or 1¼ tsp rum extract
- Pinch of salt
- 1⅓ cups unsweetened shredded dried coconut

1. Grind the graham crackers to a fine crumb in a food processor. Transfer to a large bowl.
2. Place the apricots in the food processor and process until finely chopped. Add to the crumbs. Place the dates in the food processor and process until finely chopped. Add to the crumb mixture, along with the rice syrup, cocoa, orange zest, rum or rum extract, salt, and 1 cup of the coconut. Stir well to mix.
3. Dampen hands and roll a heaping teaspoonful of the mixture into a ball. Repeat to make 36 balls.
4. Place the remaining ⅓ cup coconut in a small bowl. Roll the balls, one at a time, in the coconut to coat.
5. Refrigerate until ready to serve.

Medjools are known as the "king of dates" for their large size and exceptional sweetness. If you can't find them, substitute any pitted, dried variety.

PER COOKIE:
77 CAL

1 g pro	
13 g carb	
2.5 g fat	
2 g sat fat	
1 g fiber	
33 mg sodium	

DOUBLE CHOCOLATE CHERRY CHEWS

MAKES 3 DOZEN

- 1 cup whole wheat pastry flour
- 1/4 cup Dutch cocoa powder
- 1/2 tsp baking soda
- 1/4 tsp salt
- 1/4 cup (1/2 stick) unsalted butter, softened
- 1/4 cup trans fat-free vegetable oil spread, softened (We used Earth Balance.)
- 1/2 cup granulated sugar
- 1/2 cup packed brown sugar
- 1 large egg
- 1 tsp vanilla extract
- 1 cup pitted, unsweetened dried sweet cherries
- 2/3 cup white or dark chocolate chips

PER COOKIE:

91 CAL

1 g pro	
13 g carb	
4 g fat	
2 g sat fat	
1 g fiber	
51 mg sodium	

1. Preheat the oven to 375°F. Put the oven rack in the middle position.
2. Whisk together the flour, cocoa, baking soda, and salt in a medium bowl.
3. Place the butter and vegetable oil spread in a medium bowl. Using an electric mixer, beat until fluffy, about 1 minute. Blend in the granulated sugar and brown sugar, followed by the egg and vanilla extract. Add in the flour mixture and mix until just incorporated. Fold in the cherries and chocolate chips.
4. Drop spoonfuls of the dough (about 1 tablespoon) onto an ungreased baking sheet, spacing about 2" apart. (Work in batches.) Bake 10 minutes. Remove from the oven and let the cookies cool slightly on the baking sheet before transferring to the rack to cool completely.

PHOTO CREDITS

INDEX

Boldface page references indicate photographs. <u>Underscored</u> references indicate boxed text.

A

A1C test
function of, 15–16, <u>220</u>
numbers of, understanding, <u>15</u>, 16, 227
regular check of, 15, <u>220</u>
risk of complications of diabetes and, <u>11</u>, 227
Acarbose, 28
ACE inhibitors, 18, 217
Acid reflux, 4
Actos, 30
Acute complications of diabetes, 224–26
Aerobic exercise, <u>131</u>
Aging, 127–28, <u>127</u>, 135, <u>203</u>
Alcohol, <u>42</u>, 52, **52**, 199, 215, 321
Almond butter
Grilled Almond Butter and Berry Sandwiches, 289
Almonds
as snack, <u>61</u>
Strawberry Cream Clouds, 339
Alzheimer's disease, 217
Amaryl, 28
American Diabetes Association, <u>4</u>, 22, 75, <u>129</u>, <u>181</u>, <u>216</u>, <u>217</u>, 234
American Heart Association, 82, 129, 237
Animal protein, avoiding, <u>61</u>
Ankle-brachial index, <u>234</u>
Anthocyanins, <u>76</u>
Antidepressants, 32, 36, 179. See also *specific type*
Antihyperglycemics, 30
Apidra, 29
Appetizers
Cranberry-Apple Chutney, 262, 316
Creamy Veggie Dip, 260
Feta-Walnut Stuffed Cucumbers, 265
Honey Barbecue Drummettes, 263
Incredible Crab Canapes, 264
Spinach-Pesto Dip, 257, **257**
Three-Bean Avocado Dip, 258
215-Calorie Taco Snack, 261
Yogurt and Cucumber Dip, 259
Apple body shape, 158
Apple jelly
Banana-Chocolate Tartlets, 346

Apples
Cranberry-Apple Chutney, 262, 316
Roasted Butternut and Spinach Salad, 272, **272**
Applesauce
Red Pepper-Scallion Corn Muffins, 247
Apricots
Chocolate-Coconut Rum Balls, 353
Savory Fruit and Nut Stuffing, 295
ARBs, 18
Arm Sculptor workout, 10-minute
overview, 97, <u>97</u>
Side Plank Push-Ups, 98, **98**
Supported Curls, 97, **97**
T-Stand Rows with Kickbacks, 98, **98**
Arthritis, 5
Artichokes
Tuscan Chicken Soup, 279
Artificial sweeteners, avoiding, 68
Arugula
Watermelon Salad, 271
Asparagus
Edamame with Asparagus, Scallions, and Egg, 292
Roasted Fish with Crisp Potatoes, 324
Aspirin and stroke, 239
Atkins diet, 216
Avandamet, 30
Avandaryl, 30
Avandia, 30
Avocados
Grilled Pork Tacos with Avocado-Radish Salad, 319
Southwestern Shrimp Pizza, 330, **331**
Three-Bean Avocado Dip, 258

B

Baby greens
Leafy Grilled Chicken Salad with Creamy Balsamic Dressing, 267, **267**
Backaches, relieving, 49
Baking chocolate
Peanut Butter Cookies with Chocolate Chunks, 352
Balsamic vinegar
Balsamic Tomato and Roasted Pepper Salad, 273
Fresh Corn and Tomato Bruschetta Salad, 269

Leafy Grilled Chicken Salad with Creamy Balsamic Dressing, 267, **267**
Bananas
Banana-Chocolate Tartlets, 346
blood pressure and, lowering, 218
Crunchy Frozen Banana, 334
Grilled Banana Split, 334
Basil
Balsamic Tomato and Roasted Pepper Salad, 273
Capellini with Pine Nuts, Sun-Dried Tomatoes, and Chicken, 301, **301**
Four-Veggie Pizza, 291
Fresh Corn and Tomato Bruschetta Salad, 269
Leafy Grilled Chicken Salad with Creamy Balsamic Dressing, 267, **267**
Open-Faced Grilled Vegetable Sandwiches, 288
Roasted Fish with Crisp Potatoes, 324
Salmon and Herb Penne, 321, **321**
Beans. *See also specific type*
Black and White Bean Soup, 283
canned, 77
Dramatically Seared Green Beans, 286
fiber in, 76
Green Bean and Macadamia Nut Casserole, 287
health benefits of, 73, 76
Leafy Grilled Chicken Salad with Creamy Balsamic Dressing, 267, **267**
low-sodium, 77
Mediterranean Bean Boats, 77
nutrition of, 75–76
Open-Faced Grilled Vegetable Sandwiches, 288
in power meals, 77
protein in, 76
Roasted Vegetable Salad, 270
Rustic Bean Sauté, 77
sources, 73
Taco Salad, 77
Tex-Mex Stuffed Acorn Squash, 285, **285**
Tex-Mex Tomato Soup, 280, **281**
Three-Bean Avocado Dip, 258
Turkey Burgers with Chili Beans, 308
Tuscan Chicken Soup, 279
types of, 76
vegetarian versions, 77
White Chicken Chili, 282
Bean sprouts
Oriental Spinach Salad, 268
Sweet and Tangy Wild Salmon with Onion and Tomatoes, 325
BeaTunes, 83
Beef
Beef and Mushroom Noodles, 313
fish and seafood selection over, 59
Gingered Beef with Broccolini and Walnuts, 311, **311**
Homestyle Roast Beef, 314
Orange Beef and Broccoli, 315
Roast Beef Sandwiches, 312
Bejeweled 2 (online game), 178

Bell peppers
Balsamic Tomato and Roasted Pepper Salad, 273
Black and White Bean Soup, 283
Four-Veggie Pizza, 291
Mediterranean Breakfast Bake, 252–53
Omelet Italian-Style, 251
Open-Faced Grilled Vegetable Sandwiches, 288
Quick Thai Seafood Soup, 278
Red Pepper-Scallion Corn Muffins, 247
Roasted Butternut and Spinach Salad, 272, **272**
Roasted Vegetable Salad, 270
Spinach-Pesto Dip, 257, **257**
Sweet and Sour Chinese Pork, 317
Tex-Mex Tomato Soup, 280, **281**
Turkey Sausage and Peppers, 306
Belly fat
soda and, 51, 53
strength training to reduce, 82–83
as trouble spot, common, 170
Belly Flattener workouts
core-strengthening
Leaning Plank, 108, **108**
overview, 107
Rowing Twist, 107, **107**
Scoops, 109, **109**
Sweeping Kick, 110, **11**0
10-minute
Full-Body Roll-Ups, 100, **100**
overview, 99, 99
Windmills, 101, **101**
walking, 103–4, 105–6
Beta-carotene, 74
Beverages
alcohol, 42, 52, **52**, 199, 215, 321
coffee, 48–49, 200
ginger ale, 333
seltzer, 336
soda, 51, 53
tea, 47–48, 200
Biguanides, 29
Bikes, stationary, 147
Biologic medications, 37
Birth control pills, 237, 239
Black beans, 76
Black tea, 200
Blogs about diabetes, 23
Blood clotting disorders, 234, 237
Blood glucose (BG)
complications of diabetes and, 224
high, 225–26
low, 225, 225
medications in managing, 18
monitoring, 15–16, 15, 227–28
phone for measuring, 3
sleep deprivation and, 195
weight loss and, 12–13
Blood pressure (BP). *See also* High blood pressure
lowering
bananas, 218
positive attitude, 216

Blood pressure (BP) (*cont.*)
  lowering (*cont.*)
    potatoes, 71
    salt intake reduction, 218, <u>220</u>
    weight loss, <u>220</u>
  monitoring, 16–17
  numbers of, understanding, 16
Blood sugar levels
  coffee and, 48
  fiber and, 74
  memory and, 209
  pinto beans and, <u>76</u>
  silymarin and, 3
Blood test, <u>234</u>
Blueberries
  Berry and Peach Sundaes, 338
  Berry and Yogurt Crepes, 349
  Blueberry-Cheesecake Parfaits, 344
  Blueberry-Chocolate Parfaits, 342
  Mixed Berry Ice Pops, 336
BMI, 82, 219
Body fat, 81, 128
Body mass index (BMI), 82, 219
Body shape, 158
Body temperature and sleep, 200, 202
Body weight, <u>86</u>, 215. *See also* Obesity; Overweight;
    Weight loss
Bok choy
  Sesame Tofu with Bok Choy and Corn, 297
Bone density, 81
Bones
  diabetes and, 141
  iceberg lettuce and, 71
  vitamin D and, 49
Bookworm Adventures (online game), 178
BP. *See* Blood pressure
Bread crumbs
  Pork Kebabs Italiano, 318
  Savory Fruit and Nut Stuffing, 295
Breads
  Breakfast Bread Pudding, 248
  Chicken and Salad Pizza, 305
  Fresh Corn and Tomato Bruschetta Salad, 269
  Grilled Almond Butter and Berry Sandwiches,
    289
  Open-Faced Grilled Vegetable Sandwiches, 288
  Roast Beef Sandwiches, 312
  Turkey Burgers with Chili Beans, 308
Breakfast
  Breakfast Bread Pudding, 248
  cereals, 65–66, <u>66</u>, **67**, 68
  Chocolate Oatmeal, 250
  Cinnamon Chip Muffins, 254
  eggs for, 81–82, <u>81</u>
  importance of, 66
  Mediterranean Breakfast Bake, 252–53
  Omelet Italian-Style, 251
  "Open-Faced" Broccoli and Jack Omelet, 245, **245**
  Peach Breakfast Parfait, 246
  Red Pepper-Scallion Corn Muffins, 247
  skipping, avoiding, <u>86</u>

Sour Cream Waffles, 249
Texas Breakfast Burritos, 255
Breathing for managing stress, <u>181</u>
Broccoli
  Chicken, Broccoli, and Cashew Stir-Fry, 303, **303**
  Cream of Broccoli Soup, 277
  Gingered Beef with Broccolini and Walnuts, 311, **311**
  "Open-Faced" Broccoli and Jack Omelet, 245, **245**
  Orange Beef and Broccoli, 315
  Wok-Seared Broccoli, 298, 328
Brown sugar
  Cranberry-Apple Chutney, 262, 316
  Double Chocolate Cherry Chews, 354
  Garlic Shrimp with Spinach and Shiitake
    Mushrooms, 329
  Orange and Pear Crisp, 348
  Peanut Butter Cookies with Chocolate Chunks, 352
  Southeast-Asian-Style Eggplant, 299
  Sweet and Tangy Wild Salmon with Onion and
    Tomatoes, 325
  Sweet Potatoes with Brown Sugar-Pecan Topping,
    293
Budeprion XL 300, 34, 36–38
Bupropion SR 150, 34
Bupropion SR 200, 34
Butter
  Double Chocolate Cherry Chews, 354
  Holiday Sugar Cookies with Royal Icing, 350
B vitamins, 4–5
Byetta, 28

C

Caffeine, 48–49, 199–200
Calcium, 4
Calcium channel blocker, 217
Calories
  burning, 83, <u>84</u>, 126
  daily intake of, finding needed, 121
Cancer
  colon, 74, 219
  preventing
    black beans, <u>76</u>
    capers, 218–19
    carrots, 74
    celery, 74
    vitamin D, 49
  risk, reducing, 219
  vitamin D deficiency and, <u>48</u>
Canned food, 77
Canola oil, <u>62</u>
Capers
  in cancer prevention, 218–19
  Fresh Corn and Tomato Bruschetta Salad, 269
  in heart disease prevention, 218–19
  Salmon and Herb Penne, 321, **321**
Carbohydrates
  diet low in, 70, <u>86</u>, 216
  managing intake of, 13
  refined, avoiding, 53
  sleep and, 201–2
  sources of, 13

Carrots
    Beef and Mushroom Noodles, 313
    Black and White Bean Soup, 283
    Chicken, Broccoli, and Cashew Stir-Fry, 303, **303**
    fiber in, 74
    Homestyle Roast Beef, 314
    Peanut Noodles with Tofu, 296
    Quick Thai Seafood Soup, 278
    sugar in, 71, 74
    Tex-Mex Tomato Soup, 280, **281**
    Tuscan Chicken Soup, 279
Cashews
    Chicken, Broccoli, and Cashew Stir-Fry, 303, **303**
    Ginger Cashew Pillows, 351
Catechins, 47–48
Cauliflower
    Spiced Cauliflower Soup, 276
Celery
    high blood pressure and, lowering, 74
    Savory Fruit and Nut Stuffing, 295
    Tex-Mex Tomato Soup, 280, **281**
    Tuscan Chicken Soup, 279
Cereals, 65–66, <u>66</u>, **67**, 68, <u>74</u>
Chai tea, 47–48
Change, new theory of diabetic lifestyle
    overview, 40
    steps in
        contemplation (Step 2), 41–43
        precontemplation (Step 1), 40–41
        preparation (Step 3), 43
Cheese
    Baked Spaghetti Squash with Shrimp, 327
    Blueberry-Cheesecake Parfaits, 344
    Chicken and Salad Pizza, 305
    Cream of Broccoli Soup, 277
    Feta-Walnut Stuffed Cucumbers, 265
    Four-Veggie Pizza, 291
    Mediterranean Breakfast Bake, 252–53
    Mediterranean Salad-Wraps, 289
    "Open-Faced" Broccoli and Jack Omelet, 245, **245**
    Parmesan-Crusted Tilapia, 322
    Pork Kebabs Italiano, 318
    Portobello Parmesan, 294
    Quick Pasta Salad, 271
    Southwestern Shrimp Pizza, 330, **331**
    Stuffed Pork Roast, 316, **316**
    Tangelo Tiramisu, 347
    Texas Breakfast Burritos, 255
    Tex-Mex Stuffed Acorn Squash, 285, **285**
    Three-Bean Avocado Dip, 258
    Tuscan Chicken Soup, 279
    Watermelon Salad, 271
    Zesty Baked Fish, 323
    Zesty Skillet Turkey and Noodles, 307
Cherries
    Double Chocolate Cherry Chews, 354
    Savory Fruit and Nut Stuffing, 295
Chicken. *See* Poultry
Chickpeas
    LDL cholesterol and, lowering, <u>76</u>
    Mediterranean Salad-Wraps, 290

Chile peppers
    Chile Sautéed Shrimp, 326–27
    Creamy Veggie Dip, 260
    Southeast-Asian-Style Eggplant, 299
    Southwestern Shrimp Pizza, 330, **331**
    Texas Breakfast Burritos, 255
    Tex-Mex Tomato Soup, 280, **281**
    White Chicken Chili, 282
Chili powder
    Turkey Burgers with Chili Beans, 308
Chocolate. *See* Baking chocolate; Chocolate chips;
        Dark Chocolate shavings
Chocolate chips
    Blueberry-Chocolate Parfaits, 342
    Chocolate-Strawberry Ice Pops, 337
    Double Chocolate Cherry Chews, 354
    Grilled Banana Split, 334
Cholesterol levels. *See also* High cholesterol; LDL
        cholesterol; Triglycerides
    Atkins diet and, 216
    cholesterol intake and, 82
    HDL, 17
    lipid profile and, 17
    managing, 17
    monitoring, 17
    numbers of, understanding, 17, 217
    triglycerides and, 17
Chronic complications of diabetes, 224–25,
    226–27
Cilantro
    Edamame with Asparagus, Scallions, and Egg,
        292
    Quick Thai Seafood Soup, 278
    Roasted Fish with Crisp Potatoes, 324
    Sweet and Tangy Wild Salmon with Onion and
        Tomatoes, 325
    Tex-Mex Tomato Soup, 280, **281**
    Three-Bean Avocado Dip, 258
Cinnamon
    Breakfast Bread Pudding, 248
    Cinnamon Chip Muffins, 254
    Cranberry-Apple Chutney, 262, 316
    Peach Breakfast Parfait, 246
    Spiced Cauliflower Soup, 276
    Sweet Potatoes with Brown Sugar-Pecan Topping,
        293
Citrus juice, 48
Clementines
    Clementine and Grapefruit Compote, 345
Clotting disorders, <u>234</u>, <u>237</u>
Cocoa powder
    Chocolate-Coconut Rum Balls, 353
    Chocolate Oatmeal, 250
Coconut
    Chocolate-Coconut Rum Balls, 353
    Double Chocolate Cherry Chews, 354
    215-Calorie Taco Snack, 261
Coenzyme Q10 (CoQ10), 4
Coffee, 48–49, 200
Cognitive therapy (CT), 179
Colon cancer, 74

Complications of diabetes. *See also specific type*
  A1C test and risk of, <u>11</u>, 227
  acute, 224–26
  Alzheimer's disease, 217
  blood glucose and, 224
  chronic, 224–25, 226–27
  eye problems, 19, 232
  foot problems, 19, 230–32
  heart attack, 215
  heart disease, 215–16, <u>216</u>
  high blood pressure, 217, 227–28
  high cholesterol, 228–29
  kidney disease, 17, 229
  medical breakthroughs, 214–19
  numbers of various tests and, <u>220–21</u>
  periodontitis, <u>217</u>
  preventing, 223, 226–32
  stroke, 218, 233–39
  tips for avoiding, <u>220–21</u>
Confectioners' sugar
  Blueberry-Cheesecake Parfaits, 344
  Holiday Sugar Cookies with Royal Icing, 350
  Strawberry Cream Clouds, 339
ConsumerLab.com, 3, 34, <u>35</u>, 38
Contemplation step of diabetic lifestyle change, 41–43
Coogle, Andrea, 59–60
Cooking, 50, <u>62</u>
CoQ10, 4
Corn
  Black and White Bean Soup, 283
  Fresh Corn and Tomato Bruschetta Salad, 269
  Red Pepper-Scallion Corn Muffins, 247
  Sesame Tofu with Bok Choy and Corn, 297
Cornmeal
  Red Pepper-Scallion Corn Muffins, 247
Cortisol, 178–79, <u>195</u>
Cottage cheese
  Creamy Veggie Dip, 260
Crab
  Incredible Crab Canapes, 264
Cranberries
  Cranberry-Apple Chutney, 262, 316
Cravings, <u>195</u>
C-reactive protein, 238
Cream cheese
  Incredible Crab Canapes, 264
  Roast Beef Sandwiches, 312
  Tangelo Tiramisu, 347
CT, 179
Cucumbers
  Feta-Walnut Stuffed Cucumbers, 265
  Mediterranean Salad-Wraps, 290
  Quick Pasta Salad, 271
  Yogurt and Cucumber Dip, 259
Currants
  Breakfast Bread Pudding, 248
Curry powder
  Spiced Cauliflower Soup, 276

D

DailyMed, 8, **8**
Dairy products. *See specific type*
Dark chocolate shavings
  Banana-Chocolate Tartlets, 346
  Raspberry and Chocolate Ice Cream Pielettes, 343
DASH diet, 62–64, <u>228</u>
Dates
  Chocolate-Coconut Rum Balls, 353
Deep vein thrombosis (DVT), <u>237</u>
Dementia, <u>211</u>
Depression
  diabetes and, 22, <u>181</u>
  managing
    cognitive therapy, 179
    exercise, 177
    medications, 4–5, 179
  preventing, <u>181</u>
  vitamin D deficiency and, 50
Desserts
  Banana-Chocolate Tartlets, 346
  Berry and Peach Sundaes, 338
  Berry and Yogurt Crepes, 349
  Blueberry-Cheesecake Parfaits, 344
  Blueberry-Chocolate Parfaits, 342
  Broiled Red Grapefruit with Pomegranate Syrup, 335
  Chocolate-Coconut Rum Balls, 353
  Chocolate-Strawberry Ice Pops, 337
  Clementine and Grapefruit Compote, 345
  Crunchy Frozen Bananas, 334
  Double Chocolate Cherry Chews, 354
  Ginger Cashew Pillows, 351
  Grilled Banana Split, 334
  Holiday Sugar Cookies with Royal Icing, 350
  Mixed Berry Ice Pops, 336
  Orange and Pear Crisp, 348
  Peanut Butter Cookies with Chocolate Chunks, 352
  Raspberry and Chocolate Ice Cream Pielettes, 343
  Strawberry Cream Clouds, 339
  Tangelo Tiramisu, 347
  Vanilla Poppy Seed Biscotti, 340, **341**
  Watermelon Granita, 333, **333**
Diabeta, 28
Diabetes. *See also* Complications of diabetes;
        Diagnosis of diabetes; Managing diabetes;
        Type 2 diabetes
  blogs about, 23
  bones and, 141
  costs of, <u>6</u>
  depression and, 22, <u>181</u>
  epidemic, <u>4</u>
  erectile dysfunction and, <u>231</u>
  exercise with, 14, <u>130–31</u>
  flu shots and, 226
  gestational, 10, 59–60
  health and, maintaining, 232
  health risks of, 141
  joints and, 141
  knowledge about, 10, 41
  knowledge about own, 10–11
  laughter and, <u>207</u>

medical breakthroughs, 2–8
memory and, 209–11
obesity and, 80
overweight and, 80
self-management programs, 11, 24–25
sick-day plan, 227
sleep in preventing, 203
strength training and, 112
support, 24
treatment plan, knowing about, 11
type 1, 10, 225
weight loss and, 86–87
Diabetes educator, 11, 15
Diabetes Prevention Program, 6
Diabetic ketoacidosis, 225
Diagnosis of diabetes
emotions caused by, 2
first 5 minutes, 22
first 24 hours, 23
first week, 23–25
mental attitude and, 21–26
optimism and, 26
overwhelming feeling after, 26
redefining self after, 26
weeks after, 26
Diaries, food, 84
Diet. *See also specific food and meal*
Atkins, 216
choices and, 54–55
DASH, 62–64, 228
exercise and, 84–85
high-protein, 86
importance of healthy, 12
lifestyle and, 68
low-carb, 70, 86, 216
in managing and preventing
diabetes, 12–13, 46, 59–60, 59
heart attack, 215
heart disease, 52–53, 66, 216–17, 218
high blood pressure, 62–64, 62, 228
high cholesterol, 60–62, 61
stroke, 238
type 2 diabetes, 28, 60
medical breakthroughs, 47–53
myths
carrots are loaded with sugar, 71, 74
celery is just water, 74
iceberg lettuce has no nutrients, 71
potatoes make you fat, 70–71
variety of, 69–70
Ornish, 216
patterns, breaking out of, 120
Portfolio, 60–62
Pritikin, 59–60
review of, weekly, 123
South Beach, 216
weak spots, 123
Dietary Approaches to Stop Hypertension (DASH)
diet, 62–64, 228
Dietary fats, 17, 62, 81
Dieting foods, special, 86–87

Dietitian, 11, 13
Dijon mustard
Turkey Burgers with Chili Beans, 308
Dill
Yogurt and Cucumber Dip, 259
Dinner. *See* Beef; Fish and seafood; Pork; Poultry
Dipeptidyl-peptidase-4 (DPP-4), 30
Dips
Creamy Veggie Dip, 260
Spinach-Pesto Dip, 257, **257**
Three-Bean Avocado Dip, 258
Yogurt and Cucumber Dip, 259
DPP-4, 30
Drugs. *See* Medications
Duke University weight-loss program, 118–19
DVD home workouts
for beginners, 150–51, 151
for energy boost, 156, 156
for toning, 152–53, 153
for weight loss, 151–52, 152
DVT, 237

E

Eating strategies, 82
Edamame
Edamame with Asparagus, Scallions, and Egg, 292
Eggplants
Open-Faced Grilled Vegetable Sandwiches, 288
Southeast-Asian-Style Eggplant, 299
Eggs
Berry and Yogurt Crepes, 349
for breakfast, 81–82, **81**
Cinnamon Chip Muffins, 254
Double Chocolate Cherry Chews, 354
Edamame with Asparagus, Scallions, and Egg, 292
Holiday Sugar Cookies with Royal Icing, 350
Mediterranean Breakfast Bake, 252–53
Omelet Italian-Style, 251
"Open-Faced" Broccoli and Jack Omelet, 245, **245**
Peanut Butter Cookies with Chocolate Chunks, 352
protein in, 82
Red Pepper-Scallion Corn Muffins, 247
Sour Cream Waffles, 249
Texas Breakfast Burritos, 255
Vanilla Poppy Seed Biscotti, **340**, 341
weight loss and, 81–82
Eight O'Clock "half-caf" coffee, 49
Ellipticals, 146
Energy boosts, 129, 156, 156, 177
Erdelyi, Rosalba, 60–62
Erectile dysfunction, 231
Estrogen, 194, 196
Exenatide injection, 28
Exercise. *See also* Walking; Workouts
activity ideas, 14
aerobic, 131
after age 40, 128
arm-sculpting
Side Plank Push-Ups, 98, **98**
Supported Curls, 97, **97**
T-Stand Rows with Kickbacks, 98, **98**

Exercise(*cont.*)
  belly-flattener
    Crisscrosses, 99, **99**
    Full-Body Roll-Ups, 100, **100**
    Windmills, 101, **101**
  body-shaping
    Dead Lift and Row, 160, **160**
    Dip and Bridge, 162, **16**2
    Plié with Kick, 159, **159**
    Push-Up Jumps, 161, **161**
    Reverse Reach, 164, **164**
    Side-to-Side Hops, 163, **163**
  calorie burning and, 126
  Cardio Bust
    Bob 'n' Weave, 99
    Mountain Climbers, 97
    Side-to-Side Shuffle, 95
  core-strengthening
    Leaning Plank, 108, **108**
    Rowing Twist, 107, **107**
    Scoops, 109, **109**
    Sweeping Kick, 110, **110**
  with diabetes, 14, 130–31
  diet and, 84–85
  energy boosts and, 129, 177
  equipment, 146–47, **146–47**
  fitness and, maintaining, 93
  flexibility training, 131
  goals, 131
  health benefits of, 14, 42, 126
  importance of, 14, 137
  insulin and, 126
  interval, 90
  jumping, 135
  in managing and preventing
    aging, 127–28
    depression, 177
    diabetes, 14, 59, 89–90, 126–27
    heart attack, 215
    heart disease, 128
    high blood pressure, 129, 220
    stress, 177, 177
    stroke, 237–38
    type 2 diabetes, 28, 60
  medical breakthroughs, 126–29
  resistance training, 131, 172
  rest and, 128
  skipping, 135, 138, **138**
  before sleep, avoiding, 202
  standing, 118
  strength training
    Clock Work, 95, **95**
    Monster Squats, 96, **96**
    One-Legged Lunges, 94, **94**
  tai chi, 196
  toning
    Bench Dips, 136, **136**
    Side Lunge, 137, **137**
    Single Leg Squat, 138, **138**
    Skipping, 138, **138**
    Standing Press, 136, **136**
  for trouble spots
    Dipping Toes, 171, **171**
    Plank Extension, 172, **172**
    Standing Side-Overs, 171, **171**
    Warrior 3 to Stork, 173, **173**
  on wall
    Knee Press, 116, **116**
    Toe Reaches, 115, **115**
    Wall Bridge, 113, **113**
    Wall Scissor, 116, **116**
    Windshield Wipers, 114, **114**
  warm up
    Foot Rock-Overs, **148**, 148
    Heel Raises, **148**, 148
    Hurdles, 148
    Windmills, **148**, 148
  weight loss and, 126
  yoga
    Active Cat, 185, **185**
    Child's Pose, 189
    Cobbler's Pose, 189
    Corpse Pose, 189
    Downward Facing Dog, 186, **186**
    Extended Side-Angle, 187, **187**
    Head-to-Knee Pose, 189
    Side Plank, 188, **188**
    Warrior 3, 188, **188**
    Yogic Bicycles, 189, **189**
Eye exams, 19, 232
Eyesight. *See* Vision

F

FAST stroke treatment, 238
Fat. *See* Body fat; Dietary fats
FDA, 33, 34, 35, 36–38
Fiber
  in beans, 76
  blood sugar levels and, 74
  in carrots, 74
  in cereals, 66
  content in food, discovering, 110
  digestion and, 118
  in Portfolio Diet, 61
  satiety and, 118
Fight-or-flight mode, 195
Fish and seafood
  Baked Spaghetti Squash with Shrimp, 327
  Chile Sautéed Shrimp, 326–27
  fatty, 211
  Garlic Shrimp with Spinach and Shiitake
    Mushrooms, 329
  in heart disease prevention, 211
  Incredible Crab Canapes, 264
  memory improvement and, 211
  Parmesan-Crusted Tilapia, 322
  Quick Thai Seafood Soup, 278
  Roasted Fish with Crisp Potatoes, 324
  Salmon and Herb Penne, 321, **321**
  selecting, over poultry or meat, 59
  Southwestern Shrimp Pizza, 330, **331**
  Stir-Fried Rice Noodles with Shrimp, 328

in stroke prevention, 238–39
Sweet and Tangy Wild Salmon with Onion and Tomatoes, 325
Zesty Baked Fish, 323
Fitness, maintaining, 93
Flavonoids, 71
Flaxseed
Chocolate Oatmeal, 250
Flexibility training, 131
Flu shots, 226
Folate/folic acid, 4–5
Food. *See also specific type*
canned, 77
cravings, 195
diaries, 84
dieting, special, 86–87
frozen, 50
glycemic index and, 61
junk, 195
portions, 121, 123
satiety and, 118, 120
servings, 121, 123
trigger, 123
Food and Drug Administration (FDA), 33, 34, 35, 36–38
Foot exams, 19, 230–32
Foot problems and care, 19, 230–32
French fries, 50–51, **50**
Frozen food, 50
Fruits. *See also specific type*
Breakfast Bread Pudding, 248
health benefits of, 42, 59
Savory Fruit and Nut Stuffing, 295
in stroke prevention, 238
sugars in, 52
215-Calorie Taco Snack, 261

G

Game playing for managing stress, 178
Garbanzo beans, 76
Garlic
Garlic Shrimp with Spinach and Shiitake Mushrooms, 329
Gastroesophageal reflux disease (GERD), 201
GCs, 211
Generic medications
antidepressants, 32, 36
caution about, 31
cost savings and, 31
debate about, 34
diabetic pills, 37
Food and Drug Administration and, 33, 34, 35, 36–38
insurance companies and, 32, 34
personal experience with, 32
for Ritalin, 36
safety issues, 33, 35
for Wellbutrin, 32, 36–38
GERD, 201
Gestational diabetes, 10, 59–60
Ghrelin, 203

Ginger
Chicken, Broccoli, and Cashew Stir-Fry, 303, **303**
Garlic Shrimp with Spinach and Shiitake Mushrooms, 329
Ginger Cashew Pillows, 351
Gingered Beef with Broccolini and Walnuts, 311, **311**
Honey Barbecue Drummettes, 263
Orange Beef and Broccoli, 315
Oriental Spinach Salad, 268
Sweet and Tangy Wild Salmon with Onion and Tomatoes, 325
Ginger ale
Watermelon Granita, 333, **333**
Gingersnaps
Blueberry-Cheesecake Parfaits, 344
Glimepiride, 28
Glucocorticoids (GCs), 211
Glucophage, 4
GlucoPhone (HealthPia America), 3
Glucose, 10, 195. *See also* Blood glucose (BG)
Glucovance, 4, 29
Glyburide, 29
Glycemic index, 61
Glynase, 28
Glyset, 29
Goals
exercise, 131
nonweight, 123
SMART, 60
walking, 91, 128
weight-loss, 84
Graham crackers
Chocolate-Coconut Rum Balls, 353
Raspberry and Chocolate Ice Cream Pielettes, 343
Granola
Peach Breakfast Parfait, 246
Grapefruits
Broiled Red Grapefruit with Pomegranate Syrup, 335
Clementine and Grapefruit Compote, 345
Green Mountain "half-caf" coffee, 49
Green tea, 48, 200

H

Ham
Stir-Fried Rice Noodles with Shrimp, 328
Hazelnuts
Savory Fruit and Nut Stuffing, 295
HDL cholesterol, 17
Healing, faster, 216
Health care team, 3, 3, 11, 13, 15, 19
Heart attack, 215
Heartburn, 4
Heart disease
Atkins diet and, 216
as complication of diabetes, 215–16, 216
positive attitude and, 216
preventing and managing
capers, 218–19
diet, 52–53, 66, 216–17, 218
exercise, 128

Heart disease (*cont.*)
  preventing and managing (*cont.*)
    fish and seafood, 211
    Macadamia nuts, 50
  Pritikin diet and, 60
  vitamin D deficiency and, 49
  whole grain cereals and, 66
Heavy cream
  Strawberry Cream Clouds, 339
Hecker, Judy, 62–64
Herbs. *See specific type*
High blood pressure
  body fat and, 81
  as complication of diabetes, 217, 227–28
  DASH diet and, 62–64, 228
  managing and preventing
    celery, 74
    diet, 62–64, 62, 228
    exercise, 129, 220
    medications, 217, 220
    navy beans, 76
    positive attitude, 216
    soy milk, 61, 61
    walking, 129
  stroke risk and, 235–36, 237, 238
High cholesterol
  as complication of diabetes, 228–29
  managing and preventing
    diet, 60–62, 61
    medications, 4, 215
  stroke risk and, 235, 238
Honey
  Clementine and Grapefruit Compote, 345
  Creamy Honeydew Soup, 275, **275**
  Grilled Chicken Breasts with Plum and Walnut
      Relish, 302
  Honey Barbecue Drummettes, 263
  Mixed Berry Ice Pops, 336
  Oriental Spinach Salad, 268
  Roasted Butternut and Spinach Salad, 272, **272**
Hormones. *See* Sleep; *specific type*; Stress
Hormone therapy, 196, 237, 239
Hot flashes, 196
Humalog, 29
Humor. *See* Laughter
Humulin, 29
Hunger, 82, 196
Hyperglycemic hyperosmolar syndrome, 225
Hypertension. *See* High blood pressure

I

Ibuprofen, 5
Iceberg lettuce, 71
Ice cream
  Berry and Peach Sundaes, 338
  Raspberry and Chocolate Ice Cream Pielettes, 343
"Ideal" body weight, 86
Iletin, 29
Immune system
  boosting, 178, 196, 203
  sleep deprivation and, 195

Inactivity, price of, 129
Injectable medications, 18–19, 28, 30
Insomnia, 196, 200, 204. *See also* Sleep, deprivation
Insulin, 10, 126
Insulin injections, 18–19, 29
Insulin resistance, 59, 195. *See also* Diabetes
Interval walks, 90

J

Januvia, 30
Joints and diabetes, 141
Joslin Basics
  choices, dietary, 52–53
  diabetes complications, tips for avoiding,
      220–21
  exercise with diabetes, 130–31
  stress signals and management, 180–81
  weight loss and diabetes, 86–87
Juices, 48, 59. *See also specific type*
Jumping (exercise), 135
Junk food, 195

K

Ketoacidosis, diabetic, 225
Kidney beans, 76
Kidney disease, 17, 229
Kombucha tea, 48
Kukoamines, 71

L

Ladyfingers
  Tangelo Tiramisu, 347
Lantus, 29
Laughter
  brain and, 206–7
  diabetes and, 207
  health benefits of, 206, 208
  mood improvement and, 205
  for stress management, 177–78, 181, 205–8
LDL cholesterol
  Atkins diet and, 216
  high, 82, 226
  lowering, 50, 76, 228–29
  numbers, understanding, 17, 221, 228
  role of, 220–21
  understanding, 239
Lemongrass
  Quick Thai Seafood Soup, 278
Lemon juice
  Creamy Veggie Dip, 260
  Mixed Berry Ice Pops, 336
  Open-Faced Grilled Vegetable Sandwiches, 288
  Roasted Butternut and Spinach Salad, 272, **272**
  Watermelon Granita, 333, **333**
Lente, 29
Lettuce. *See also* Salads
  iceberg, 71
  Roast Beef Sandwiches, 312
Lexapro, 4–5
Lifestyle, 68, 129. *See also* Change, new theory of
      diabetic lifestyle

Lime juice
  Creamy Honeydew Soup, 275, **275**
  Grilled Pork Tacos with Avocado-Radish Salad, 319
  Quick Thai Seafood Soup, 278
  Roasted Fish with Crisp Potatoes, 324
  Southeast-Asian-Style Eggplant, 299
  Tex-Mex Tomato Soup, 280, **281**
Lipid profile, 17
Lipitor, 4
Longevity, 42, 50, 216
Lotrel, 217
Lunch. *See* Salads; Sandwiches; Soups

M

Macadamia nuts
  Green Bean and Macadamia Nut Casserole, 287
  in heart disease prevention, 50
Managing diabetes
  blood glucose monitoring, 15–16, 15
  blood pressure monitoring, 16–17
  cholesterol level monitoring, 17
  diet, 12–13, 46, 59–60, 59
  exercise, 14, 59, 89–90, 126–27
  eye exams, 19
  foot exams, 19
  key steps to, 10–11
  medications, 4, 18–19, 28–30, 29
  microalbumin test, 17–18
  other steps, 19
  Personal Diabetes Goal Tracker, 20
  vitamin D, 49
Maraschino cherries
  Berry and Peach Sundaes, 338
Margarine
  Orange and Pear Crisp, 348
Marshmallows
  Grilled Banana Split, 334
Matthews, Karen, 120–21
Meals, monitoring, 118. *See also specific type*
Meat. *See specific type*
Medications. *See also* Generic medications; *specific type*
  antidepressants, 32, 36, 179
  biologic, 37
  erectile dysfunction and, 231
  Food and Drug Administration and, 35
  injectable, 18–19, 28, 30
  insomnia and, 204
  in managing
    arthritis, 5
    blood glucose, 18
    depression, 4–5, 179
    diabetes, 4, 18–19, 28–30, 29
    heartburn/acid reflux, 4
    high blood pressure, 217, 220
    high cholesterol, 4, 215
    type 2 diabetes, 28–30, 29
  microalbumin test and, 18
  mix-ups, avoiding, 5–6, 5
  multivitamins and, 4
  reactions to, 7
  safety issues, 5–7, 5, 33, 35
  schedule, maintaining, 8
  side effects, 3–4, 7
  sleep, 196
  soundalikes, 5
  understanding diabetic, 18–19
Meglitinides, 29
Melatonin, 200
Melons
  Creamy Honeydew Soup, 275, **275**
Memory, 203, 209–11, 211
Metabolic syndrome, 51, 81
Metformin, 28–29
Microalbumin test, 17–18, 221, 229–30
Micronase, 28
Miglitol, 29
Migraine with aura, 237
Milk. *See also* Soy milk
  Berry and Yogurt Crepes, 349
  Breakfast Bread Pudding, 248
  Cinnamon Chip Muffins, 254
  Cream of Broccoli Soup, 277
  Feta-Walnut Stuffed Cucumbers, 265
  Green Bean and Macadamia Nut Casserole, 287
  Holiday Sugar Cookies with Royal Icing, 350
  "Open-Faced" Broccoli and Jack Omelet, 245, **245**
  Sour Cream Waffles, 249
  Texas Breakfast Burritos, 255
Milk thistle (*Silybum maranum*), 3, **3**
Mint
  Fresh Corn and Tomato Bruschetta Salad, 269
  Mixed Berry Ice Pops, 336
  Southeast-Asian-Style Eggplant, 299
  Yogurt and Cucumber Dip, 259
Mirepoix, 74
Mood
  improving, 178, 203, 205
  sleep deprivation and, 195
Muffins
  Cinnamon Chip Muffins, 254
  Red Pepper-Scallion Corn Muffins, 247
Multivitamins, 4
Mushrooms
  Beef and Mushroom Noodles, 313
  Four-Veggie Pizza, 291
  Garlic Shrimp with Spinach and Shiitake Mushrooms, 329
  Green Bean and Macadamia Nut Casserole, 287
  Oriental Spinach Salad, 268
  Portobello Parmesan, 294
  Quick Thai Seafood Soup, 278
Music, 83, 83, 129
Mustard greens
  Spiced Cauliflower Soup, 276
MyWalkingMusic.com, 83

N

Napping, 204
Naproxen, 5
Nateglinide Oral, 29
National Stroke Association, 238

National Weight Control Registry database, 134
Navy beans, _76_
Negative thoughts, avoiding, 178
Neuropathy, 230
Nexium, 4
Night sweats, 196
Noodles. *See also* Soba noodles
    Beef and Mushroom Noodles, 313
    Stir-Fried Rice Noodles with Shrimp, 328
    Zesty Skillet Turkey and Noodles, 307
NordicTrack C2155 treadmill, 146–47
Notes from Joslin
    A1C test, _11_
    diet and lifestyle, _68_
    exercise, importance of, _137_
    fish and memory improvement, _211_
    fitness, maintaining, _93_
    generic medications, _37_
    laughter's health benefits, _208_
    overwhelming feeling after diagnosis, _26_
    recordkeeping of diabetic tests, _43_
    resistance training, _172_
    SMART goals, _60_
    strength training and diabetes, _112_
    stroke treatment, FAST, _238_
    support for weight loss, _123_
    tai chi health benefits, _196_
    whole grains and weight loss, _74_
Novolin, 29
NovoLog, 29
NP, 3, _3_, 11
Numbers of various tests, knowing about, 10–11,
    220–21
Nurse practitioner (NP), 3, _3_, 11
Nutrition. *See* Diet; *specific food*
Nuts. *See also specific type*
    in Portfolio Diet, 61
    Savory Fruit and Nut Stuffing, 295
    as snack, _61_

O

Oatmeal
    Blueberry-Chocolate Parfaits, 342
Oats. *See also* Rolled oats
    Chocolate Oatmeal, 250
    Parmesan-Crusted Tilapia, 322
    Turkey Meatballs, 309
Obesity, 80, 192
Olive oil, _62_
Olives
    Baked Spaghetti Squash with Shrimp, 327
    Chicken-Olive Sauté, 304
    Mediterranean Salad-Wraps, 290
    Roasted Vegetable Salad, 270
    Texas Breakfast Burritos, 255
Omeprazole, 36
onePAC, 8
Onions
    Baked Spaghetti Squash with Shrimp, 327
    Beef and Mushroom Noodles, 313
    Black and White Bean Soup, 283

Chicken and Salad Pizza, 305
Chicken-Olive Sauté, 304
Cream of Broccoli Soup, 277
Creamy Veggie Dip, 260
Four-Veggie Pizza, 291
Fresh Corn and Tomato Bruschetta Salad, 269
Grilled Chicken Breasts with Plum and Walnut
    Relish, 302
Homestyle Roast Beef, 314
Leafy Grilled Chicken Salad with Creamy Balsamic
    Dressing, 267, **267**
Mediterranean Salad-Wraps, 290
Open-Faced Grilled Vegetable Sandwiches, 288
Pork Kebabs Italiano, 318
Roast Beef Sandwiches, 312
Roasted Butternut and Spinach Salad, 272, **272**
Roasted Vegetable Salad, 270
Savory Fruit and Nut Stuffing, 295
Southeast-Asian-Style Eggplant, 299
Southwestern Shrimp Pizza, 330, **331**
Spiced Cauliflower Soup, 276
Sweet and Sour Chinese Pork, 317
Sweet and Tangy Wild Salmon with Onion and
    Tomatoes, 325
Tex-Mex Tomato Soup, 280, **281**
Turkey Burgers with Chili Beans, 308
Turkey Meatballs, 309
Turkey Sausage and Peppers, 306
Tuscan Chicken Soup, 279
White Chicken Chili, 282
Ophthalmologist, 19
Optimism, 26
Orange juice
    Cranberry-Apple Chutney, 262
    Grilled Chicken Breasts with Plum and Walnut
        Relish, 302
    Orange Beef and Broccoli, 315
    Wok-Seared Broccoli, 298, 328
Oranges
    nutrition of, 72
    Orange and Pear Crisp, 348
    Oriental Spinach Salad, 268
    sugar in, 52
Oregano
    Baked Spaghetti Squash with Shrimp, 327
    Chicken and Salad Pizza, 305
    Grilled Pork Tacos with Avocado-Radish Salad, 319
    Salmon and Herb Penne, 321, **321**
    Tuscan Chicken Soup, 279
Orinase, 30
Ornish Diet, 216
Osteoporosis, 49, 135
Overweight, 80, 219

P

Pain tolerance, increasing, 178
Parsley
    Black and White Bean Soup, 283
    Feta-Walnut Stuffed Cucumbers, 265
    Zesty Skillet Turkey and Noodles, 307
Partner, weight-loss, 84, 121

Pasta
   Capellini with Pine Nuts, Sun-Dried Tomatoes, and
      Chicken, 301, **301**
   Quick Pasta Salad, 271
   Salmon and Herb Penne, 321, **321**
Patient personality, identifying, 24
Peaches
   Berry and Peach Sundaes, 338
   Peach Breakfast Parfait, 246
Peanut butter
   Peanut Butter Cookies with Chocolate Chunks, 352
   Peanut Noodles with Tofu, 296
   215-Calorie Taco Snack, 261
Pear body shape, 158
Pears
   Orange and Pear Crisp, 348
Peas
   Stir-Fried Rice Noodles with Shrimp, 328
Pecans
   Sweet Potatoes with Brown Sugar-Pecan Topping,
      293
Pedometers, 122, 128
Peggle (online game), 178
People's Pharmacy, 32
Peppers. *See* Bell peppers; Chile peppers; Roasted
      peppers
Perfection, healthy striving for, 177
Perimenopause, 196
Periodontitis, 217
Personal Diabetes Goal Tracker, 20
Pesto
   Four-Veggie Pizza, 291
   Spinach-Pesto Dip, 257, **257**
Phyllo dough
   Mediterranean Breakfast Bake, 252–53
Physician, 11
Picante sauce
   Three-Bean Avocado Dip, 258
Pills, diabetes, 18, 29, 37. *See also* Medications
Pineapples
   Grilled Banana Split, 334
   Sweet and Sour Chinese Pork, 317
Pine nuts
   Capellini with Pine Nuts, Sun-Dried Tomatoes, and
      Chicken, 301, **301**
   Tex-Mex Stuffed Acorn Squash, 285, **285**
Pinto beans, 76
Pioglitazone, 30
Pizza
   Chicken and Salad Pizza, 305
   Four-Veggie Pizza, 291
   Southwestern Shrimp Pizza, 330, **331**
Plant sterols, 61–62
Plums
   Grilled Chicken Breasts with Plum and Walnut
      Relish, 302
Podiatrist, 19
Podrunner, 83
Pomegranate juice
   Broiled Red Grapefruit with Pomegranate Syrup,
      335

Poppy seeds
   Vanilla Poppy Seed Biscotti, **340**, 341
Pork
   Grilled Pork Tacos with Avocado-Radish Salad,
      319
   Pork Kebabs Italiano, 318
   Stuffed Pork Roast, 316
   Sweet and Sour Chinese Pork, 317
Portfolio Diet, 60–62
Portions, 121, 123
Positive attitude, 26, 178, 215–16
Posture, good, 82
Potassium, 71, 76, 218
Potatoes
   cooking, 50
   french fries, 50–51, **50**
   health benefits of, 70–71
   myth about nutrition of, 70–71
   nutrition of, 70
   Rainbow Fries, 51
   Roasted Fish with Crisp Potatoes, 324
   Roasted Vegetable Salad, 270
   skins of, 50
   Sweet Potatoes with Brown Sugar-Pecan Topping,
      293
   Texas Breakfast Burritos, 255
Poultry
   Capellini with Pine Nuts, Sun-Dried Tomatoes, and
      Chicken, 301, **301**
   Chicken, Broccoli, and Cashew Stir-Fry, 303
   Chicken and Salad Pizza, 305
   Chicken-Olive Sauté, 304
   fish and seafood selection over, 59
   Grilled Chicken Breasts with Plum and Walnut
      Relish, 302
   Honey Barbecue Drummettes, 263
   Leafy Grilled Chicken Salad with Creamy Balsamic
      Dressing, 267, **267**
   Texas Breakfast Burritos, 255
   Turkey Burgers with Chili Beans, 308
   Turkey Meatballs, 309
   Turkey Sausage and Peppers, 306
   Tuscan Chicken Soup, 279
   White Chicken Chili, 282
   Zesty Skillet Turkey and Noodles, 307
Pramlintide injection, 30
Prandase, 28
Prandin, 30
Precontemplation step of diabetic lifestyle change,
      40–41
Precose, 28
Prediabetes, 6, 81
Pregnancy and statins, 215
Preparation step for diabetic lifestyle change, 43
Prescriptions. *See* Medications
Prevention recipes, 243. *See also specific food and
      meal*
Prilosec, 4, 36
Pritikin Diet, 59–60
Progesterone, 194, 196
Prolactin, 200

Protein
    animal, avoiding, 61
    in beans, 76
    diet high in, 86
    in eggs, 82
Prozac, 4–5
Pu-erh tea, 48

R

Rabinowitz, Nancy, 123
Radicchio
    Roasted Butternut and Spinach Salad, 272, **272**
Radishes
    Grilled Pork Tacos with Avocado-Radish Salad, 319
Raspberries
    Berry and Peach Sundaes, 338
    Grilled Almond Butter and Berry Sandwiches, 289
    Mixed Berry Ice Pops, 336
    Raspberry and Chocolate Ice Cream Pielettes, 343
Ray, Susan, 119
RD, 13
Refined carbohydrates, avoiding, 53
Registered Dietitian (RD), 13
Repaglinide, 30
Resistance training, 131, 172. *See also* Strength
        training
Resistant starch, 70
Rest and exercise, 128
Retinopathy, 232
Reyther, Lupe, 122
Rice
    Orange Beef and Broccoli, 315
"Ringxiety," 179
Ritalin, 36
Roasted peppers
    Chicken and Salad Pizza, 305
    Mediterranean Salad-Wraps, 290
    Turkey Burgers with Chili Beans, 308
Rolled oats. *See also* Oats
    Crunchy Frozen Banana, 334
    Ginger Cashew Pillows, 351
Rooibos tea, 47
Room temperature and sleep, 200–201
Rosemary
    Chicken-Olive Sauté, 304
    Roasted Vegetable Salad, 270
Rosiglitazone, 30
Rx Essentials (Nature Made), 3–4

S

Sage
    Savory Fruit and Nut Stuffing, 295
    Tuscan Chicken Soup, 279
Salad greens
    Mediterranean Salad-Wraps, 290
Salads
    Balsamic Tomato and Roasted Pepper Salad, 273
    Fresh Corn and Tomato Bruschetta Salad, 269
    iceberg lettuce, 71
    Leafy Grilled Chicken Salad with Creamy Balsamic
        Dressing, 267, **267**

Oriental Spinach Salad, 268
    Quick Pasta Salad, 271
    Roasted Butternut and Spinach Salad, 272, **272**
    Roasted Vegetable Salad, 270
    spinach, 62, **63**
    Taco, 77
    Watermelon Salad, 271
Salmon
    Parmesan-Crusted Tilapia, 322
    Salmon and Herb Penne, 321, **321**
    Sweet and Tangy Wild Salmon with Onion and
        Tomatoes, 325
Salt, 77, 217–18, 220
Sandwiches
    Grilled Almond Butter and Berry Sandwiches, 289
    Mediterranean Salad-Wraps, 290
    Open-Faced Grilled Vegetable Sandwiches, 288
    Turkey Burgers with Chili Beans, 308
Satiety, 118, 120
Saying no for managing stress, 181
Scallions
    Chicken, Broccoli, and Cashew Stir-Fry, 303, **303**
    Edamame with Asparagus, Scallions, and Egg, 292
    Gingered Beef with Broccolini and Walnuts, 311, **311**
    Green Bean and Macadamia Nut Casserole, 287
    Grilled Pork Tacos with Avocado-Radish Salad, 319
    Mediterranean Breakfast Bake, 252–53
    Orange Beef and Broccoli, 315
    Peanut Noodles with Tofu, 296
    Quick Thai Seafood Soup, 278
    Red Pepper-Scallion Corn Muffins, 247
    Tex-Mex Stuffed Acorn Squash, 285, **285**
    Turkey Burgers with Chili Beans, 308
    Zesty Baked Fish, 323
    Zesty Skillet Turkey and Noodles, 307
Scallops
    Quick Thai Seafood Soup, 278
Sedentary lifestyle, 129
Seeds. *See specific type*
Self-management programs, 11, 24–25
Seltzer, Mixed Berry Ice Pops, 336
Servings, 121, 123
Sesame seeds
    Oriental Spinach Salad, 268
    Peanut Noodles with Tofu, 296
    Sesame Tofu with Bok Choy and Corn, 297
Sexual health, 231
Sherry
    Orange Beef and Broccoli, 315
    Southeast-Asian-Style Eggplant, 299
Shrimp
    Baked Spaghetti Squash with Shrimp, 327
    Chile Sautéed Shrimp, 326–27
    Garlic Shrimp with Spinach and Shiitake
        Mushrooms, 329
    Southwestern Shrimp Pizza, 330, **331**
    Stir-Fried Rice Noodles with Shrimp, 328
Sick-day plan for diabetics, 227
Side dishes. *See* Vegetables
Silymarin, 3
Sitagliptin, 30

Skipping (exercise), 135, 138, **138**
Sleep
    aging and, <u>203</u>
    alcohol and, 199
    bedmates and, 194
    body temperature and, 200, 202
    caffeine and, 199
    carbohydrates and, 201–2
    deprivation, 191–94, <u>195</u>, 196
    in diabetes prevention, <u>203</u>
    eating before, avoiding, 201
    exercise before, avoiding, 202
    health benefits of, <u>203</u>
    hormones and, fluctuating, 194, 196
    hunger and, 196
    immune system improvement and, <u>203</u>
    insomnia and, 196, <u>200</u>, 204
    medications, 196
    melatonin and, <u>200</u>
    memory and, <u>203</u>
    mood and, <u>203</u>
    napping and, 204
    obesity and, 192
    overactive mind and, 192–93
    prolactin and, <u>200</u>
    ritual, developing, 202–4
    room temperature and, 200–201
    schedule of sleep and wake, 203–4
    smoking and, <u>201</u>
    snoring and, 194
    tips for good night's, <u>193</u>, 197–204
    tryptophan and, 201
    weekend sleep-ins and, 193–94
    weight loss and, <u>203</u>
Sleep apnea, <u>237</u>
Smoking, <u>42</u>, <u>201</u>, 215, 237
Snacks. *See also* Appetizers
    almonds as, <u>61</u>
    empty-calorie, avoiding, 52–53
    healthy, 53, **53**
    nuts as <u>61</u>
    215-Calorie Taco Snack, 261
    walking versus eating, 120
Snoring, 194
Soba noodles
    Chicken, Broccoli, and Cashew Stir-Fry, 303, **303**
    Peanut Noodles with Tofu, 296
Soda, 51, 53
Sodium, 77, 217–18, <u>220</u>
Soft drinks, 51, 53
Soups
    base, 74
    Black and White Bean Soup, 283
    Cream of Broccoli Soup, 277
    Creamy Honeydew Soup, 275, **275**
    Quick Thai Seafood Soup, 278
    satiety and, 120
    Spiced Cauliflower Soup, 276
    Tex-Mex Tomato Soup, 280, **281**
    Tuscan Chicken Soup, 279
    White Chicken Chili, 282

Sour cream
    Blueberry-Cheesecake Parfaits, 344
    Creamy Veggie Dip, 260
    Sour Cream Waffles, 249
    Spinach-Pesto Dip, 257, **257**
    Tex-Mex Tomato Soup, 280, **281**
South Beach Diet, 216
Soy, 61
Soy milk
    Chocolate-Strawberry Ice Pops, 337
    in high cholesterol management, 61, <u>61</u>
Soy sauce
    Beef and Mushroom Noodles, 313
    Chicken, Broccoli, and Cashew Stir-Fry, 303, **303**
    Edamame with Asparagus, Scallions, and Egg, 292
    Garlic Shrimp with Spinach and Shiitake Mushrooms, 329
    Gingered Beef with Broccolini and Walnuts, 311, **311**
    Honey Barbecue Drummettes, 263
    Orange Beef and Broccoli, 315
    Oriental Spinach Salad, 268
    Peanut Noodles with Tofu, 296
    Quick Thai Seafood Soup, 278
    Southeast-Asian-Style Eggplant, 299
    Stir-Fried Rice Noodles with Shrimp, 328
    Sweet and Sour Chinese Pork, 317
    Sweet and Tangy Wild Salmon with Onion and Tomatoes, 325
    Wok-Seared Broccoli, 298, 328
Spices, 202. *See also specific type*
Spinach
    Garlic Shrimp with Spinach and Shiitake Mushrooms, 329
    Oriental Spinach Salad, 268
    Roasted Butternut and Spinach Salad, 272, **272**
    salads, <u>62</u>, **63**
    Spinach-Pesto Dip, 25, **257**
SportsArt E83 elliptical, 146
Squash
    Baked Spaghetti Squash with Shrimp, 327
    Mediterranean Breakfast Bake, 252–53
    Roasted Butternut and Spinach Salad, 272, **272**
    Tex-Mex Stuffed Acorn Squash, 285, **285**
Standing, 118
Starch, 70
Starlix, 29
Statins, 61–62, 215
Stationary bikes, 147
Strawberries
    Chocolate-Strawberry Ice Pops, 337
    Strawberry Cream Clouds, 339
Strawberry sorbet
    Grilled Banana Split, 334
Strength training
    belly fat reduction and, 82–83
    diabetes and, <u>112</u>
    10-minute workout
        Clock Work, 95, **95**
        Monster Squats, 96, **96**

Strength training (*cont.*)
  10-minute workout (*cont.*)
    One-Legged Lunges, 99, **99**
    overview, 94, <u>94</u>
  weight loss and, 82–83
Stress
  addressing biggest offenders of, 211
  from cell phone ringing, 179
  eating as a result of, 178–79
  fight-or-flight mode and, <u>195</u>
  glucocorticoids and, 211
  health risks, 178
  hormone, 178–79, <u>195</u>
  managing
    breathing, <u>181</u>
    exercise, 177, <u>177</u>
    game playing, 178
    laughter, 177–78, <u>181</u>, 205–8
    saying no, <u>181</u>
    tree therapy, 177
    yoga, 183–84, <u>189</u>
  medical breakthroughs, 176–79
  pressure and, managing, 211
  signals, <u>180</u>
  source of, identifying, 211
  from workload anxiety, 178
Stroke
  aspirin and, 239
  as complication of diabetes, 218, 233–39
  preventing, 237–38
  risk of, 235–36, <u>237</u>
  tests for diagnosing, <u>234</u>
  treating, 236–37, <u>238</u>
Sugar. *See also* Brown sugar; Confectioners' sugar
  in carrots, 71, 74
  Holiday Sugar Cookies with Royal Icing, 350
  in oranges, 52
  in soda, 53
  sweets and, 52–53
Sugar alcohols, avoiding, 68
Sulfonylurea, 28
Sunflower seeds
  Roasted Butternut and Spinach Salad, 272, **272**
Support, weight-loss, <u>123</u>
Sweet potatoes
  Sweet Potatoes with Brown Sugar-Pecan Topping, 293
Sweets, 52–53. *See also* Desserts
Symlin, 30
Systolic blood pressure, 218

T

Tahini
  Yogurt and Cucumber Dip, 259
Tai chi, <u>196</u>
Tangelos
  Tangelo Tiramisu, 347
Tea, 47–48, 200
Teva Pharmaceuticals, 37
Thiamin, <u>76</u>
Thisilyn (Nature's Way), 3

Thyme
  Portobello Parmesan, 294
  Roasted Butternut and Spinach Salad, 272, **272**
  Tuscan Chicken Soup, 279
Tilapia
  Parmesan-Crusted Tilapia, 322
Tissue plasminogen activator (tPA), 236
Tofu
  Peanut Noodles with Tofu, 296
  Sesame Tofu with Bok Choy and Corn, 297
  stir-fry, <u>61</u>
Tolazamide, 30
Tolbutamide, 30
Tolinase, 30
Tomatoes
  Baked Spaghetti Squash with Shrimp, 327
  Balsamic Tomato and Roasted Pepper Salad, 273
  Capellini with Pine Nuts, Sun-Dried Tomatoes, and Chicken, 301, **301**
  Chicken and Salad Pizza, 305
  Chicken-Olive Sauté, 304
  Four-Veggie Pizza, 291
  Fresh Corn and Tomato Bruschetta Salad, 269
  Leafy Grilled Chicken Salad with Creamy Balsamic Dressing, 267, **267**
  Omelet Italian-Style, 251
  Pork Kebabs Italiano, 318
  Portobello Parmesan, 294
  Quick Pasta Salad, 271
  Roast Beef Sandwiches, 312
  Roasted Fish with Crisp Potatoes, 324
  Salmon and Herb Penne, 321, **321**
  Southwestern Shrimp Pizza, 330, **331**
  Sweet and Tangy Wild Salmon with Onion and Tomatoes, 325
  Tex-Mex Stuffed Acorn Squash, 285, **285**
  Tex-Mex Tomato Soup, 280, **281**
  Three-Bean Avocado Dip, 258
  Turkey Sausage and Peppers, 306
  Tuscan Chicken Soup, 279
  Zesty Skillet Turkey and Noodles, 307
Tomato sauce
  Honey Barbecue Drummettes, 263
  Southwestern Shrimp Pizza, 330, **331**
  Turkey Burgers with Chili Beans, 308
  Turkey Meatballs, 309
Toning
  DVD home workout, 152–53, <u>153</u>
  maximizing metabolism workout
    Bench Dips, 136, **136**
    overview, 135, <u>135</u>
    Side Lunge, 137, **137**
    Single Leg Squat, 138, **138**
    Skipping, 138, **138**
    Standing Press, 136, **136**
  1-minute workout, <u>93</u>, <u>96</u>, <u>100</u>
  walking program, 93, <u>93</u>
Tortillas
  Grilled Pork Tacos with Avocado-Radish Salad, 319
  Mediterranean Salad-Wraps, 290
  Texas Breakfast Burritos, 255

Tex-Mex Tomato Soup, 280, **281**
215-Calorie Taco Snack, 261
tPA, 236
Trader Darwin's silymarin, 3
Treadmills, 146, **147–48**
Treatment plan for diabetes, knowing about, 11
Tree therapy for managing stress, 177
Trigger foods, 123
Triglycerides, 17, 81, 211, 216
Tryptophan, 201
Turkey. *See* Poultry
Type 1 diabetes, 10, 225
Type 2 diabetes
  calories and, excessive, 60
  description of, 10
  hyperglycemic hyperosmolar syndrome and, 225
  managing and preventing
    diet, 28, 60
    exercise, 28, 60
    insulin, 18
    medications, 28–30, 29
    pinto beans, 76
    tai chi, 196
    vegetables, 72
    weight loss, 28
  silymarin and, 3
  walking and, 127

U

United States Pharmacopeia (USP), 5
University of Alabama weight-loss program, 119–21
University of Colorado weight-loss program, 121–22
University of Vermont weight-loss program, 122–23
USDA Dietary Guidelines, 72
USP, 5

V

Vanilla
  Vanilla Poppy Seed Biscotti, **340**, 341
Vegetables. *See also specific type*
  dark green, 72–73
  Dramatically Seared Green Beans, 286
  Edamame with Asparagus, Scallions, and Egg, 292
  Four-Veggie Pizza, 291
  Green Bean and Macadamia Nuts Casserole, 287
  Grilled Almond Butter and Berry Sandwiches, 289
  health benefits of, 42, 59
  intake of, increasing, 72–73
  Mediterranean Salad-Wraps, 290
  Open-Faced Grilled Vegetable Sandwiches, 288
  orange, 73
  Peanut Noodles with Tofu, 296
  Portobello Parmesan, 294
  Roasted Vegetable Salad, 270
  Savory Fruit and Nut Stuffing, 295
  Sesame Tofu with Bok Choy and Corn, 297
  Southeast-Asian-Style Eggplant, 299
  starchy, 73
  in stroke prevention, 238
  Sweet Potatoes with Brown Sugar-Pecan Topping, 293

Tex-Mex Stuffed Acorn Squash, 285, **285**
  in type 2 diabetes prevention and
    management, 72
  Wok-Seared Broccoli, 298, 328
Velosulin, 29
Vision
  carrots and, 74
  iceberg lettuce and, 71
  refined carbohydrates and, avoiding, 53
Vision Fitness R2050 stationary bike, 147
Visualizing workout, 129
Visual Medication Schedule, 8
Vitamin A, 71
Vitamin B_1, 76
Vitamin B_{12}, 4
Vitamin C, 218
Vitamin D, 5, 48, 49–50

W

Walking
  Belly Flattener workouts, 103–4, 105–6
  Calorie-Burner workout, 92
  Energy-Booster workout, 92
  equipment, 90
  goals, 91, 128
  health benefits of, 129, 140
  heart health and, 128
  high blood pressure and, managing, 129
  interval, 90
  logs, 128
  music and, 83, 83
  pedometers and, 122, 128
  programs
    Maximize Your Metabolism, 135–38, 135,
      136–38
    Shape Up Fast, 139–40, 139
    Walk Off Weight, 134, 134
  snacking versus, 120
  10-minute workouts, 92, 92–93
  test run before starting program, 42–43
  time for, 90
  with toning, 135–38, 135, **136–38**
  Toning workout, 93, 93
  triglycerides and, reducing, 216
  type 2 diabetes and, 127
  uphill, 83–84
  weight loss and, 83–84, 83, 89–90
Walnuts
  Berry and Peach Sundaes, 338
  Chocolate Oatmeal, 250
  Feta-Walnut Stuffed Cucumbers, 265
  Gingered Beef with Broccolini and Walnuts, 311,
    311
  Grilled Chicken Breasts with Plum and Walnut
    Relish, 302
Warm up before workout, **148**, 148
Watermelon
  Watermelon Granita, 333, **333**
  Watermelon Salad, 271
Weight gain and aging, 127, 135
Weight lifting. *See* Strength training

Weight loss
    blood glucose and, 12–13
    blood pressure and, lowering, <u>220</u>
    body fat and, 81
    calorie burning and, 83, <u>84</u>
    celery and, 74
    diabetes and, <u>86–87</u>
    DVD home workout, 151–52, <u>152</u>
    eating strategies and, 82
    eggs and, 81–82
    exercise and, 126
    goals, 84
    "ideal" body weight and, <u>86</u>
    medical breakthroughs, 80–85
    partner, 84, 121
    posture and, good, 82
    real-life results
        Matthews, Karen, 120–21
        Rabinowitz, Nancy, 123
        Ray, Susan, 119
        Reyther, Lupe, 122
    sleep and, <u>203</u>
    strength training and, 82–83
    support and, 123
    in type 2 diabetes management and prevention, 28
    university programs
        Duke University, 118–19
        overview, 117–18
        University of Alabama, 119–21
        University of Colorado, 121–22
        University of Vermont, 122–23
    walking and, 83–84, <u>83</u>, 89–90
    whole grains and, <u>74</u>
Wellbutrin, 32, 34
Wellbutrin XL 300, 36–38
Wheat germ
    Ginger Cashew Pillows, 351
White tea, 47
White wine
    Salmon and Herb Penne, 321, **321**
Whole grains
    in cereals, 66, 68, <u>74</u>
    Red Pepper-Scallion Corn Muffins, 247
    weight loss and, <u>74</u>
Workouts. *See also* Exercise; Toning
    body-shaping
        Dead Lift and Row, 160, **160**
        Dip and Bridge, 162, **162**
        overview, 157–58, <u>158</u>
        Plié with Kick, 159, **159**
        Push-Up Jumps, 161, **161**
        Reverse Reach, 164, **164**
        Side-to-Side Hops, 163, **163**
    fat-burning cardio routines
        Chutes and Ladders, <u>166</u>
        overview, 165
        Pyramids, <u>168</u>
        Roller Coaster, <u>167</u>
    home
        benefits of, 149
        DVDs, 150–53, 156
        in specific rooms, <u>154–55</u>
    joint-friendly
        45-Minute Fat-Burning Plan, 144, <u>144</u>
        machines for, 146–47, **146–47**
        overview, 141
        60-Minute Weight Loss Workout, 145, <u>145</u>
    music and, 129
    10-minute
        arm sculptor, 97–98, **97–98**, <u>97</u>
        belly flattener, 99–101, **99–101**, <u>99</u>
        benefits of, 90–91
        Cardio Bursts, <u>95</u>, <u>97</u>, <u>99</u>
        strength training, 94–97, **94–97**, <u>94</u>
        walking, 92, <u>92–93</u>
        yoga stress buster, <u>189</u>
    for trouble spots
        Dipping Toes, 171, **171**
        overview, 169–70, <u>170</u>
        Plank Extension, 172, **172**
        Standing Side-Overs, 171, **171**
        Warrior 3 to Stork, 173, **173**
    visualizing, 129
    wall
        Knee Press, 116, **116**
        overview, 111–12, <u>112</u>
        Toe Reaches, 115, **115**
        Wall Bridge, 113, **113**
        Wall Scissor, 116, **116**
        Windshield Wipers, 114, **114**
    warm up before, **148**, <u>148</u>

Y

Yoga
    in stress management, 183–84, <u>189</u>
    workout
        Active Cat, 185, **185**
        Downward Facing Dog, 186, **186**
        Extended Side-Angle, 187, **187**
        overview, 184, <u>184</u>
        Side Plank, 118, **118**
        10-minute stress buster, <u>189</u>
        Warrior 3, 188, **188**
        Yogic Bicycles, 189, **189**
Yogurt
    Berry and Yogurt Crepes, 349
    Creamy Honeydew Soup, 275, **275**
    Crunchy Frozen Banana, 334
    Peach Breakfast Parfait, 246
    Red Pepper-Scallion Corn Muffins, 247
    Sour Cream Waffles, 249
    Spinach-Pesto Dip, 257, **257**
    Yogurt and Cucumber Dip, 259

Z

Zocor, 4
Zoloft, 4–5, 36
Zucchini
    Four-Veggie Pizza, 291
    Open-Faced Grilled Vegetable Sandwiches, 288
    Tuscan Chicken Soup, 279